SERIOUS ELECTRIC BASS

This book is dedicated to:
My daughters, Adriana and Cristina, and all of my students.

Special thanks to:
Aaron Stang and everyone at Warner Bros. Publications, Rick Gordon,
Dean Taba, Tim Emmons, Liz Story, Arlo Chan, Dick Grove,
Dr. Russell Di Bartolo, June Lehman and Kathy Piazza.

Yamaha basses courtesy of Jerry Andreas, Yamaha Corporation America
Modulus basses courtesy of Jane McNail, Modulus Guitars

Project Managers: Aaron Stang and Albert Nigro
Engraving and Layout: Joel Di Bartolo
Technical Editors: Albert Nigro and Rick Fansler
Art Design: Frank Milone / Joseph Klucar

Contents

Foreword
by
Michael Manring

If you're serious about the electric bass, this is the book for you!

In *Serious Electric Bass* you'll find all you need to know about chords, scales and modes: not only how to play them, but also how they function and how to use them in real musical situations. Joel Di Bartolo, who spent over 20 years in the LA studio scene (18 of them on *The Tonight Show starring Johnny Carson*), has done us bassists a great favor by putting together *all* the harmonic information we need in a coherent and easy to read form organized specifically for the bass guitarist. A veritable encyclopedia of harmonic patterns, *Serious Electric Bass* de-mystifies the world of scales and chords and will help you understand all of the tonal patterns used in music today.

The great thing about Joel's approach in *Serious Electric Bass* is the comprehensive way he connects harmonic information to knowledge of the fingerboard. Every scale and chord is presented together with its corresponding fingering patterns and shapes. This will greatly expand your conception of the instrument by helping you to develop the ability to visualize various forms of scale and chord patterns on the bass. Joel also explains the harmonic functions of each scale and how specific scales relate to specific chords. These are the missing pieces of information for students who have a basic grasp of a number of scales but not much idea about when and how to use them. *Boy, I wish I had this book when I was a student!*

Also included is some extremely valuable information about setting up and maintaining your bass. I've found that the ability to perform minor repairs and adjustments on your instrument is absolutely essential for any working musician. While there is, of course, no substitute for the work of a trained and talented instrument technician, you just never know when something will go wrong when there isn't one around—like just before the last set at a gig way out in the boondocks! I definitely suggest paying close attention to the information presented in the first chapter and developing an active relationship with the day-to-day health of your bass.

One word of caution: I wouldn't recommend planning on blazing through this book in a few weeks. There is a wealth of information here and it all deserves careful and patient study. Plan on keeping *Serious Electric Bass* around for many years to refer and re-refer to as your understanding of and fluency in these patterns develops. I hope your copy, like mine, will end up nicely worn in, sitting in a place where it is easily accessible in you practice area.

Using a gradual and steady approach, I think you'll find that *Serious Electric Bass* will help you develop an understanding of the information that you need for any kind of musical situation you might find yourself in. The real benefit to having a thorough understanding of harmonic patterns on the bass is that it will help to support your creative process. As you develop a greater understanding of the mechanics of harmony and the ability to visualize tonal patterns on the fingerboard, you are building tools for developing your own personal sense of musical expression and opening the way to making some very cool music!

Best of luck,
Michael

Introduction

You are soloing all day, every day!

"I'm soloing all day, every day? What are you joking?"

No, I'm not joking. Every day, from the time you get up in the morning until the time you go to sleep at night, you are taking solos—language solos—for our purposes, English solos, the language you are reading and understanding right now. Unless you've written and memorized a script the night before, every word you say during the day is said as a result of something you happen to be thinking or in response to something said to you. You might start a conversation by saying "How are you?," or you might respond to same question that is asked of you by saying "I'm fine." Clear question, clear answer.

You can do this because you understand every word that you say and every word that is said to you. In fact, when you are speaking, you rarely think about each individual word. You don't have to any more. You know how to combine the sounds of the language into words, phrases and sentences that are understood by people who speak the same language. If you can't find the exact word to convey what you are trying to say, you can either ask for help or go and look it up yourself. If someone says something that you don't quite understand, you can ask them to say it in different ways until you understand it perfectly. No problem. You've been taking language solos for years!

If you can think it, you can say it. If you can hear it and understand it, you can respond to it.

The building blocks that create both spoken and musical languages are very similar. Check out this list.

1. Both use the same alphabet. English uses A to Z. Music uses A to G.
2. Both can be written down and read by others.
3. Both have a basic vocabulary. English has simple words. Music has simple scales and triads—a basic sonic vocabulary.
4. Both have expanded vocabularies that add clarity, variety and impact to what you are saying or playing. English has "big words." Music has exotic sounding scales and chords.
5. Both require that things be spelled a specific way to be understood. The word bass is always spelled b-a-s-s. An F chord is always spelled F-A-C.
6. English has phrases. Music has melodic and rhythmic phrases.
7. English has statements. Music has the melody.
8. English has stories. Music has songs.
9. Stories have paragraphs which divide them up. Songs have sections that divide them up—the intro, letter A, letter B, coda.
10. English has dialects. You can tell if someone is from Tennessee or New York! Music has styles.
11. Plays have scripts that you memorize. Our music has chord progressions, bass lines and solos that you memorize. As your sonic vocabulary and your technique on the bass grow, you'll be able to write your own scripts using every ounce of creativity you have.

Your ability to communicate clearly, effectively and creatively depends entirely upon how well you understand the language you are speaking. Our language, as musicians, is the language of music. This book was written to help you to enhance you ability to think, speak, hear and understand the language of music on the bass.

The "Gee, I Did It Myself" Guide to Setting Up & Adjusting Your Bass

This chapter explains how you can set up your electric bass correctly and keep it that way. Being able to adjust your bass to suit your particular style of playing will not only provide you with a great measure of control over how your bass feels, but will also save you money at the guitar shop on minor adjustments and repairs.

You can easily learn the types of adjustments and repairs that will be discussed, and you will only need to make a small investment in tools and supplies. Major repairs such as re-fretting, complete electronic modification and adjustments that you are either unwilling or unable to do should be handled by a reputable repair shop.

Here's a list of the tools you will need to complete these adjustment procedures. You may purchase them at either a hardware store or a store that specializes in electronic supplies.

1. A small pair of wire cutters, approximately 4 inches long, for cutting strings to proper length when changing strings.

2. Phillips or slot screwdrivers or allen (hex) wrenches used for intonating strings, raising or lowering bridges (string height), and removing the neck of your bass. The choice and size of the tool required for any of these particular tasks will differ from bass to bass. For example, some basses need phillips screwdrivers to intonate the strings; others need slot screwdrivers. European and Japanese basses need allen wrenches in metric sizes to raise and lower the bridges; American made basses call for allen wrenches sized in inches. Old Fender basses require jeweler's screwdrivers to do the job.

3. A slot screwdriver, an allen wrench in metric or inch sizes or a socket wrench— depending upon the make of the bass—to adjust the truss rod (make the neck flatter or more curved).

Most hardware stores sell fold out sets of allen wrenches in either metric or inch sizes for $3 to $4 per set. Although these sets usually have more sizes of allen wrenches than you will ever need, I recommend that you buy allen wrenches in sets because it's real easy to lose a single, tiny wrench in the bottom of your bass bag. Also, for about $20 an all–in–one set of tools, called the "Guitar Tool," at most guitar stores. This tool has a wire cutter, slot and phillips screwdrivers plus all the common sizes of allen wrenches— in both metric and inch sizes—in one convenient package.

4. A can of contact cleaner for cleaning volume and tone controls.

   Be sure that the product is safe for use on or near plastics—it should say so on the label. If you buy and use one that is unsafe, you could cause severe damage to both the electronic components and the finish of your bass.

5. 4–O (0000) steel wool or 600-grit emery cloth used for smoothing out the back of the neck and for cleaning guitar cords with brass plugs.

6. An electronic tuner for intonating the strings. Buy this at a music store on your way home from the hardware store.

N.B. 1: Check over your bass and have the correctly sized tools on hand. Keep them in your bass bag all the time. When you are in dire need of a particular tool, usually in the middle of a gig, you'll find that the tool that works on someone else's instrument won't work on yours. Uh, oh!

READ THE ENTIRE DISCUSSION OF A REPAIR BEFORE TRYING IT!

Section 1: Changing Strings

Changing strings? What could be so difficult about changing strings? Well, nothing is very hard about it. But…if you install a set of strings incorrectly, you face the possibility of having buzzing low strings or of having a string pop off a tuning peg or of having a string break at a most inconvenient moment. You'll need wire cutters for this job.

1. If you are replacing an entire set of strings, you should *replace one string at a time.* This keeps the neck under tension and prevents it from flexing too much. After removing a string, look into the peg, and you will see a small hole—this is where the end of the new string goes.

2. Thread the new string through the bridge and cut the string about 6 inches beyond the empty peg.

3. Put the end of the string into the hole in the peg and start winding.

When changing a string whose tuning peg is furthest away from the fingerboard, like the G string on a Fender, you might not have 6 inches of string beyond the peg—so don't cut the string at all. If you don't put the end of the string into the hole in the peg, you are courting disaster because it could pop off the peg while you are playing. This will make you the object of humiliating and disparaging remarks from the other players in the band that will haunt you the rest of your life! (Just joking!) Be sure that the string is wound onto the peg smoothly from top to bottom and that the string does not overlap itself as this could cause the string to unravel or break. Besides, it looks better, too.

4. If you have reached the bottom of the peg and still have more string to wind, remove the string from the peg and cut ½ to 1 inch off the end of the string, and try again. Because the configuration of the tuning pegs differs from bass to bass (on a Fender, the G string is the longest; on a Music Man, the G string is the shortest), you will have to experiment to find out the exact amount of string to cut off. Once you have changed strings a few times, you will know how much to cut off before winding them on their pegs. On an electric bass, unlike on a guitar, winding the strings all the way to the bottom of the peg is of the utmost importance because it provides the correct downward pressure on the nut and a bit more tension on the string itself. This will help minimize buzzes and rattles that bass strings, especially fat, low ones, often have.

5. Gently tug at a new string after it is brought up to pitch for the first time. New strings tend to stretch a lot before they settle in. For example, an E string will sometimes lose a whole step or more. Re-tune the string and repeat the process until the string stops going real flat. The strings will stretch a bit more as you play, but not for long.

A Checklist for Changing Strings:

(Have you read all of Section 1? This checklist won't do you much good if you haven't!)

1. What you'll need:
   a. a pair of wire cutters
   b. a tuner
   c. a new string or set of strings

2. What to do:
   a. Replace one string at a time.
   b. Cut the string about 6 inches beyond the empty peg.
   c. Put the end of the string into the hole in the peg, and wind it onto the peg from top to bottom with no overlaps.
   d. If the string is too long, cut off ½ to 1 inch, and try again.
   e. Be sure that the string is wound all the way to the bottom of the peg.
   f. Gently tug at a new string after it has been brought up to pitch for the first time, retune, and repeat the process until the string stops going flat.

Section 2: Intonating The Bridge

Tuning pegs get the strings in tune with each other.

On the other hand, adjusting the bridge or saddle of a string gets the string in tune with itself.

In tune with itself?

Check this out! With your bass plugged into your tuner, play a one-octave G on the G string (12th fret), and notice where the tuner registers the pitch. Now, play the harmonic in the same spot by just touching the string, not allowing it to touch the fingerboard, and notice where the tuner registers the pitch. If the two notes are not exactly the same pitch according to your tuner, the string is out of tune with itself, and you must adjust the bridge (saddle).

You should intonate the bridge every time you change strings, especially if you are changing brands or gauges. Even if you are replacing an old set of strings with an identical set from the same manufacturer, you should check the intonation at the bridge because it's possible that even with modern manufacturing techniques, a string's gauge may be off just enough to require readjustment.

To do this job, you will need your tuner; or if you don't own a tuner yet, you will need a remarkably good ear sensitive to differences in pitch of five cents or less. (Tuners measure pitch in cents—100 cents to the half step.) You can purchase good, compact tuner at a guitar shop for around $50 – $75. Watch for sales. Try to find an automatic, chromatic one that will respond to pitch changes without having to change a switch on the tuner every time you change pitch—a real time saver. Also, a tuner will come in very handy when you are trying to tune up while the drummer is checking out a new bass drum or some new cymbals! Depending on the type of bridge on your bass, you will need a phillips or a slot screwdriver or an allen (hex) wrench to adjust the set screw for each individual saddle.

1. Plug your bass into the **input** jack of your tuner and turn up the volume knob all the way. With a two pickup bass, turn up both volume controls; or if your bass has a pan pot, turn it to the center position (both pickups on).
2. Starting with the open G string, play the octave G harmonic and remember where the tuner registers. (Most tuners use either 0 or 440 as the reference point for a note being in tune.) Now, play the note G and see if the meter on the tuner returns to the same spot as the fingered note did.
3. If the fingered note is **sharp** to the harmonic, turn the screw—usually found at the very bottom of the bridge assembly—**clockwise** a quarter turn. (The saddle will move toward the rear of the bridge assembly.)
4. If the fingered note is **flat** to the harmonic, turn the screw **counterclockwise** a quarter turn. (The saddle will move toward the front of the bridge assembly.) If the saddle doesn't move, push on the head of the screw with the tool you are using until the saddle is seated firmly against the back of the bridge assembly.

5. Compare the two pitches (fingered note and harmonic) again. Although their points on the meter may have changed, you will notice that the difference between the two pitches has decreased. Continue in this manner until both the fingered note and the harmonic give matching readings on the tuner. During this process, it doesn't matter if the tuner isn't reading 0 or 440. As long as the two notes give the same reading, you are all right. By applying this procedure to each string, each string should be fairly well in tune with itself.

Fine Tuning Your Bass

To truly fine tune your bass, especially one with a two-octave neck, you should intonate each string at the octave and a fifth (high D on the C string) as well as at the octave. After you have intonated the octave and its harmonic to your satisfaction, move up to the octave and a fifth (19th fret), and repeat the process.

Now, return to the octave fret and if those notes still match, move on to the next string. If they don't, repeat the process at the octave, and recheck the octave and a fifth. Continue in this manner until the notes match at both points on the neck.

If it isn't possible to get the two points to match, one of two things could be wrong. The string itself could be untrue (loose or uneven windings), or the frets of your bass might be slightly off. In either case, try to find an average between the two, and move on to the next string.

N.B. 2: Often, your tuner will measure the octave and a fifth fingered note as being sharper than the octave fingered note. As long as the octave and a fifth fingered note is the same as its harmonic and the octave fingered note does the same, you are OK.

This procedure may seem rather involved; but as with changing strings, the more you do it the faster and easier it becomes. There is nothing worse than playing an exposed line high up on the bass and having it be out of tune. "But I just tuned my bass!," you say. This "two-point" intonating procedure will not only bring the upper register of your instrument into perfect tune with the rest of the fingerboard, but it will also benefit your low strings a lot.

The upper register of the E string, or the B string on a 5-string bass, usually sounds flabby; that is, the notes just don't seem to center in. Using the two–point intonating method usually cures this problem, allowing you to play notes high up on low strings that sound clear and well-centered.

N.B. 3: This section has dealt with Fender-style bridges only (i.e., those bridges with the adjustment screws located at the end of the bridge assembly). If your bass has an intonating procedure that requires you to remove the string from the saddle, loosen an allen screw, move the saddle by hand, tighten the allen screw, bring the string up to pitch, and only then check its intonation, or if the bass requires some other equally ingenious (read "tedious") method, check with your dealer or repair shop if you aren't sure how to do it. The Fender-style bridge is the most common one on the market. Although this section can't begin to cover every bass bridge ever made, the remarks concerning matching fingered notes and harmonics on your tuner do apply to all types of bridges.

N.B. 4: This section is pretty involved. Be sure you understand all of it before moving ahead.

A Checklist for Intonating the Bridge:

1. What to remember:

   a. Tuning pegs get the strings in tune with each other.

   b. Intonating the bridge gets each string in tune with itself.

   c. Intonate the bridge every time you change strings.

   d. The two–point intonating procedure will not only improve the pitch of your instrument, but it will also improve its sound.

2. What you'll need:

   a. a tuner

   b. a cord

   c. a screwdriver (either slot or phillips) or an allen wrench

3. What to do:

   a. Plug your bass into the tuner, and turn up all of the volume controls.

   b. Starting with the G string, play both the octave (12th fret) and the G harmonic in the same spot. Compare the two readings on the tuner.

   c. If the fingered note is **sharp** to the harmonic, turn the screw **clockwise.**

   d. If the fingered note is **flat** to the harmonic, turn the screw **counterclockwise.**

   e. Continue comparing tuner readings and adjusting the screw until the tuner readings match. Move on to the next string.

   f. To fine tune your bass, repeat steps b through e at the octave and a fifth (19th fret). Compare the notes at the 19th fret with those at the 12th fret. Make any necessary changes.

Section 3: Adjusting The Truss Rod

The truss rod—the metal rod built into the neck of every wood neck bass—keeps the neck straight when the strings are brought up to full tension (i.e. when the bass is in tune). Depending upon the particular bass, the screw or socket used for the adjustment of the truss rod is located at the base of the neck where the neck joins the body or in the peghead, oftentimes concealed under a metal or plastic plate that you must remove with a small phillips screwdriver.

As the location of the adjusting screw varies from bass to bass, so does the tool needed to accomplish the task. Old Fenders require a slot screwdriver to be used at the base of the neck; new Fenders use an allen wrench in the peghead. Most newer basses use an allen wrench in the peghead; some others require a socket wrench.

For those of you who own basses with graphite necks, read on to discover what you are missing out on. Graphite necks don't have truss rods!

The neck of your bass is not perfectly flat. If it were, the bass would be impossible to play. As you played a note, the string would hit all the frets at once, resulting in nothing but noise. A slight warp or bow, as it is more commonly called, is required to make the bass playable.

To check the bow in the neck of your bass, hold down the E string at both the first and last frets. With the full length of the string this close to the fretboard, the bow will be easy to see. Also, you should check the bow on the G string side of the neck. When both ends of the string are being held down, the space between the string and the frets should be about the same as on the E string side. If it isn't, the neck might be twisted and should be checked at your repair shop.

No adjustments to the truss rod need to be made if...

1. near the middle of the neck, the space between the string and the fretboard is about $\frac{1}{16}$ of an inch;

2. when playing the instrument, there is little or no fret buzz; and

3. the bass is comfortable to play.

Adjustments to the truss rod may not be necessary if...

the bow of the neck is OK and yet

1. the bass produces a lot of fret noise; or

2. it feels hard to play.

Here are some reasons why adjustment of the truss rod may not be necessary:

1. Fret noise on a single note at any point on the neck:

This usually is caused by a worn or damaged fret. Playing hard, especially when using round wound strings, wears out frets rather quickly. To check frets for wear, pull the string over the noisy fret to the side, and look for gouges, cuts or indentations. If damage to the frets is light, it's time to take your bass into the shop for a fret "dressing"—filing and polishing. If the damage is severe and widespread, a complete fret replacement is in order. When looking for a good repair shop, be sure to ask friends if they have had a similar job done and if they were happy with the work.

2. Condition of the strings:

If, after checking for fret wear, you find that the frets are in good condition yet you still suffer from fret noise, the strings themselves may be the cause of the problem. As strings age, the constant mashing against the frets will cause their undersides to flatten out, eliminating the possibility of a good, quiet contact with the frets. Dirty or dead strings have lost the responsiveness they had when new, and no amount of pulling or pounding will bring them back to life. Boiling dirty, old strings cleans out the windings, making them useful for a short while. If your strings have flat spots or are real old, change them—and a good deal of the noise will go into the trash can with the old strings.

3. Improper string height:

If your frets and strings are OK and the noise problem persists, your strings may be too low. With the bass volume all way the down, test for string height. Play chromatically up one string until the buzzing starts. Raise the bridge of that string ever so slightly (a quarter turn or so), and test for buzzes again. If all is well, move on to the next string. If not, continue raising the set screws little by little until the buzzing goes away. A small amount of fret buzz is OK; you don't want to raise the strings up so high that the bass is hard to play.

4. Hard to play notes close to the nut:

If this is happening, the nut is probably too high. Also, most new basses suffer from this problem. If you have changed from a light gauge set of strings to a medium or heavy set, the grooves cut into the nut may not be wide enough to accommodate the new strings. The new strings will ride up too high in the nut. Unless you have a light touch with a rattail file, let the repair shop lower the nut for you. One swipe too many and you will have to need the entire nut replaced.

Repair shops love do-it-yourselfers!

5. Improper fretting technique:

Too little or too much left-hand pressure will cause the frets to buzz. When playing lightly, you don't need to grind the strings into the frets. Save that for hard playing. You must find a balance between your left-hand fretting technique and your right-hand plucking technique that suits the style of music you are playing. Try to play notes directly behind each fret. If the fingernails on your left hand are too long, you will not be able to make good string to fret contact. Playing the bass is not a pretty thing!

Adjustments to the truss rod are necessary if...

you've decided that none of the above apply to your particular situation.

Here are some reasons why the adjustment of the truss rod are necessary:

1. Excessive fret noise or buzzing:

The neck is probably too flat.

2. Excessive left hand pressure required to play:

The neck is probably bowed too much. If it resembles something that would be put to better use on an archery court, it's time to act!

3. Changing string gauges:

Heavy strings, when brought up to pitch, place more tension on a neck set up for lighter ones. This causes the neck to bow too much. Conversely, when light strings are used in place of heavy ones, the neck will flatten out because the amount of tension required to bring them up to pitch is less than for the heavier strings you were using.

4. Changes in the weather:

An increase in the humidity will cause the neck to bow as excess moisture is absorbed into the wood. Drier than normal weather will make the neck flatten out. The weather will become an important factor in the play–ability of your bass if you travel around to different locations or live in a place that experiences drastic seasonal changes.

5. Changing your style of playing:

When changing from a light style of playing to a more aggressive one, you will need more bow in the neck to avoid noises and choked notes. If you prefer a lighter style of playing, a flatter neck will suit you better. I am referring to your general style of playing, not to stylistic changes required when moving from one type of song to another—for example, pop to slap to jazz.

If you have determined that the truss rod should be adjusted, here's how to go about it. Keep in mind that all of the following remarks regarding the direction in which the truss rod screw is to be turned refer to your bass in its normal playing position—the peghead of the bass pointing to your left. If you play a left–handed bass, reverse the turning directions.

1. Lower the pitch of all the strings at least one whole step.
2. If the truss rod adjustment screw is located at the base of the neck and you want to
   a. make the neck **flatter**—turn the screw **clockwise** (away from you), or
   b. **increase the bow** of the neck—turn the screw **counterclockwise** (toward you). (If access to the screw is difficult, you must remove the neck, turn the screw, reattach the neck, bring the strings up to pitch and then check things out...Sorry.)

3. If the adjustment screw is located in the peghead and you want to

    a. make the neck **flatter**—turn the screw **counterclockwise** (toward you); or

    b. **increase the bow** of the neck—turn the screw **clockwise** (away from you). No matter where the adjustment screw is located, use caution while you turn the screw. When either flattening the neck or increasing the bow of the neck, sometimes only a quarter turn of the screw will produce the desired result. Too much force on a tight truss rod could strip its threads, rendering it and the neck useless. Every once in a while, especially with a new instrument, the truss rod may never have been adjusted, and you could find yourself turning the screw a good deal before you feel that anything has been accomplished. In either case, stop turning the screw as soon as you feel resistance with the tool. Bring the strings back up to pitch and recheck the bow of the neck. If all looks well and the neck feels good when you are playing, your job is done.

4. If the neck has not settled far enough—or has settled too far—in the direction you wanted it to go, repeat steps 1 and either step 2 or 3 until you are happy with the result.

5. In case the truss rod screw is stuck, here are two methods that may free it up:

    a. Hold the body of the bass tightly against your body with one arm, grab the peghead with your other hand, and gently rock the neck back and forth. Try turning the screw again; or

    b. Have a friend hold the body of the bass securely against a tabletop. As you bend the neck in the desired direction, try turning the screw in the proper direction.

    When using either of these two methods, be careful that you don't force the screw.

    Occasionally, a neck that has not been adjusted in a while will return to its original shape a day or two after you have adjusted it. Don't panic! Some bass necks, especially brand new ones that have never been adjusted and very old ones that haven't been adjusted in years, need a little more coaxing. Just repeat the adjustment procedure, and this time it should stay in place. If it doesn't, and nothing you can do seems to solve the problem, take the bass to your (one hopes) friendly repair shop.

About repair shops...

A professional shop is equipped to handle all kinds of seemingly unsolvable problems. If you aren't happy with the work the shop has done for you, ask to have the job redone. A reputable repair shop will always try to satisfy you or, in case it can't, the repairman will be able to explain why the job you want done can't be done. Also, as the technicians at the shop learn how you like your instrument to behave, they will give you excellent service every time you return. If a shop can't or won't work with you, move on to another shop.

Remember—word of mouth is the best recommendation for a repair shop.

A Checklist for Adjusting the Truss Rod:

1. What to remember:

a. The truss rod is used to find and hold the correct bow in the neck.

b. The neck needs to have a slight amount of bow in it for the bass to be playable.

2. What you'll need:

a. Either a slot screwdriver, an allen wrench, or a socket wrench; plus

b. a small phillips screwdriver if the adjustment screw is hidden under a plate.

3. What to do:

a. Check the bow of the neck.

b. If the bow of the neck is OK, reread items 1–5 on pages 7–8. Make the necessary repairs or adjustments.

c. If the truss rod is the problem (see items 1–5 on pages 8–9), lower the strings at least one whole step, and locate the truss rod adjustment screw.

    1. If the screw is located at the base of the neck, turn the screw clockwise to flatten the bow and counterclockwise to increase it.

    2. If the screw is located in the peghead, turn the screw counterclockwise to flatten the bow and clockwise to increase it.

d. Gently turn the screw a quarter to a half turn. Bring the strings back up to pitch, and check the neck.

e. If you've gone too far, turn the screw a bit in the opposite direction.

f. If the truss rod is frozen in place, check out item 5 on page 10. Be extra careful!

g. If the neck returns to its original shape in a day or two, repeat the procedure.

h. If nothing you can do solves the problem, take the bass to a good repair shop.

4. Apology:

Sorry about all the "Ifs." Every bass neck is different. No two pieces of wood behave in the same manner.

Section 4: Adjusting The Tilt (Angle) Of The Neck

The angle of the neck may be adjusted only on basses with bolt-on necks. Having worked your way through the previous 7 ½ pages, you would think that your bass would be in perfect playing condition by now. But there are times when no amount of truss rod adjusting or string lowering or raising will create a smooth, even feel all over the neck. Usually when this happens, the notes above the octave on any string (the upper register) are a bit harder to play than those below the octave. Adjusting the tilt of the neck should solve the problem.

If you own a bass with a "through-the-body" design (neck and body are one piece) and you have this problem, only very fine adjustments of both the truss rod and string height can solve it. For you bolt–on neck owners, this adjustment may be done in one of two ways.

If your bass has a neck-tilting screw built in:

A newer Fender, an old Music Man, or any other bass that has a small hole in the neck mounting plate found on the back of the instrument, has a neck-tilting screw built in. Basses with this feature usually have three rather than four screws holding the neck onto the body.

1. Lower the pitch of the strings so they flop on the fingerboard. Loosen the neck mounting screws two or three full turns.

2. Insert yet another size allen wrench. The wrench that just fits into the hole is, more often than not, the correct size. (If your instrument requires a particular size allen wrench to adjust the truss rod and another size to raise or lower the strings, this is the third size allen wrench you will need. Buy a whole set.) While standing the bass up on a table or on your lap, use one hand to press the neck into the body. The screws will stick out of the back of the bass. With your other hand, slowly turn the screw clockwise until you feel resistance. Turn the wrench another one-half turn and you should see the neck raise slightly.

3. Remove the allen wrench, tighten the screws, bring the bass back up to pitch and check to see if the problem has been solved. If not, repeat the procedure.

4. If you have gone too far, lower the strings, loosen the neck and turn the screw a bit in the opposite direction. Tighten everything up and check it again. Things should be OK this time.

Your bass does not have a neck-tilting screw built in:

Unfortunately, most basses don't have that neat little hole in the neck mounting plate. So…

1. Loosen the strings (you don't have to take them off of the pegs) and remove the neck from the bass. When removing the neck, just turn the screws far enough to get the neck off. (Leaving the screws in the body of the bass will make re–attaching the neck easier.)

2. Find a book of matches and cut off a quarter of the cover. Place the piece of matchbook cover in the bottom of the neck slot.

3. Screw the neck back on, making sure that the torque on each screw is about the same. Bring the strings up to pitch and check out the feel of the neck in the upper register. If it feels good, your job is done.

4. If it doesn't, you must repeat the entire tedious process all over again, adding or subtracting another piece of matchbook cover until the upper register of the neck feels better.

"Why a piece of matchbook cover?," you ask. Well, legend has it that over the years as repair technicians were doing this job, they reached for the closest thing at hand to act as a thin shim. Nine times out of ten it was a book of matches. Clever, huh? You may use anything that you think will work—a thin piece of metal or a piece of inner tube, etc. Because a piece of paper or rubber can't give you as precise an adjustment as the built–in tilter described above, you may have to adjust the height of the strings ever so slightly to finish the job. This may seem like a lot of trouble to go through, but the result of fine tuning the neck will make your bass feel better under your hands than it has ever felt.

A Checklist For Tilting The Neck:

1. What to remember:

a. Tilting the neck brings the upper register of the bass closer to the strings.

b. The entire neck will have a uniform feel.

2. What you'll need:

a. Your set of allen wrenches and a phillips screwdriver.

b. A book of matches or some other shim if your bass doesn't have a tilter built in.

3. What to do:

a. If your bass has a tilter built in:

    1. Loosen both the strings and the neck mounting screws.

    2. Insert the allen wrench, and turn it in the proper direction.

    3. Tighten up the neck, bring the strings up to pitch, and check it out.

    4. If you've gone too far, repeat the process.

b. If your bass does not have a tilter built in:

    1. Loosen the strings and remove the neck.

    2. Place a $\frac{1}{2}$ inch piece of matchbook cover in the bottom of the neck slot.

    3. Replace the neck, bring the strings up to pitch, and check it out.

    4. If you don't notice a change, repeat step 1, and place another piece of matchbook cover or whatever type of shim you are using on top of the first one. Repeat step 3.

    5. If you've gone too far, use thinner shims.

Section 5: Cleaning Noisy Volume And Tone Controls

Most of the noise, pops and squawks you encounter when turning the knobs on your bass are caused by the dirt, dust and sweat that accumulates in them over time. Your can of contact cleaner will cure 99% of these problems. Pots (i.e. potentiometers, volume and tone controls) rarely wear out. It's the grime that creeps into them that makes you think you have a $100 repair bill staring you in the face.

1. All you have to do is remove the knobs with either a slot screwdriver or an allen wrench, insert the thin plastic straw that came with the can of cleaner into the spray button and squirt the cleaner down into the pot.

2. If you can gain access to the body of the pot by either removing the cover on the back of the bass or by removing the mounting plate on the front of the bass, you will be able to do a more thorough job of cleaning by squirting the spray directly into the pot.

3. Rotate the shaft of the pot back and forth a few times, and—like magic—the noise is history. If you haven't cleaned the pots for a while, a repeat application could be necessary. Replace the knobs and you're in business!

4. If the noise won't go away, you may have to replace a pot or two. If you know how to solder, find out the value of the pots and replace them yourself. If you don't, go to the repair technician.

Section 6: Smoothing Out The Back Of The Neck

Over time, the finish on the back of the neck builds up a layer of dirt and "crud" using your own sweat as glue. Wiping off your bass every time you finish playing will certainly keep this build up to a minimum. As the finish wears, dirt will creep in no matter how careful you are in your cleaning. For those of you who have removed the finish from the back of the neck, the problem is even worse. The unprotected wood expands and contracts with changes in temperature and humidity and soaks up dirt like a sponge—the neck feels sticky all the time.

Here's where your 4–0 steel wool or emery cloth comes in.

1. With either the steel wool or the emery cloth in your hand (be sure to use a large enough piece to cover the neck from edge to edge), cup your hand around the neck and lightly rub the entire length of the neck being careful to follow its contour.

2. Check the neck after a few passes, you don't want to take the finish off! The neck will feel smooth as silk, probably better than it did when it was new.

Section 7: Cords

Very simply, buy the best cords you can afford. According the 2nd edition of the *Yahama Sound Reinforcement Handbook:*

> Hum, crackles, [or buzzes] can all be caused by a cable [guitar cord]. If you think about it, regardless of how high the quality of your…[bass, amplifier, speakers and effects]… may be, the entire system can be degraded or silenced by a bad cable. You should never try to save money by cutting corners with cable.

> All wire is not the same, nor are all look alike connectors made the same way. Even if the overall diameter, wire gauge and general construction are similar, two cables may have significantly different electrical and physical properties such as resistance, capacitance between conductors, inductance between conductors [an open, full range, quiet sound], overall flexibility, durability, and the ability to withstand crushing or sharp bends [will the cord last more than a week]…[1989, p.281]

Run this experiment. Using the same bass and amp and without changing the settings, listen to a bad cord then replace it with a good one. Not only will you hear a difference in improved tone quality and volume, but also in how much more quiet it is (i.e. improved signal to noise ratio).

Avoid cords with molded plugs.

Molded (plastic) plugs can't be fixed if they break and are usually attached to cheap, bad-sounding cable.

Avoid coil cords.

The rubber will be flexible for years while the thin wire inside fatigues and breaks.

Avoid extra long cords.

Not only does the sound of your bass lose high end after 18 feet or so of length, you are also guaranteed to have someone in the band trip over it perhaps sending you, him and your gear flying all over the stage. Not a pretty sight! If you really need to be far away from your amp, invest in a wireless system. Again, buy the best you can afford.

…Finally

You are going to enjoy playing your bass a lot more if it feels good in your hands. The simple procedures described in this chapter will not only allow you to come up with your own personal "feel" for your bass, but they will also save you a lot of money. As you become more confident making these and other adjustments to your bass, the instrument will become "yours." Time spent wondering why your bass doesn't work will be replaced with time spent getting into your music.

Things to have in your bass case all the time:

Your personal checklist

- A tuner.

- A couple of cords—you never know when a cord may decide not to work.

- A new set of strings—you never know when a string might break.

- Tools for adjusting your bass—check off the tools you need for each bass you own and keep them in the case with that bass. If you own more than two instruments, copy this page.

Bass #1: _____

Number of strings: _____

Adjusting the bridge:

- Intonating the bridge:
    - ❏ phillips screwdriver
    - ❏ slot screwdriver
    - ❏ allen wrench
    - ❏ inch size: ____
    - ❏ metric size: ____

- Setting string height:
    - ❏ allen wrench
    - ❏ inch size: ____
    - ❏ metric size: ____
    - ❏ jeweler's screwdriver size:____

Adjusting the truss rod:

- ❏ slot screwdriver
- ❏ allen wrench
- ❏ inch size: ____
- ❏ metric size: ____
- ❏ socket wrench size: ____

Bass #2: _____

Number of strings: _____

Adjusting the bridge:

- Intonating the bridge:
    - ❏ phillips screwdriver
    - ❏ slot screwdriver
    - ❏ allen wrench
    - ❏ inch size: ____
    - ❏ metric size: ____

- Setting string height:
    - ❏ allen wrench
    - ❏ inch size: ____
    - ❏ metric size: ____
    - ❏ jeweler's screwdriver size: ____

Adjusting the truss rod:

- ❏ slot screwdriver
- ❏ allen wrench
- ❏ inch size: ____
- ❏ metric size: ____
- ❏ socket wrench size: ____

2

The 1st Position

This chapter introduces the 1st position—probably the most important position on the neck because it is used for bass parts more than any other position on the bass.

It starts with your first (index) finger on the first fret of the bass—A♭ (G♯) on the G string, E♭ (D♯) on the D string, B♭ on the A string, and F on the E string. (C on the B string.)

I know that you've been playing in this area of the bass for a while and can find your way around it pretty well. But I'll bet you don't know that this position is unique in several ways:

- All the open strings are available for use in scale and chord patterns.
- The notes on the E string (4-string basses) or on the B string (5-string basses) in this position are not found any other place on the neck.
- Without having to shift you hand, you can play more scales, chords in this position than you can in any other position on the neck.
- You can play in the 1st position every scale and chord you know now or will learn.
- Almost all the fingerings for scale and chords in this position are unique to this position.

Here are the notes in the 1st position (include the notes on the B string if you have one):

Playing with all four fingers of the left hand

You will enhance your playing a great deal if you use all four fingers on the left hand. Because all your fingers are available for playing notes, you will cut dramatically the amount of shifting you have to do; and you will reduce a lot of ugly fret and string noise.

If you don't usually play in this portion of the neck with all four fingers of your left hand, here are a few simple exercises to help you get used to it. Exercises 1 through 9 on the next page go up and down one string. Although notes given are on the A string, practice each exercise on all four (five) strings. Exercises 10 and 11 cover four strings. Repeat each exercise until you are comfortable with it, then move on.

A few things to remember:

1. Stay as relaxed and loose as you possibly can. Don't squeeze the neck.

2. When you play a note with your second finger, keep your first finger down on the neck in playing position. When you play a third-finger note, your first and second fingers should be down on the neck as well. For fourth-finger notes, all four fingers should be in their proper playing position. In the time it takes you and your left hand to become accustomed to playing this way, you'll feel your left hand becoming more flexible, stronger and less tense as all of your fingers learn to support one another. You will find it easier to control your fingers, especially your third and fourth fingers, if your hand is acting as a unit.

3. Keep your fingers and your thumb arched—just as they would be if you didn't have the bass in your hand. You don't walk around with you fingers perfectly straight and your thumb bent back, do you? Strive to play the bass with your whole body as comfortable and relaxed (read *normal*) as possible.

   If you are standing, distribute your weight evenly on both feet. If you are sitting on a chair or stool, *don't slouch.* (Sorry if I sound like your dad here.) If you are suffering an excessive amount of aches and pains, your body is telling you that you are doing something wrong. If you work to erase every bit of tension from your body as you play, it will usually cure what ails you.

4. Keep an eye on your little finger. Don't let it curl up when you aren't using it. That's a sign of tension. Be careful to keep you little finger over the neck at all times. It won't do you much good dangling in midair! As you lift up any finger on your left hand it shouldn't pop up off the fingerboard—another sign of a tense hand. Keep your fingers above and close to the string, ready to play.

5. If you are having trouble keeping your hand open in this part of the neck, practice the exercises up higher on the fretboard, and move back down the neck as you become more comfortable. Use any four-note group you like. Your goal is to become as relaxed and free in the low end of the neck as you are up at the high end.

4-Finger Exercises (Remember to repeat each exercise until you're comfortable with it!!)

The Chromatic Scale

Here's the chromatic scale (a scale in which a half step [one fret] separates each note) using all the notes found in the 1st position on a 4-string bass. Be sure to use all four fingers of the left hand and to have a smooth, relaxed touch. Keep your hand open!

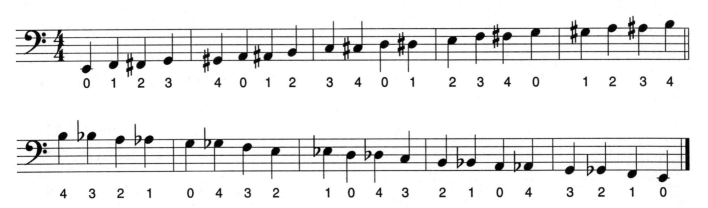

Eight complete one octave chromatic scales are available in the 1st position on a 4-string bass starting with the E chromatic scale. (There are 12 on a 5-string starting with low B.)

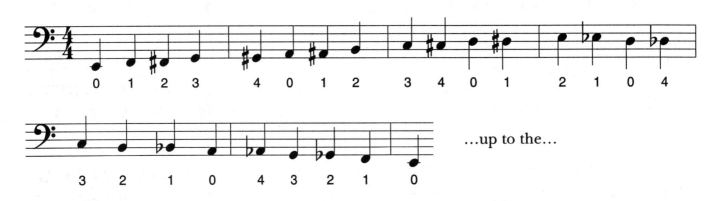

...up to the...

...B chromatic scale.

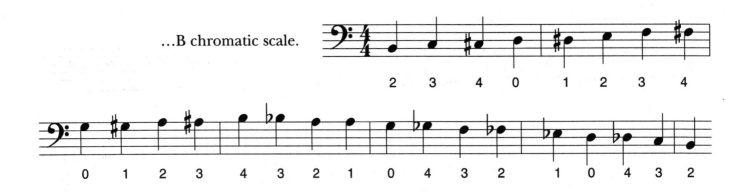

Be sure to practice the six remaining chromatic scales, too: F, F#, G, Ab, A and Bb.

Remember that in the 1st position you will be using **all four fingers and open strings—no shifting.**
So, the F# scale will start with your 2nd finger, G with your 3rd and Ab with your 4th.
For those of you with 5-string basses, add the B, C, Db, D and Eb chromatic scales to the list.

This exercise covers the entire 1st position on a 4-string bass. While practicing, keep all four fingers of your left hand over the string you are playing. Practice the exercise slowly at first until you are very comfortable, and only then increase your speed.

Exercise 12:

1st Position Intervals

Interval Facts:

1. The term "interval" is used to describe the distance between two notes.

2. Intervals are defined by both *type* (2nds, 3rds, 4ths, etc.) and by *quality* (major, minor, perfect, augmented and diminished).

3. The distance between the letters of the alphabet used in music (A–B–C–D–E–F–G) determines the **type** of interval. For example, C *up* to G is called a 5th because the note G is five letters *above* the note C (C–d–e–f–G); C *down* to G is a 4th (C–b–a–G)—four letters *below* the note C.

Example 3:

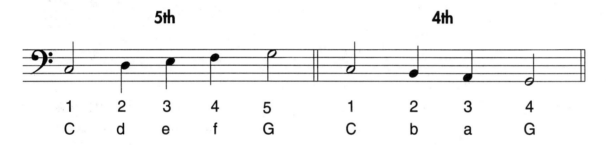

4. The **type** (or number) of the interval does not change as its quality changes. For example, D *up* to A will always be some kind of a 5th no matter if sharps or flats are used; G *down* to F will always be some kind of a 2nd. Remember that the number given to an interval is determined by the number of spaces between its letters, not by the accidentals (flats – ♭, double flats – ♭♭, sharps – ♯ or double sharps – 𝄪) attached to it.

Example 4:

5. The **quality** of an interval (major, minor, augmented or diminished) is determined by the number of half steps (semitones) contained in the interval. For example, a major 3rd—three letters apart—contains four semitones; a minor 3rd, also three letters apart, has three semitones. A 5th—five letters apart—has seven semitones in it; a diminished 5th has six.

An augmented interval is commonly called a plus (+) or sharp (♯) interval (e.g. an aug5th can be called either a +5 or a ♯5). A diminished fifth is often called a flat five (a dim5th is the same as a ♭5). Minor intervals are sometimes called flat (e.g. a m7th = ♭7).

Example 5:

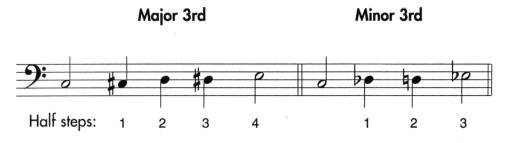

Example 6:

Major and Minor Intervals

Every interval commonly used, from a minor 2nd (one half step or one fret) to a 13th (21 half steps), includes a specific number of half steps. Just as feet and inches measure the exact distance between two points, you use **type** and **quality** to measure the exact distance between two notes.

6. All 2nds, 3rds, 6ths, 7ths, 9ths, 10ths and 13ths are either major or minor intervals. All unisons, 4ths, 5ths, octaves and 11ths are perfect intervals.

Example 6:

Major and Minor Intervals

continued on next page

More Major and Minor Intervals

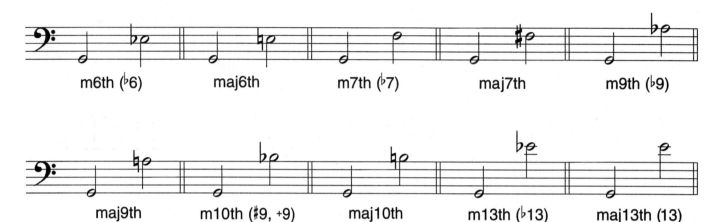

m6th (♭6)   maj6th   m7th (♭7)   maj7th   m9th (♭9)

maj9th   m10th (♯9, +9)   maj10th   m13th (♭13)   maj13th (13)

N.B. 1 When someone asks you to play a 7th, he or she almost always want you to play a minor 7th, not a major 7th. Whether you are being asked to play the 7th interval as part of a line (melodically) or as part of a chord (harmonically), you will find that the minor 7th interval is used both in bass lines and in chords (e.g., m7th and dom7th chords) much more than the major 7th interval. As a result, the term "7th" as used in popular music means minor 7th. A major 7th interval or chord is asked for by name; same for dim7th.

N.B. 2 The m10th interval is usually designated as a ♯9 or a +9 in chords. According to Interval Fact 4 on page 22, the quality of the interval does not affect the type of the interval. In the example above, the +9 interval should be spelled G to A♯. The problem is that most people don't like using certain note names, A♯ being one of them. It's not that those notes aren't used in melodies, scales and chords, it's just that B♭ is easier to say than A♯ for most people. Some other difficult notes are E♯, B♯, F♭, C♭ or any note that has either a double sharp or a double flat attached to it. +9's (♯9) are favorite targets for this type of enharmonic change.

Example 6a:

Perfect Intervals

unison   4th   5th   octave   11th

N.B. 3 The term, "perfect," isn't used in pop or jazz music very much. A perfect 5th is called a "5th," a perfect 4th is called a "4th," and so on. The term is usually reserved to describe a "normal" or "regular" 4th, 5th, octave or 11th that has not been raised or lowered a half step (augmented or diminished). Be aware that the term exists and remember what it means, so in case someone asks you to play a "perfect" interval of some sort, your reply won't be "Huh...?".

7. When any **major interval** is **lowered** by a **half step,** it becomes **minor.**

Example 7:

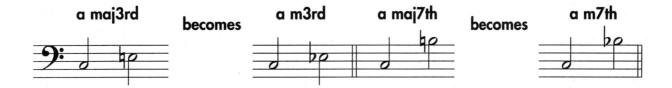

8. When any **minor** or **perfect interval** is lowered a **half step,** it becomes **diminished.**

Example 8:

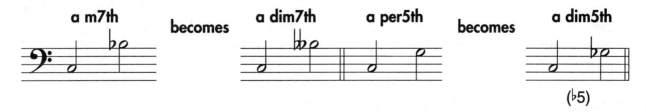

9. When any **perfect or major interval** is **raised a half step,** it becomes **augmented.**

Example 9:

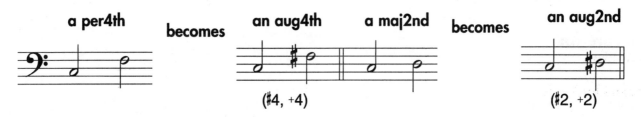

10. *Remember that the reverse of items 7 through 9 is also true.*
   a. When any **minor interval** is **raised a half step,** it becomes **major.** (See Example 7.)
   b. When any **diminished interval** is **raised a half step,** it becomes either **minor** or **perfect.** (See Example 8.)
   c. When any **augmented interval** is **lowered by a half step,** it becomes either **perfect** or **major.** (See Example 9.)

11. This diagram will help you to visualize the half step relationships that exist between major, minor, perfect, augmented and diminished intervals regardless of type (2nd, 3rd, 4th, etc.).

    If, for example, you start from Major and go down the left side of the diagram, as the major interval is lowered half step by half step, it becomes Minor, and finally Diminished. Go up the way you came and, by adding half steps, you'll arrive back at the major interval. You may start at any point on the diagram to see how the quality of an interval is changed by raising or lowering it a half step. Cool.

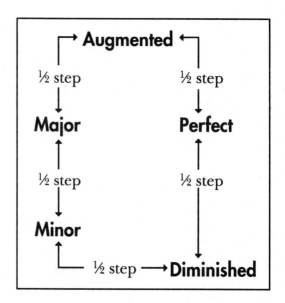

1st Position Interval Exercises

These exercises work their way from major 2nds (aka whole steps) up to octaves, all in the first position. We have already covered minor 2nds (aka half steps)in the chromatic scale exercises. You may not be used to some of the fingerings, but I ask that you do follow them. Not only do these exercises help you to hear the different intervals, they also provide a great work–out for your left hand and also get you used to using all four fingers of your left hand.

Be sure to:

- Relax your whole body;

- Keep your hand open with your thumb and fingers curved as normal;

- Keep a steady tempo;

- Keep your note lengths the same. It doesn't matter if the notes are long, short or anything in between—they should all be the same length!; and, most of all,

- **Relax!** If you feel any tension in either hand, stop playing wait until you feel loose again. Perhaps while you are waiting, you could figure out the cause of the tension.

But first...Enharmonic notes in the 1st position

These exercises will also help you to become more comfortable with enharmonic notes. Enharmonic notes share the same pitch yet have different names—B♯= C, F♭= E. Here are all of the enharmonic notes found in the first position. Double sharps (𝄪) and double flats (♭♭) aren't used in popular music very much these days but you should be aware of their existence, what they mean and how to use them. Unlike most people, you will be comfortable using B♯'s and F♭'s!

N.B. 4: The most commonly used notes, those with naturals, sharps and almost all flats, are shown as half notes. Notes used less often, double sharps and double flats, are shown as quarter notes. Say each note as you play it.

And now...on to the exercises

Fingerings are given for the first half of every exercise. Reverse them for the second half. More often than not, sharps are used going up and flats are used going down. Traditionally, that's how chromatic intervals are written. **Be sure to use the printed fingerings.**

Exercise 13:   Major 2nds

Exercise 14:   Minor 3rds

Exercise 15: Major 3rds

Exercise 16: Perfect 4ths

Move your left hand back and forth for each note—all four fingers should be moving and supporting each other as described in item 2 on page 18. Don't *barre* the strings—fretting two more notes with one finger of your left hand. This exercise calls for a flexible left wrist!

Exercise 17:   Augmented 4ths (♯4 or ⁺4) and Diminished 5ths (♭5)

Exercise 18:   Perfect 5ths

Exercise 19:   Minor 6ths

Exercise 20:   Major 6ths

Exercise 21:   Minor 7ths   (Again, move your left hand for each note. Don't *barre* the strings.)

Exercise 22:   Major 7ths

Exercise 23:   Octaves

3

Major Scales & Chords In the 1st Position

The Major Scale

Major scale facts:

1. Interval construction: 1 = a whole step (2 frets)   1/2 = a half step (1 fret)

	root	maj2	maj3	per4	per5	maj6	maj7	octave
Intervals above root:								
Intervals between scale steps:	1	1	1/2	1	1	1	1/2	

2. Melodic numbering of scale steps:

Scale steps are numbered from bottom to top with the second scale step referred to as the "second" (above the root); the third scale step being the "third", etc. Here is the *melodic* spelling of the scale—a melody or a song:

1   2   3   4   5   6   7   octave

3. Harmonic numbering of scale steps:

When used in chords, however, scale step 2 functions as the 9th of the chord, step 4 as the 11th and scale step 6 as the 13th. Remember – 2 = 9, 4 = 11 and 6 = 13. For example, $B^{\flat 7}$, D^9 and F^{13} are common chord symbols. Here's the *harmonic* spelling of the major scale:

1   9   3   11   5   13   7   8 (octave)

Learning scales harmonically as well as melodically will be a great help when dealing with chords.
We'll learn all scales and modes both ways!

4. Major scale tetrachords:

A major scale, or any other scale for that matter, may be divided in half forming two four note groups—each group called a tetrachord. The *lower tetrachord* contains the first four notes of the scale while the *upper tetrachord* contains the last four.

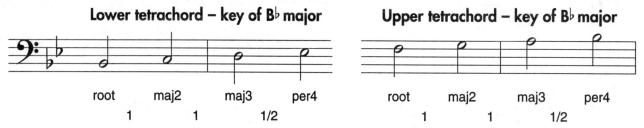

Do you notice that each tetrachord has the same interval structure? This particular group of intervals—whole step–whole step–half step—is called a *major tetrachord.*

In a major scale, the lower and upper tetrachords are separated by a whole step. As we study other scales and modes, we will also study their tetrachords. They will prove to be invaluable aids in line playing and soloing.

Major tetrachords come in a variety of shapes on the fingerboard. Study the fingerboard patterns below and you'll discover that combinations of only three major tetrachord shapes create eight one-octave major scales in the 1st position—all 12 keys on a 5-string bass!

The fingering for Shape 1 is: 0(open string)–2–4–0; Shape 2: 2–4–1–2; Shape 3: 3–0–2–3.

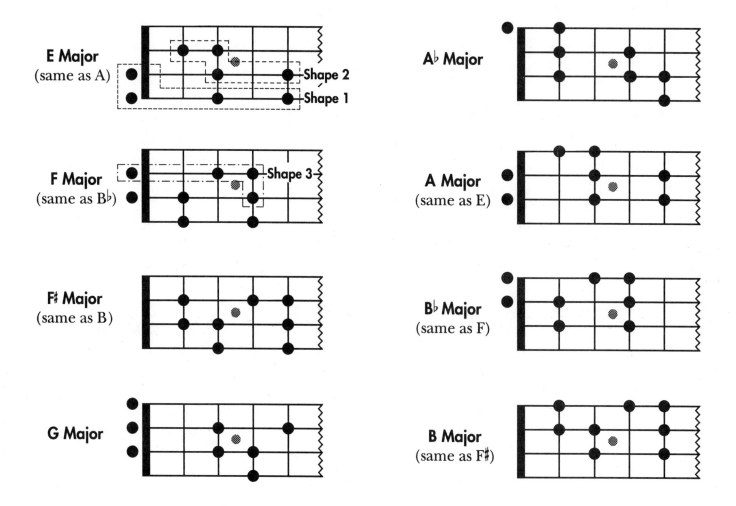

1st Position Major Scale Exercises

- Play all of the exercises with a relaxed left hand.

- Right hand picking should alternate between your index and middle fingers.

- *Subdivide!*

  Subdividing takes simple counting to a new level. Rather than just counting "1–2–3–4" to yourself as you play, subdividing breaks down each beat of the music you are playing into two, four or three parts that enable you to play with increased rhythmic accuracy and, most importantly, a good feel. Depending on the type of music you are playing, each quarter note (one beat) is counted as either eighth notes, sixteenth notes or eighth note triplets. Subdividing silently fills in the *space between the beats*—the *"inside beats"*—providing you with a solid, comfortable cushion for playing music.

  Check out these examples of common subdivisions. As you play through each subdivision, count out loud until you are comfortable with it; then repeat each one counting to yourself. For Examples 1 through 4, only eight quarter notes are played. A few styles of music are listed for each type of subdivision.

1. Simple counting – No subdivision – Bet you can't guess what style of music this is. (I can't either!)

2. Straight eighth notes – rock, pop, metal, reggae, country, classical, etc.

3. Straight sixteenth notes – same as above.

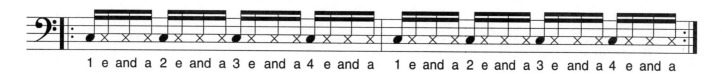

4. Triplets – pop and jazz ballads, rhythm 'n' blues, slow blues, slow shuffles, etc.

5. Tied triplets – Medium to fast tempos for blues, shuffles, etc.

1 and a   2 and a   3 and a   4 and a   1 and a   2 and a   3 and a   4 and a

6. Another way of looking at Example 5 – Same feel, however. Notice the meter change.

1   an   2   an   3   an   4   an   1   an   2   an   3   an   4   an

This is how you'll usually see a shuffle or blues line written out. The top of the bass part might be marked either "Shuffle" or "Shuffle feel." You'll sometimes see a marking like this: All of them mean that the part is to be played with a triplet feel.

Eighth notes   **Dotted eighth and sixteenth notes**

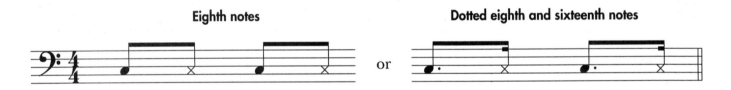

or

Why do some bands "feel" better to you than others? It's because all of the players in the band you like are locked onto the feel (time, groove or style) of the music they are playing. All of the bass lines, the keyboard, guitar and drum patterns and fills, plus the solos are *"in the pocket."* The players are clear on the concept—the subdivisions. Those bands that don't feel too good to you are more than likely made up of players who aren't so clear. If you've ever heard a rock band trying to play jazz or a jazz band trying to play rock, you know what I'm talking about. The rock musicians can't play the swing feel—eighth note triplets—characteristic to jazz music while the jazz musicians can't play the rock feel—straight eighth or sixteenth notes—needed for rock, pop, metal, reggae, latin or classical music, for that matter. These *inside beats,* the subdivisions which *define the style,* will make or break a performance if they aren't paid proper attention.

If you ask a favorite player about subdividing, you might hear something like "Oh, I just feel it." Great…where does that leave you? Don't get discouraged. The players who make you feel so good have learned, through *a lot of listening and a lot of practice,* exactly what the feel—the subdivisions they play without thinking about them—should be for the style of music that they are playing.

Listening to a lot of different styles of music (rock, jazz, blues, etc.) and figuring out the subdivisions that make each style come alive will open up your mind the incredible variety of music that's out there for you to have fun playing.

Practicing subdividing is easy. Doing so will help you to master any style of music you want to play. You'll get much more work if your playing feels good.

Play these 1st position exercises with the subdivisions indicated. Keep the subdivision in your head for each exercise. A metronome set to the actual subdivision may be helpful at first. **Use the printed fingerings.** Keep a steady tempo. Each exercise should be played non-stop from beginning to end. If you've got a 5-string bass, add the low B, C, C♯, D and E♭ scales.

Exercise 1: • Jazz feel

   • Eighth-note triplet subdivision

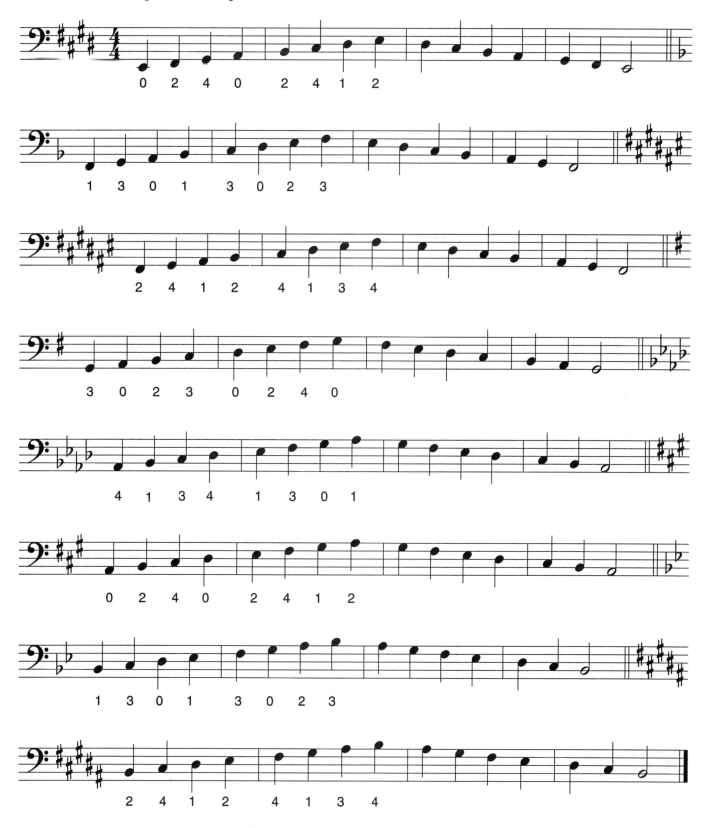

Exercise 2:

- Jazz feel
- Eighth-note triplet subdivision

Exercise 3:

- Rock feel
- Straight eighth note subdivision

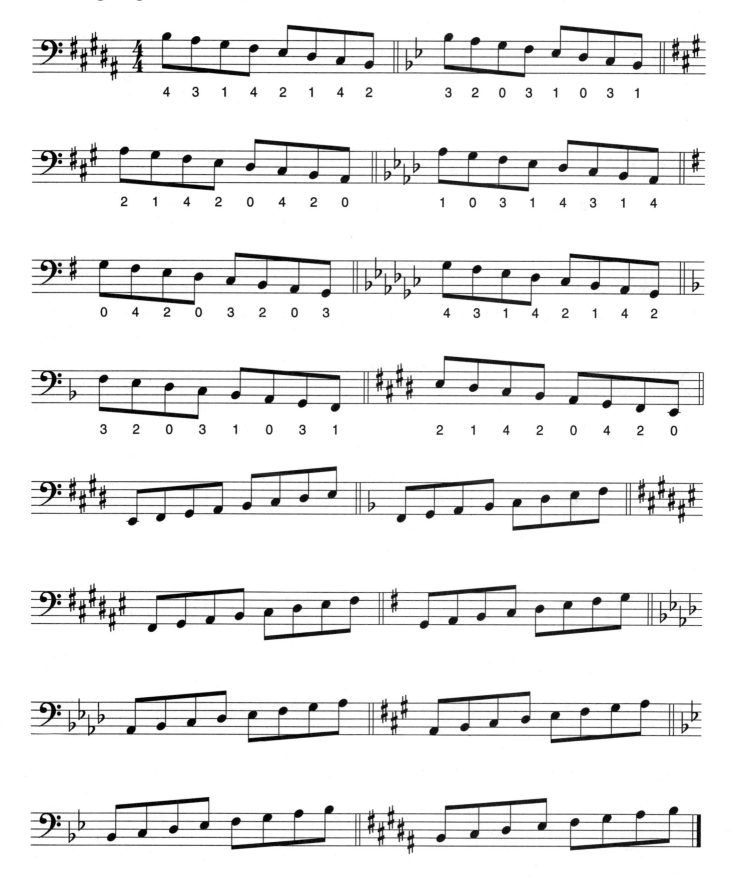

Exercise 4:

- Latin feel
- Straight eighth note subdivision

Exercise 5:

- Rock feel • Straight sixteenth note subdivision
- I've left out the fingerings. You should know them by now!
- Try these variations: 1: ♫♪ ♫♪ 2: ♪♫ ♫♪ 3: ♫♪ ♫♪

Exercise 6:

- Shuffle feel
- Eighth-note triplet subdivision
- This exercise changes keys in whole steps

simile

Exercise 7:

- Shuffle feel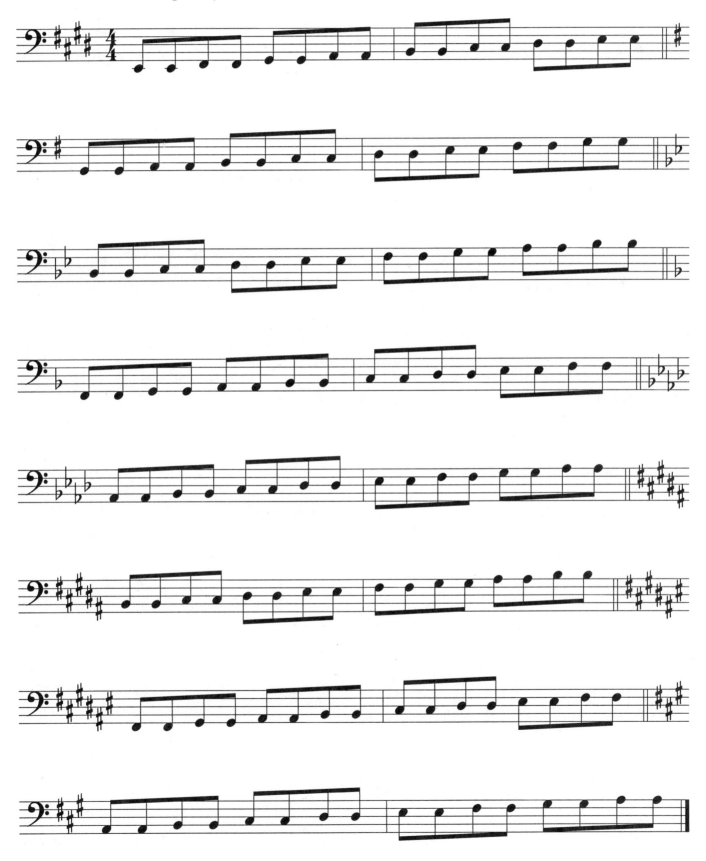

- This exercise changes keys in minor thirds

Exercise 8:

- Jazz feel
- Eighth-note triplet subdivision

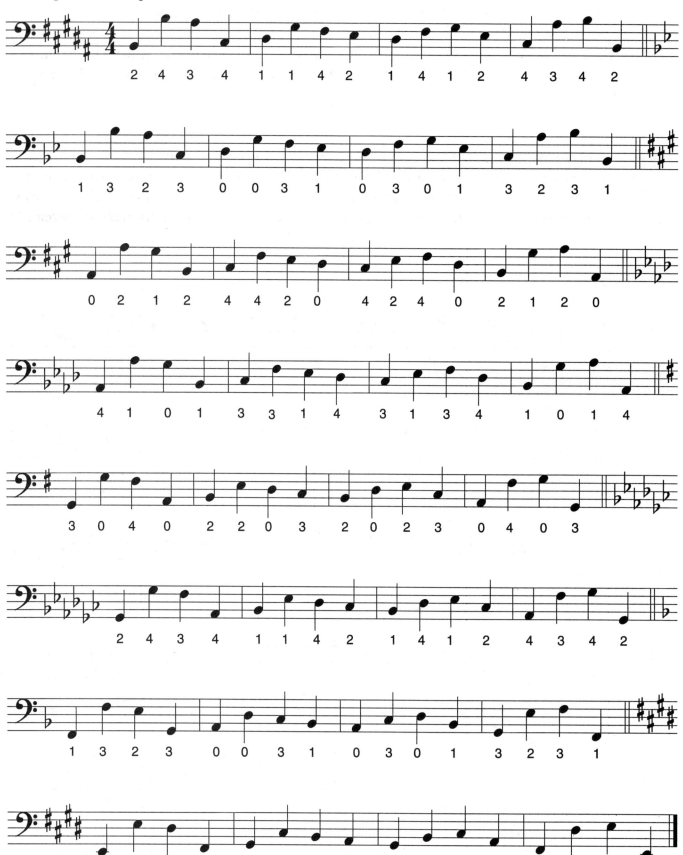

The eight exercises you've just practiced point out a few things about the 1st position and about your playing. Among them:

1. no shifts are needed to play in ten keys: E, F, F♯, G♭, G, A♭, A, B♭, B and C♭;

2. unlike the rest of the neck, where the same fingering pattern could work for all one octave major scales no matter what the key, *five unique sets of fingerings* are required to play Exercises 1 through 8 in the 1st position;

3. if playing with all four fingers of your left hand seems a bit cumbersome in this end of the neck, remember that if you get it together in the 1st position the rest of the neck will be a piece of cake!

As promised in the beginning of Chapter 2, it is possible to play in *every key* in the 1st position. Although you can't play a full octave of the five remaining keys—on a 4-string bass—when restricting yourself to the 1st position, you are able to play portions of them. Here they are. (Those of you with 5- or 6-string basses should have been playing complete one octave scales in every key already!)

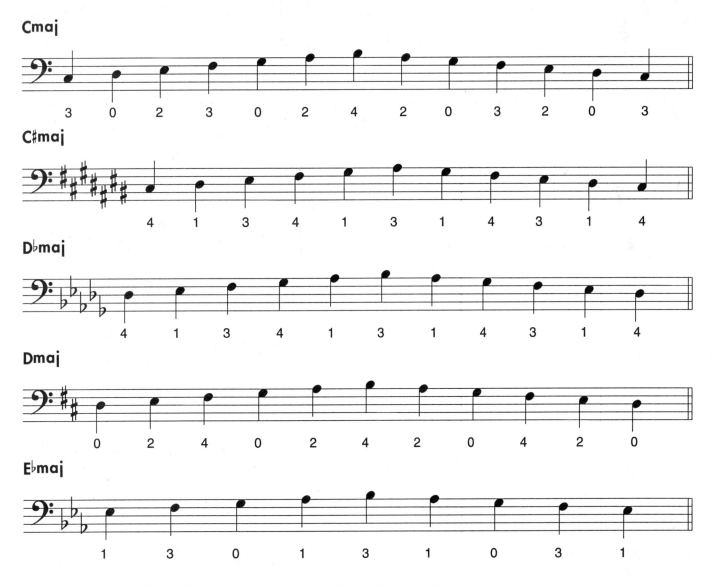

That's a total of 15 keys in one position, all without having to move your hand. Amazing!

Major Scales Covering The Entire 1st Position

You've known or have figured out by now that it's possible to play major scales in the 1st position that cover more that an octave on a 4-string bass. The E major scale may be played a fifth beyond the octave—from low E, the open E string, up to B on the G string. For the keys of F, F#, G♭, G, A♭, A, B♭ and B major in the 1st position, there are notes in those scales that go below the root in addition to notes above the octave. For example, in F major you are able to play a half step below the root and a fourth above the octave. Although it's not possible to play complete one octave scales (root to octave) for the remaining major keys, namely C, C#, D♭, D and E♭, it is possible to play notes below the roots of those keys. In the key of C major, you can only play up to B on the G string, but you can play down to the E below C.

Practicing scales (chords, too) this way helps to break the root-to-octave pattern of playing while at the same time allowing the you to gain complete mastery of every scale and chord in the 1st position. If you are playing a 5-string or a 6-string bass and learn all of your scales and chords covering the entire 1st position, you'll find octaves worth of stuff you never knew existed!

continued on next page

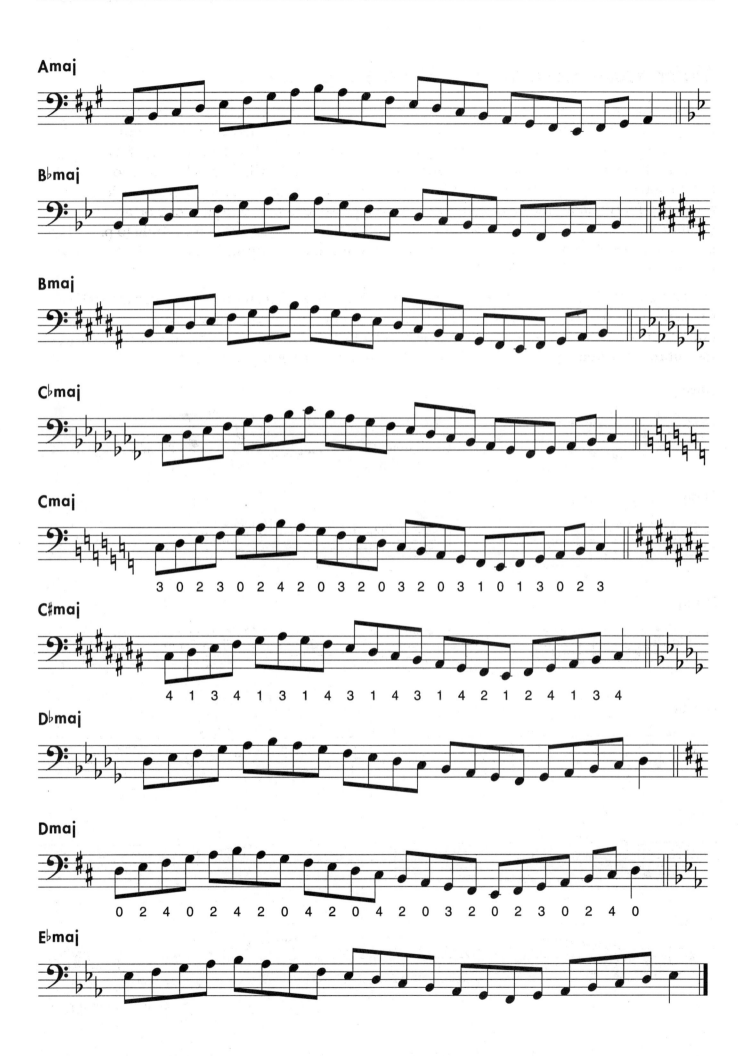

Major Chords In The 1st Position

Some definitions:

- **interval:** the distance between two notes. Remember? If you don't, see page 22.

- **chord:** a combination of more than two notes (i.e. three or more notes) played together.

- **triad:** a chord made up of three notes. It consists of any note of the scale, plus the 3rd and 5th scale steps above it.

- **tonic triad:** a triad built from the first note of a scale. In the example above, the B♭ triad is the tonic triad.

- **major triad:** a triad with a major 3rd and a perfect 5th above the root. The tonic triad of a major scale is a major triad. Check out the B♭ triad one more time.

- **major 7th chord:** a major triad with a major 7th added above the root. The tonic 7th chord of a major scale is a major 7th chord. Common symbols: maj7, Ma7 and ma7.

- **arpeggio:** a chord in which each note is played individually rather than all at once. Chords on the bass are usually played as arpeggios.

- **inverted chord:** a chord in which a note other than the root is the lowest note. A chord with its 3rd as the lowest note is said to be in *1st inversion;* a chord with its 5th as the lowest note is in *2nd inversion.*

Root position **1st inversion** **2nd inversion**

- **major triad exercises in the 1st position:** a series of exercises that should be practiced *a lot.* Don't forget that there are five unique fingerings for chords as well as scales in the 1st position. If you've got more than 4 strings, use them all!

Major triad exercises in the 1st position:

Exercise 10:

- Major triads up and down in half steps.

Exercise 11:

- Can you name the chords in the second half of this exercise?

Exercise 12: This one goes around the cycle of fifths.

Exercise 13: How does each note function in each triad?   Root, 3rd, 5th??

Exercise 14:

- In this last exercise, the chords move up and down in minor thirds.

Your own 1st position major scale and chord ideas:

One more definition:

- **improvising:** the act of using your knowledge of the material at hand—in this case, major triads—to come up with *your own* melodic and harmonic ideas. Free improvisation applied the material you are studying now and will study in the future not only increases your understanding of that material, but also gives you the confidence to actually use everything you are learning in any musical situation.

  Big stuff!

4

On To Some Serious Shifting

Shifting? What's the big deal?

Well...it's no big deal if you always shift to the spot on the neck you are aiming for and never make a mistake. I'll bet that you start to think hard about shifting when you see that huge leap coming up in the part you are reading.

More than likely when you are playing a bass line or soloing over a song you are pretty sure of but not really sure of, you will grab a spot in the neck and hold on for dear life until you have to move your hand and then hope you land in the right place! This series of exercises will help you to get your shifting together. All you have to think about is shifting. No songs!

A few pointers before you get started:

- Be sure that your left hand and arm are completely relaxed.

- Make your shifts *quickly* no matter what the tempo. Your left hand needs to be in place before your right hand plays the note. If you move your left hand slowly, you will usually be OK at slow tempos but will fall behind at faster ones. You don't want your left hand busting the groove do you? Quick shifting also eliminates a lot of fret noise. Shifts should be seen but not heard!

- One finger on your left hand should be lightly touching the string as you shift.

- Listen very carefully to your playing—make sure that the note you are shifting to is the same length as the note you shifted from. Don't shift until the last nanosecond!

- Keep your hand open while shifting. Your fingers should cover four frets all of the time.

There are a number of possible shifting combinations for each exercise. Practice all of them! Keep an eye on your hand at first then, as you become more comfortable with the particular shift you are working on, take your eyes off of the bass and increase your speed.

Exercise 1: One Note On the D string. (Keep your hand open!)

1st finger: 1—2 / 1–3 / 1– 4 • 2nd finger: 2–1 / 2–3 / 2-4

3rd finger: 3–1 / 3–2 / 3-4 • 4th finger: 4–1 / 4–2 / 4–3

Exercise 2: Two Notes On the D string. (Cover four frets all of the time!)

> 1st finger: 1–1 / 1–2 / 1–4 • 2nd finger: 2–1 / 2–2 / 2–3
>
> 3rd finger: 3–1 / 3–2 / 3–3 / 3–4 • 4th finger: 4–1 / 4–2 / 4–3 / 4–4

Exercise 3: Up One String On the A string. (Shift quickly!)

> 1st finger: 1–1 / 1–2 / 1–3 / 1–4 • 2nd finger: 2–1 / 2–2 / 2–3 / 2–4
>
> 3rd finger: 3–1 / 3–2 / 3–3 / 3–4 • 4th finger: 4–1 / 4–2 / 4–3 / 4–4

Exercise 4: On *every* string.

• Find and play every occurrence of every note on your bass. For example, find every F, then find every F♯, then every G, etc., until you've covered every chromatic pitch. Don't forget the notes high up on the E string or the B string—for those of you with a 5-string bass.

Exercise 5: Up Two Strings On the A and D strings.

1st finger: 1–1 / 1–2 / 1–3 / 1–4 • 2nd finger: 2–1 / 2–2 / 2–3 / 2–4

3rd finger: 3–1 / 3–2 / 3–3 / 3–4 • 4th finger: 4–1 / 4–2 / 4–3 / 4–4

Exercise 6: Across Three Strings On the E and D strings. (Cover all four frets!)

1st finger: 1–1 / 1–2 / 1–3 / 1–4 • 2nd finger: 2–1 / 2–2 / 2–3 / 2–4

3rd finger: 3–1 / 3–2 / 3–3 / 3–4 • 4th finger: 4–1 / 4–2 / 4–3 / 4–4

Exercise 7: **Across Four Strings** On the E and G strings. (Keep your hand open!)

1st finger: 1–1 / 1–2 / 1–3 / 1–4 • 2nd finger: 2–1 / 2–2 / 2–3 / 2–4

3rd finger: 3–1 / 3–2 / 3–3 / 3–4 • 4th finger: 4–1 / 4–2 / 4–3 / 4–4

Exercise 8: **Same Finger** On *any* string. (Shift quickly!)

- This time, start anyplace on the fingerboard; use any combination of strings.
- Change keys. Check out the chords—maj7, dom7, aug7, m(maj7), m7, m7(♭5).
- Be creative. Use as much of the neck as you can.
- Don't get caught doing this exercise in public.

1–1 • 2–2 • 3–3 • 4–4

5

Major Scales & Chords Outside of the 1st Position

Finally, out of the 1st position! Great. Now you can use the good ol' major scale fingering that starts with your second finger all over the bass and be done with the major scale. Cool. Hold on…what if you want to play some sort of major scale stuff and your second finger isn't in the right place? What then? You could always make some awkward shift and break up the musical line; or, you could come up with another way to finger it. You're in luck! Below you'll find one old and eight new ways to play a one octave major scale—old sound, new direction.

Learning a variety of new ways to play old material will allow you to play your music by using the sound of the music—that's what it's all about is, isn't it?—rather than by always using patterns. Your playing will blossom.

Shifts are indicated by double-headed arrows—the shifts up are the same as they are down. In one case, three finger technique (upright bass) and four finger technique (electric bass) are combined to facilitate smooth shifting. In the eighth fingering given for the major scale, the 5th and 6th scale steps are played with the first and fourth fingers (upright technique) rather than with the first and third fingers (our usual electric bass technique), opening up your first finger to play the 7th step of the scale on the next string very easily. Compressing and expanding your hand in this manner streamlines moving from one string to another. The symbol that indicates three finger technique or "compression" looks like an inverted V — ∧. The fingerboard charts will help you to visualize these new fingerings. Practice these fingerings all over your bass.

Major Scale Fingerboard Charts

1. Up one string – Starting with an open string (Use all of your open strings!)

```
0  1  3  4     1  3     1  2
                        2  3
                        3  4
```

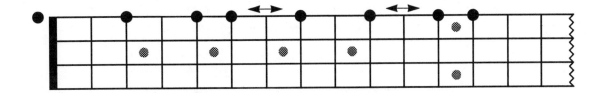

2. Up one string – Starting with a fingered note

1   3↔1   2   4↔1   3   4

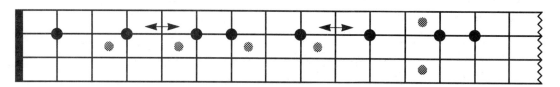

3. Two strings

1↔1   3   4   1↔1   3   4

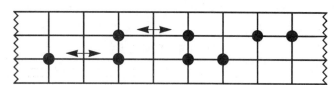

4. Three strings – your old favorite

2   4   1   2   4   1   3   4

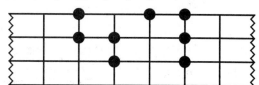

5. Three strings

2   4   1   2↔2   4   1   2

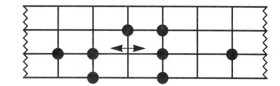

6. Three strings

4   1   3   4   1↔1   3   4

7. Three strings

4   1↔1   2   4   1   3   4

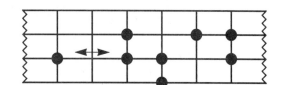

8. Four strings

4   1   3   4   1   ∧   4   1   2

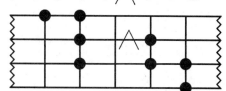

This fingering is unique in that it goes *up* in pitch but *down* the neck. I like it a lot.

9. Two string pairs – Keys of F, B♭ and E♭

1   3   0↔2   4   1   3   4

Major Scale Exercises

Use as many of the new fingerings as you can. While the fingering you choose may have to be altered a bit to accommodate the different exercises, keep the shape of the fingering intact. For example, if you have chosen fingering 2, be sure to go up and down one string. Cover the entire neck. Practice in every key. Each exercise is written out in two keys. The row of note names below each exercise lists the remaining keys. Cross them out as you practice.

Exercise 1:

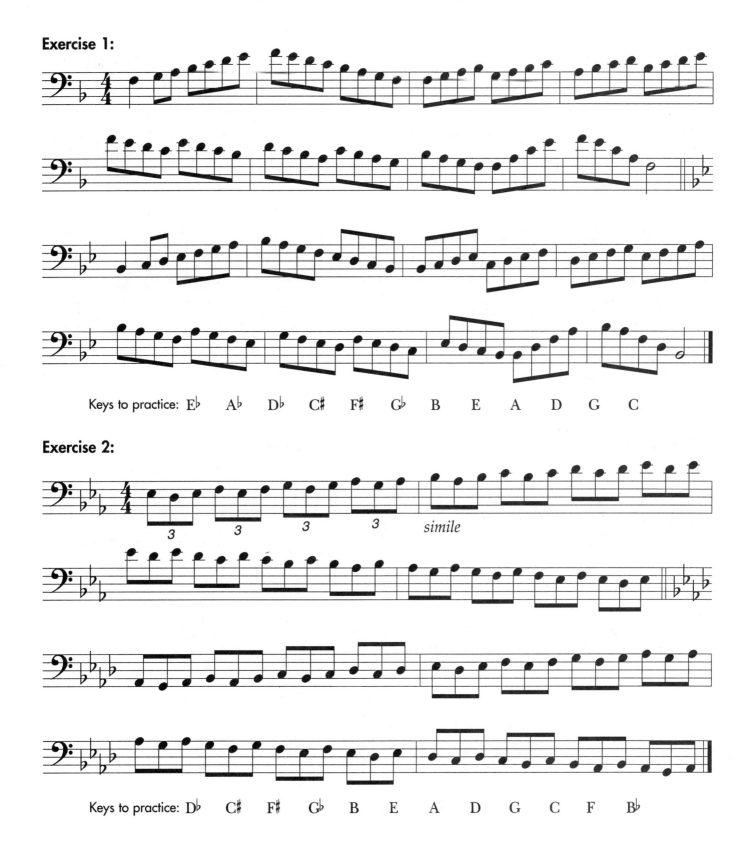

Keys to practice: E♭ A♭ D♭ C♯ F♯ G♭ B E A D G C

Exercise 2:

Keys to practice: D♭ C♯ F♯ G♭ B E A D G C F B♭

Exercise 3:

Keys to practice: C♯ G♭ B E A D G C F B♭ E♭ A♭

Exercise 4:

Keys to practice: A D G C F B♭ E♭ A♭ D♭ C♯ F♯ G♭

Exercise 5:

Keys to practice: G C F B♭ E♭ A♭ D♭ C♯ F♯ G♭ B E

Exercise 6:

Keys to practice: F B♭ E♭ A♭ D♭ C♯ F♯ G♭ B E A D

Maj7th chords

In Exercise 7, each bar starts on the E string. The first bar of each line covers three strings and uses the maj7th chord fingering that begins with your second finger, no shifts (#4 on p. 58). The fingering for the second bar of each line covers four strings and starts with your fourth finger (#8 on p. 58). Check out the compression shift between beats 1 and 2 and the stretch between your 2nd and 3rd fingers in beat 3.

Exercise 7:

continued on next page

2 1 4 1 4 3 4 3 4 3 4 1 2   4 3 1 4 2 1 2 1 2 1 2 3 4

simile

Exercise 8:

Use both fingerings. Fingering **1** is pattern **4**, fingering **2** is pattern **8** (p. 58).

1: 2 1 4 3 3 4 1 2 etc.
2: 4 3 2 1 1 2 3 4 etc.

3 4 1 2 2 1 4 3 etc.
1 2 3 4 4 3 2 1 etc.

Exercise 9:

- This one uses a variation of scale fingering pattern **3** on page 58.

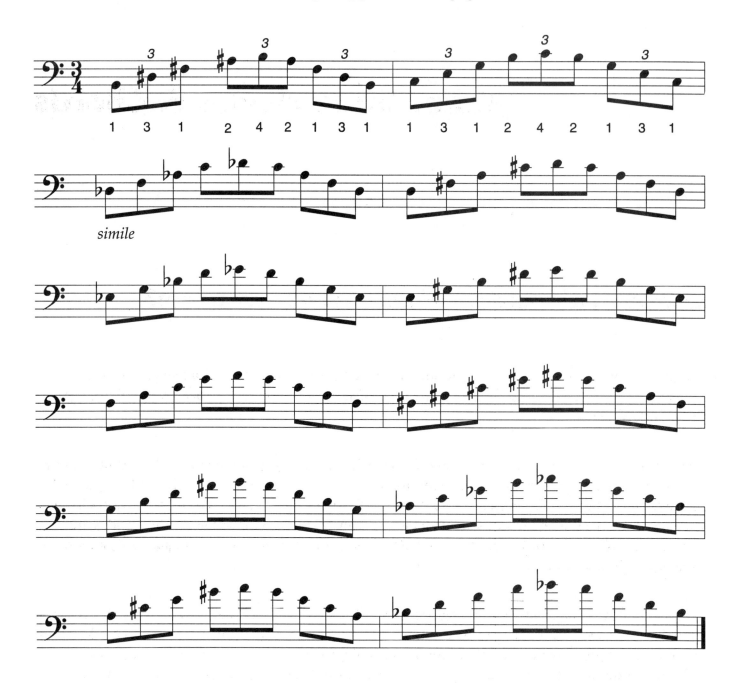

Exercise 10:

- The shapes of scale fingering patterns **4, 8** and **3** have been used for the last three exercises. Come up with new ideas using the shapes of the remaining scale patterns shown on pages 57 and 58.

- Be sure to cover the entire neck of your bass. Some basses have more frets and more strings than others. Play up as high and as low as your bass has frets. If your bass has more than four

6

Major Scale Modes & Chords

What are major modes and where do they come from?

Just like the major scale, major scale modes are specific sets of whole and half steps. Do you remember the interval construction of the major scale? If you don't, turn back to the first page of Chapter 3—p. 33.

The modes of the major scale are created by starting on each note of a major scale and playing up an octave—seven notes—resulting in seven modes (one mode per scale step). Don't be confused by the fact that these new scales are called modes. Because the modes share the same notes in the same specific order as the major scale from which they are derived, it's obvious that modes are merely a specific group of interrelated *or diatonic scales*. In popular music, pop, jazz, etc., a mode is a scale, a scale is a mode.

Each mode of the major scale—the major scale itself included—has a name attached to it. As the name "major scale" implies a specific set of whole and half steps, so to do the ancient Greek names that have been given to each mode of the major scale. No matter what major key you are dealing with, the mode names, their scale steps, their tonic chords and their intervals above the root remain the same, giving each mode its own unique melodic and harmonic character.

Using the key of F major, this example graphically illustrates the derivation of the major scale modes. Remember that the mode names and the scale steps to which they are attached are the same for *every* major key!

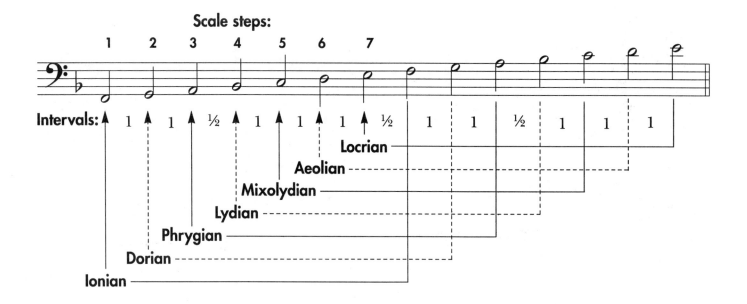

POP QUIZ #1

Which notes do the following modes start with?

1. Key of C major – Aeolian mode ___
2. Key of B♭ major – Dorian mode ___
3. Key of E major – Mixolydian mode ___
4. Key of F♯ major – Ionian mode ___
5. Key of B major – Lydian mode ___

6. Key of G major – Lydian mode ___
7. Key of D major – Phrygian mode ___
8. Key of A major – Locrian mode ___
9. Key of D♭ major – Dorian mode ___
10. Key of E♭ major – Mixolydian mode ___

Super important!

When playing, writing or talking about a specific mode, the starting note or tonic of the mode is given first, followed by the type of mode. For example, "C" Aeolian means an Aeolian mode starting on the note "C."

Which major keys do the following modes come from?

1. C Lydian ___
2. F Locrian ___
3. E♭ Ionian ___
4. C♯ Mixolydian ___
5. E Locrian ___

6. D Mixolydian ___
7. A Phrygian ___
8. B Dorian ___
9. G♭ Lydian ___
10. C Locrian ___

11. B♭ Dorian ___
12. G Aeolian ___
13. C♯ Locrian ___
14. A♭ Phrygian ___
15. F♯ Mixolydian ___

Major Mode Chords

The major modes contain four types of 7th chords—the maj7, the m7, the dominant7 and the m7(♭5). Like the maj7 chord that was discussed in Chapter 3, the quality of these diatonic chords is determined by the interval make up of the modes from which they are derived. Remember that each of these 7th chords is made up of the root, 3rd, 5th (a triad) and 7th of the mode.

1. Major 7th chord
Root, maj3rd, per5th (a maj triad) and maj7th
Ionian and Lydian modes

2. Minor 7th chord
Root, m3rd, per5th (a min triad) and m7th
Dorian, Phrygian and Aeolian modes

3. Dominant 7th chord
Root, maj3rd, per5th (a maj triad) and m7th
Mixolydian mode

4. Minor 7th (♭5) chord
Root, m3rd, dim5th (a dim triad) and m7th
Locrian mode

I Ionian mode – maj7th chord

II Dorian mode – m7th chord

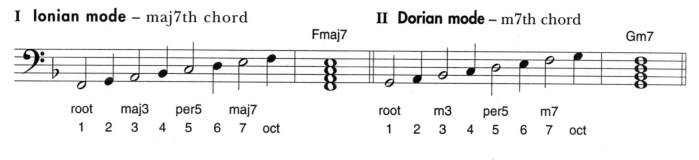

III Phrygian mode – m7 chord

IV Lydian mode – maj7th chord

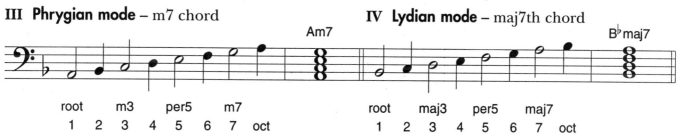

V Mixolydian mode – dom7th chord

VI Aeolian mode – m7th chord

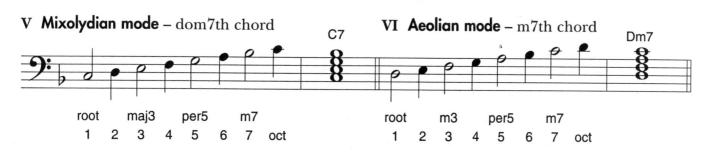

VII Locrian mode – m7 (♭5) chord

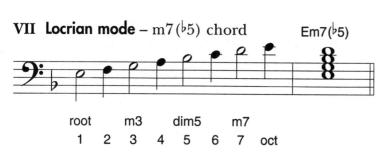

Here are the diatonic 7th chords in F major. Find a keyboard and play them over enough times so that your ear becomes very familiar with both the sound of the chords as a group and with the sound of each individual type of chord. Play them is as many keys as you can.

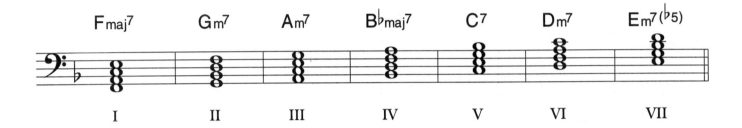

Why the Roman numerals?

1. You've probably noticed that Roman numerals precede the mode names on the previous page and appear under the chords in the example above. For many years, Roman numerals have been used in traditional harmony to indicate which scale step a particular mode name is attached.

2. For our purposes, the Roman numerals serve a much more important function as they signify the chord that each mode produces. All the music that you hear is based on chord progressions—the movement from one chord to another. Chord progressions are described using numbers such as II–V–I or I–IV–III–VI–II–V–I and derive their numbering from the chords produced by the modes found in the major scale. The numbers of the chords match the numbers of the modes they come from—e.g. the Dorian mode is the second mode of the major scale, so the II chord in a song is a m7 based on the Dorian mode.

As each mode always implies a specific chord, each chord always implies a specific mode.

So...

the **maj7** chord from the **Ionian mode** is *always* the **I chord** in major,

the **m7** chord from the **Dorian mode** is *always* the **II chord** in major,

the **m7** chord from the **Phrygian mode** is *always* the **III chord** in major,

the **maj7** chord from the **Lydian mode** is *always* the **IV chord** in major,

the **dom7** chord from the **Mixolydian mode** is *always* the **V chord** in major,

the **m7** chord from the **Aeolian mode** is *always* the **VI chord** in major, and

the **m7($\flat$5)** chord from the **Locrian mode** is *always* the **VII chord** in major. Remember an Am7($\flat$5) chord is sometimes called by it's classical name—half-diminished. Its symbol is a small circle with a line through it – ∅ (e.g., A∅).

This means that in a II7–V7–I7 progression in a major key, a m7 chord (II7 – Dorian) moves to a dom7 chord (V7 – Mixolydian) to a maj7 chord (I7 – Ionian). Can you figure out the chords and modes used in the I7–IV7–VII7–III7–VI7–II7–V7–I7 progression?

3. Sometimes lower case Roman numerals are used for minor chords. A m7 chord would be written ii^7, iii^7, vi^7 or vii$^{\varnothing}$ rather than II^7, III^7, VI^7 or VII$^{\varnothing}$. The chord progression on the bottom of previous page would look like this: I^7–IV^7–vii$^{\varnothing}$–iii^7–vi^7–ii^7–V^7–I^7.

Pop Quiz #2

Name the following chords: (Be sure to give the complete chord name—Gm7, E7, etc.)

1. ii^7 chord in F _____
2. IV^7 chord in E$\flat$ _____
3. vii$^{\varnothing}$ chord in B$\flat$ _____
4. V^7 chord in C$\sharp$ _____
5. iii^7 chord in G _____
6. V^7 chord in C$\flat$ _____
7. I^7 chord in D _____
8. ii^7 chord in F$\sharp$ _____
9. vii$^{\varnothing}$ chord in A$\flat$ _____
10. vi^7 chord in A _____
11. iii^7 chord in G$\flat$ _____
12. vi^7 chord in E _____
13. IV^7 chord in B _____
14. I^7 chord in D$\flat$ _____
15. ii^7 chord in C _____

Name the chords for the ii^7–V^7–I^7 progressions in the keys listed:

1. C major _____
2. A$\flat$ major _____
3. E major _____
4. D$\flat$ major _____
5. F$\sharp$ major _____
6. E$\flat$ major _____
7. B major _____
8. C$\sharp$ major _____
9. A major _____
10. G$\flat$ major _____
11. G major _____
12. B$\flat$ major _____
13. F major _____
14. D major _____
15. C$\flat$ major _____

Using the Roman numerals, make up your own chord progressions and figure them out in every key. How about using the I–IV–vii–iii–vi–ii–V–I given at the top of the page?

Why are major scale modes and chords so important?

The modes of the major scale and the chords they produce provide all of the basic melodic (modes) and harmonic (chords) material used in every style of music—pop, jazz, blues, rock and so on. Every song you have ever played or will play includes major scale modes and chords.

More Super Important Information!

Having just spent the last five pages explaining how the modes and chords of the major scale are related, I am now going to tell you that *all the modes we are now studying can and do exist as separate, unique scales out there in the world of harmony.* Any of the modes can be used as the tonic scale for a song. For example, the Mixolydian mode serves as the basis for the blues whereas many famous jazz pieces have been built around the Dorian mode. The unique melodic and harmonic character of each mode will be discussed in this chapter. We'll start with the Dorian mode. (The Ionian mode has already been covered in Chapters 3 and 5.)

The Dorian Mode

Dorian mode facts:

1. Derivation:

The Dorian mode is built from the second scale step of the major scale.

Scale steps: 1   2

2. Interval construction:

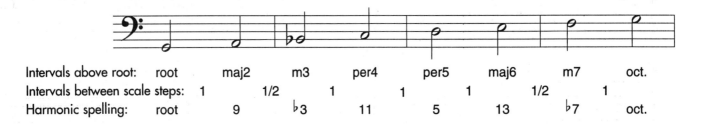

Intervals above root:	root	maj2	m3	per4	per5	maj6	m7	oct.
Intervals between scale steps:	1	1/2	1	1	1	1/2	1	
Harmonic spelling:	root	9	♭3	11	5	13	♭7	oct.

3. Scale type and tonic chord:

The Dorian mode is considered to be minor scale as there is a minor 3rd above the root. Its tonic chord is a m7 or a m6—for example, Gm^7 and Gm^6. Other possible chord symbols (using G as the root) are Gm^9, Gm^{11} and Gm^{13}.

4. Intervals above the root that define the Dorian mode:

- m3rd   • maj6th (13)   • m7th

5. Most common uses:

- It provides the "2" chord and scale found in ii^7 - V^7 - I progressions.
- It is used as the tonic chord—the key of—many jazz and pop tunes.

6. Tetrachord construction:

The Dorian mode is made up of two minor tetrachords a whole step apart.

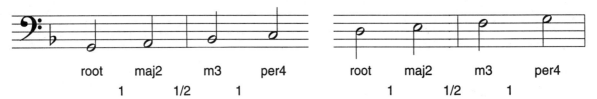

	root	maj2	m3	per4		root	maj2	m3	per4
		1	1/2	1			1	1/2	1	

The minor tetrachord is the second type of tetrachord we've encountered.
Remember the major tetrachords found in the major scale? If you don't, see page 34.

Dorian mode exercises in the 1st position:

Here is the Dorian mode in 14 keys covering the entire 1st position. Because no fingerings are provided, be sure to keep your left hand open and use all four fingers. Practice a mode and chord in one key until you are comfortable with the fingering, and then move on to the next key. Your goal is to play the next three pages non-stop! As you play, listen to the sound of the mode and chord. Pay attention to the notes that make this mode unique, namely the 3rd, 6th and 7th.

E Dorian

Em7(6)

F Dorian

Fm7(6)

F♯ Dorian Practice this one in G♭, too. Name each note as you play.

F♯m7(6)

G Dorian

Gm7(6)

continued on next page

A♭ Dorian

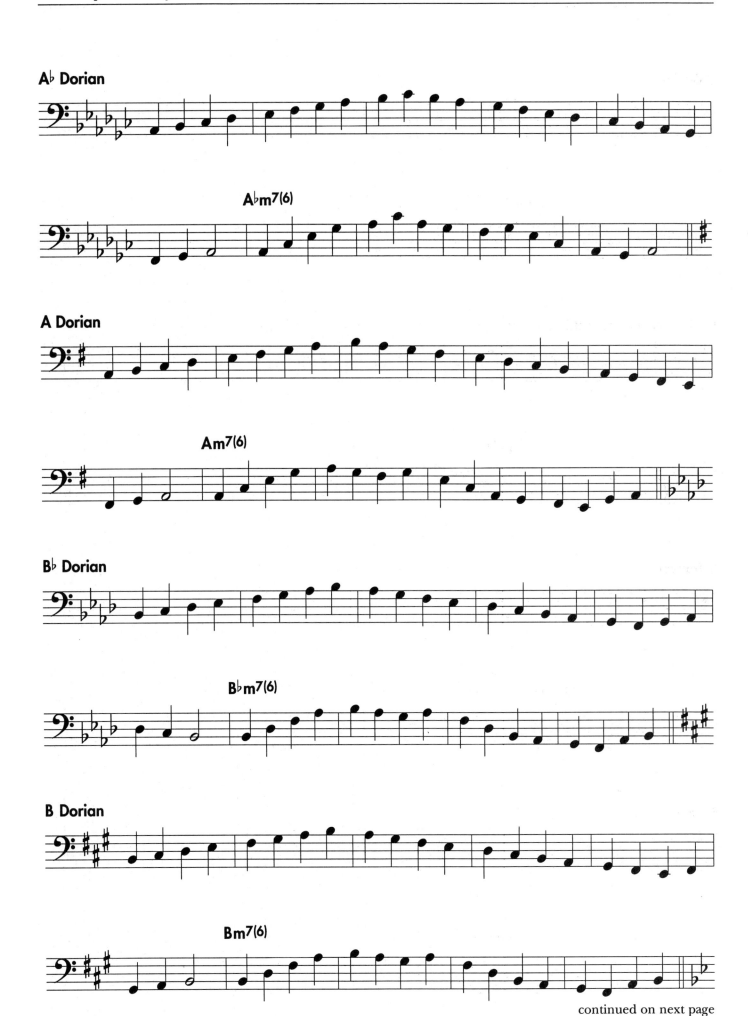

A♭m7(6)

A Dorian

Am7(6)

B♭ Dorian

B♭m7(6)

B Dorian

Bm7(6)

continued on next page

C Dorian

Cm7(6)

C♯ Dorian Practice this one in D♭, too. Name each note as you play.

C♯m7(6)

D Dorian

Dm7(6)

E♭ Dorian

E♭m7(6)

The Dorian mode outside of the 1st position:

Here are some ideas for playing a one octave Dorian mode outside of the 1st position. Practice these and then come up with some of your own. Play over the entire fingerboard.

1. Up one string – Starting with an open string

0 1 2 ◄►1 3 ◄►1 2 4

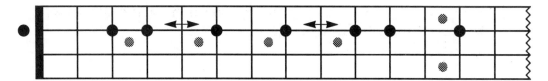

2. Up one string – Starting with a fingered note

1 3 4 ◄►1 3 ◄►1 2 4

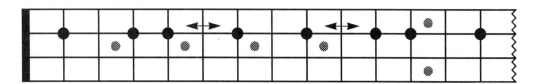

3. Two strings

1 ◄►1 2 4 1 ◄►1 2 4

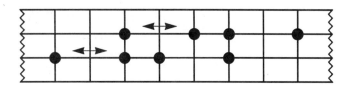

4. Three strings

1 ◄►1 2 4 1 3 4 1

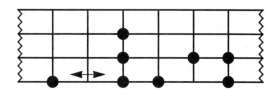

5. Three strings

1 3 4 1 /\ 4 1 2 4

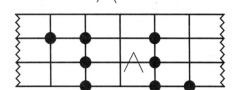

6. Four strings

4 1 2 4 1 3 4 1

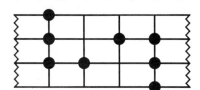

Compare this one with major scale pattern 8 on page 58.

7. Two string pairs – F♯, B and E Dorian only

1 3 0 ◄►2 4 1 2 4

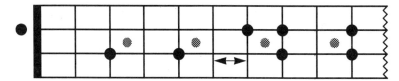

Dorian mode exercises outside of the 1st position:

Practice the following Dorian mode exercises in every key. The row of notes below each exercise contains all of the starting pitches for the mode. Either circle or cross out each note in the list as you practice through each of the exercises.

Use as many of the fingerings as you can for each exercise. For Exercises 2, 3 and 4, you will have to alter some of the fingerings a bit; but try to retain the general shape of the fingering you have chosen. For example, if you want to play Exercise 2 up one string, you will have to come up with your own fingering. Just be sure to play up and down one string!

Exercise 1: Dorian mode

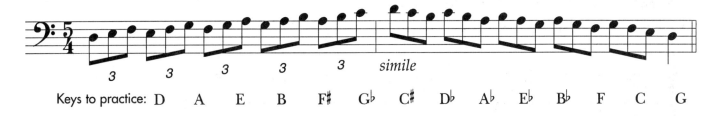

Keys to practice: D   A   E   B   F♯   G♭   C♯   D♭   A♭   E♭   B♭   F   C   G

Exercise 2: Dorian mode in thirds

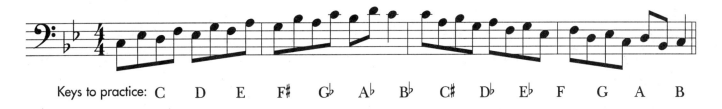

Keys to practice: C   D   E   F♯   G♭   A♭   B♭   C♯   D♭   E♭   F   G   A   B

Exercise 3: m7 chord

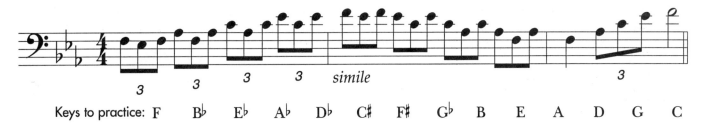

Keys to practice: F   B♭   E♭   A♭   D♭   C♯   F♯   G♭   B   E   A   D   G   C

Exercise 4: m6 and m7 chords

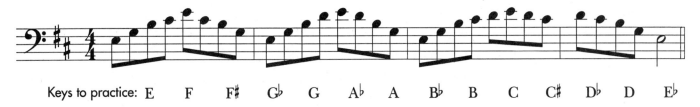

Keys to practice: E   F   F♯   G♭   G   A♭   A   B♭   B   C   C♯   D♭   D   E♭

Your own Dorian mode, m6 and m7 chord ideas:

• Be creative with the Dorian mode and its chords!

• Use the *whole* neck of your bass. Combine 1st position fingerings with fingerings that cover the rest of the neck. Include the notes in the mode below the root, too.

The Mixolydian Mode

Wait a minute…we've skipped the Phrygian and Lydian modes! Since the Mixolydian mode is part of America's most popular chord progression—the ii[7] – V[7] – I—we'll cover it now and get to the remaining modes later.

Mixolydian mode facts:

1. Derivation:

The Mixolydian mode is built from the fifth scale step of the major scale.

Scale steps: 1 2 3 4 5

2. Interval construction:

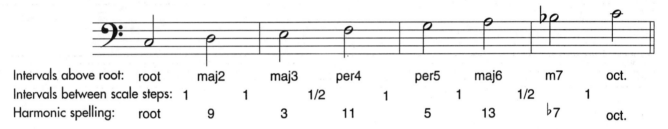

Intervals above root:	root	maj2	maj3	per4	per5	maj6	m7	oct.
Intervals between scale steps:	1		1	1/2	1	1	1/2	1
Harmonic spelling:	root	9	3	11	5	13	♭7	oct.

3. Scale type and tonic chord:

The Mixolydian mode is considered to be a dominant scale because it contains a maj3rd in combination a m7th above the root. The m7 (♭7) above the root distinguishes the Mixolydian mode from the major scale. Its tonic chord is a dom7th—for example: G[7]. Other possible chord symbols—using G as the root—are G[9], G[11] and G[13].

4. Intervals above the root that define the Mixolydian mode:

- maj3rd   • maj6th   • m7th

5. Most common uses:

- It provides the "5" chord and scale found in almost all ii[7] - V[7] - I progressions.
- It is the tonic chord and scale for many jazz, pop and blues tunes.

6. Tetrachord construction:

The Mixolydian mode is made up of major and minor tetrachords that are a whole step apart.

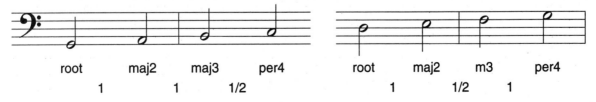

	root	maj2	maj3	per4		root	maj2	m3	per4
		1	1	1/2			1	1/2	1

Mixolydian mode exercises in the 1st position:

Now's your chance to use your head. Play all fifteen (when you include G♭, D♭ and C♭) of the Mixolydian modes and their tonic chords in the first position in the same way the Dorian mode 1st position exercises are written out on page 71 through 73.

Here's the plan:

1. Start on the root of the mode and play up as high as you can in the 1st position;
2. Then, play down the mode as low as you can go;
3. Next, play back up to the root;
4. Do the same thing with the tonic chord—the dom7 chord. Add the 13th (the 6th scale step) occasionally.

These two examples will help to get you going. If you've got more than 4 strings, use all of them!

Do you know what major keys these Mixolydian modes are related to?

Now improvise, using the Mixolydian mode in every key in the 1st position.

The Mixolydian mode outside of the 1st position:

Here are some ideas for playing a one octave Mixolydian mode outside of the 1st position. Practice these, and then come up with some of your own. Play over the entire fingerboard.

1. Up one string – Starting with an open string

0 1◄►1 2 4◄►1 2 4

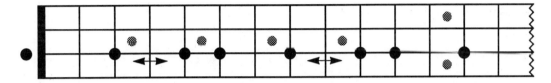

2. Up one string – Starting with a fingered note

1 3◄►1 2 4◄►1 2 4

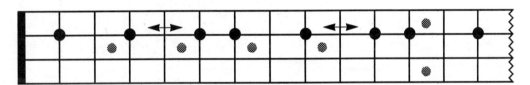

3. Two strings

1◄►1 3 4 1◄►1 2 4

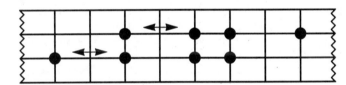

4. Three strings

2 4 1 2 4 1 2 4

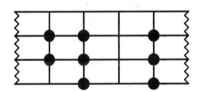

5. Three strings

1◄►1 3 4 1 3 4 1

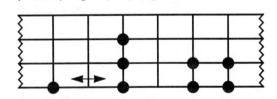

6. Three strings

4 1 3 4 1◄►1 2 4

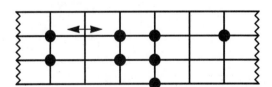

7. Two string pairs – F, B♭ and E♭ Mixolydian

1 3 0◄►2 4 1 2 4

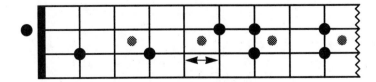

8. Four strings (See #8, p.58 & #6, p.74)

4 1 3 4 1 3 4 1

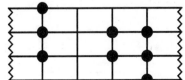

Mixolydian exercises outside of the 1st position:

Practice these exercises in every key. To help you keep track of your progress, starting pitches for each exercise are provided. Use as many of the fingerings given on page 79 as you can. Again, be sure to stick with the shape of the fingering you have chosen. Cover the entire neck—all the way to the top and down to the bottom on every string.

Exercise 1: Mixolydian mode

Keys to practice: C♭ C♯ D♭ D E♭ E F F♯ G♭ G A♭ A B♭ B

Exercise 2: dom7 chord

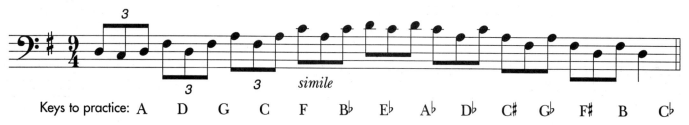

Keys to practice: A D G C F B♭ E♭ A♭ D♭ C♯ G♭ F♯ B C♭

Exercise 3: Mixolydian tetrachords in every key

Your own Mixolydian mode and dom7 chord ideas:

- Improvise your brains out! Pay particular attention to the dom7.

- Integrate 1st position fingerings with those that cover the rest of the neck. Use the *whole* fingerboard. Include notes below the root of the mode, too.

The Phrygian Mode

Phrygian mode facts:

1. Derivation: The Phrygian mode is built from the third scale step of the major scale.

Scale step: 1   2   3

2. Interval construction:

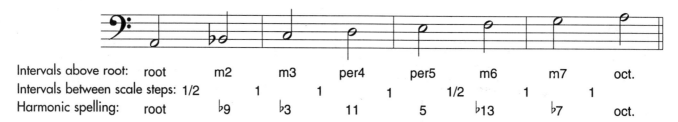

Intervals above root:	root	m2	m3	per4	per5	m6	m7	oct.
Intervals between scale steps:	1/2	1	1	1	1/2	1	1	
Harmonic spelling:	root	♭9	♭3	11	5	♭13	♭7	oct.

3. Scale type and tonic chord:

With its m3rd above the root, the Phrygian mode is the second minor scale created from the major scale. The m2 (♭9) and the m6 (♭13) distinguish the Phrygian mode from the Dorian mode. Its tonic chord is a ,m7. A more accurate description is: m7(♭9, ♭13). Both the m2 (♭9) and the m6 (♭13) above the root give this mode a somewhat Spanish flavor.

4. Intervals above the root that define the Phrygian mode:

- m2nd (♭9)   • m3rd   • m6th(♭13)   • m7th

5. Most common use:

- It provides the "3" chord (the most common substitute for a "1" chord) for progressions in major keys. Although the ♭9 is usually left out of both keyboard and guitar voicings—the root and ♭9 clash too much when played together—it sounds fine in walking bass lines.

6. Tetrachord construction:

The Phrygian mode is made up of two Phrygian tetrachords a whole step apart.

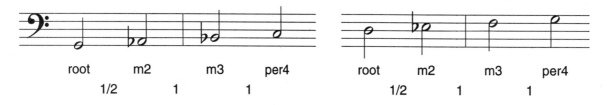

root	m2	m3	per4		root	m2	m3	per4
	1/2	1	1			1/2	1	1

The Phrygian tetrachord is the third type of tetrachord we've studied. Add this one to the major and minor tetrachords you already know!

Phrygian mode exercises in the 1st position:

For starters, play the Phrygian mode in every key using the same plan that was used for the Dorian and Mixolydian modes in the 1st position. Remember how it goes?

1. Starting from the root, play up the mode as far as you can in the 1st position;
2. Then, play the mode down as far as you can;
3. Then, play back up to the root;
4. Next, do the same with the tonic chord, in this case the m7. Add the ♭9 and the ♭13 where you can.
5. Practice C♯ and G Phrygian, then move on to the remaining modes and chords.

C♯ Phrygian

C♯m7

G Phrygian

Gm7

Keys to practice: C   D   D♯   E♭   E   F   F♯   G♯   A   A♯   B♭   B

Do you know what major keys the starting pitches for these Phrygian modes are related to?

Now, using the Phrygian mode in the 1st position, make up your own lines. Including the ♭9 and the ♭13 in your improvisations will lock the sound of this mode into your head.

The Phrygian mode outside of the 1st position:

Here are some ideas for playing a one-octave Phrygian mode outside of the 1st position. Practice these, and then come up with some of your own. Play over the entire fingerboard.

1. Up one string – Starting with an open string

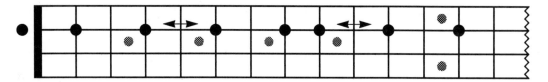

2. Up one string – Starting with a fingered note

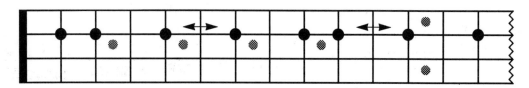

3. Two strings

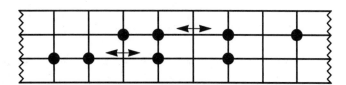

4. Three strings

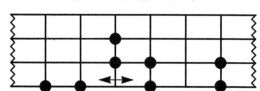

5. Three strings

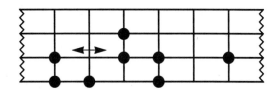

6. Four strings (See #8, p.58, #6, p.74, #8, p.79)

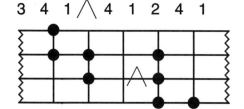

7. Two string pairs – F♯, B and E Phrygian

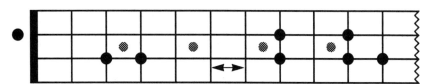

8. Three strings

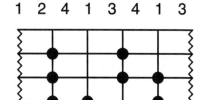

Phrygian mode exercises outside of the 1st position:

Practice these exercises in every key. To help you keep track of your progress, starting pitches for each exercise are provided. Use as many of the fingerings given on page 84 as you can. Again, be sure to stick with the shape of the fingering you have chosen.

Exercise 1: Phrygian mode

Keys to practice: G   C   F   A♯   B♭   D♯   E♭   G♯   C♯   F♯   B   E   A

Exercise 2: Phrygian mode – oblique motion (one note stays the same, the others move)

Keys to practice: F♯   C♯   G♯   D♯   A♯   F   C   G   D   E♭   A   E   B

Exercise 3: m7(♭9, ♭13)

Keys to practice: E   F   F♯   G   G♯   A   A♯   B   C   C♯   D   D♯   E♭

Your own Phrygian mode and m7(♭9, ♭13) ideas:

• Turn the Phrygian mode inside out!

• Mix 1st position fingerings with those found on page 84. Pay particular attention to the ♭9th and the ♭13th. Cover the entire fingerboard from bottom to top. Go below the root.

The Lydian mode

Lydian mode facts:

1. Derivation:

The Lydian mode is built from the fourth scale step of the major scale.

Scale step: 1 2 3 4

2. Interval construction: (The Lydian mode has no minor intervals above the root!)

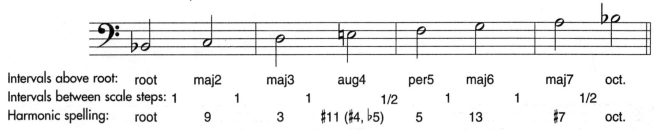

Intervals above root:	root	maj2	maj3	aug4	per5	maj6	maj7	oct.
Intervals between scale steps:	1	1	1	1/2	1	1	1/2	
Harmonic spelling:	root	9	3	♯11 (♯4, ♭5)	5	13	♯7	oct.

3. Scale type and tonic chord:

With a maj3rd and a maj7th above the root, the Lydian mode is the first major mode created from the major scale. The + or ♯4(♯11) found in this mode distinguishes it from the Ionian mode—the major scale. The tonic chord of the Lydian mode is the maj7(♯11) but it is often written as maj7(♭5)—for example, Gmaj7(♯11) or Gmaj7(♭5).

4. Intervals above the root that define the Lydian mode:

- maj3rd • aug4th (+4 or ♯4, ♯11 aka ♭5) • maj7th

5. Most common uses:

- It provides the "4" chord in songs written in major keys.
- As the tonic chord in any jazz or pop tune that can take the added spice that the ♯11 gives to the chord. Some jazz players *always* add the ♯11 to maj7th chords!

6. Tetrachord construction:

The Lydian mode is made up of whole-tone and major tetrachords a half step apart.

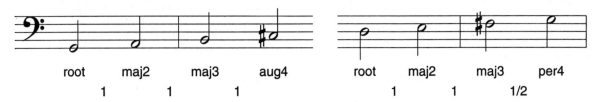

root	maj2	maj3	aug4	root	maj2	maj3	per4
	1	1	1		1	1	1/2

The whole-tone tetrachord is the fourth type of tetrachord we've come across. Add this one to the major, minor and phrygian tetrachords you already know!

Lydian mode exercises in the 1st position:

Play the Lydian mode in every key using the same scheme that has been used for the modes studied so far in the 1st position.

1. Starting from the root, play up as far as you can go in the 1st position;
2. Then, play down the mode as far as you can going below the root for all keys except E;
3. Then, play back up to the root;
4. Next, do the same with the tonic chord, in this case the maj7(#11) (maj7♭5). Add the #11(♭5) where you can.
5. Practice C and F Lydian, then move on to the remaining modes and chords.

C Lydian:

F Lydian:

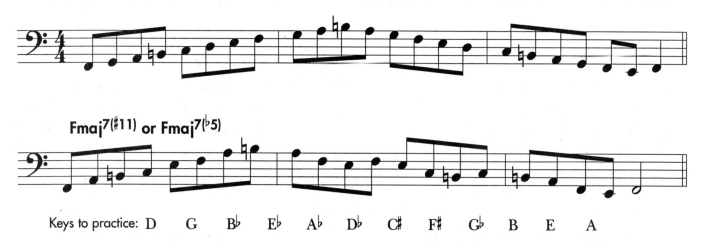

Keys to practice: D   G   B♭   E♭   A♭   D♭   C#   F#   G♭   B   E   A

Do you know what major keys the starting pitches for these Lydian modes are related to?

Now, make up your own lines using the Lydian mode in the 1st position. Include the #11 and the maj7th in your ideas.

The Lydian mode outside of the 1st position:

Here are some ideas for playing a one-octave Lydian mode outside of the 1st position. Practice these, and then come up with some of your own. Be sure to cover the entire bass.

1. Up one string – Starting with an open string

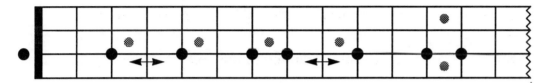

2. Up one string – Starting with a fingered note

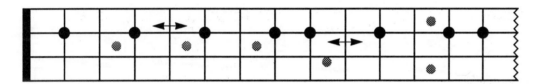

3. Two strings

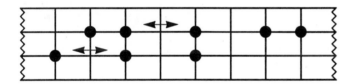

4. Three strings

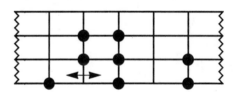

5. Three strings

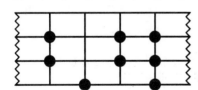

6. Three strings

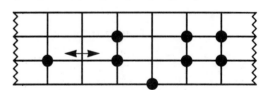

7. Two string pairs – F, B♭ and E♭ Lydian

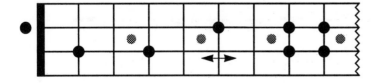

8. Four strings (See #8 on page 58.)

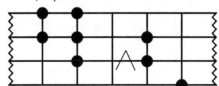

Lydian mode exercises outside of the 1st position:

Practice these exercises in every key. To keep track of your progress, use the list of starting pitches following each exercise. Play each exercise with as many of the fingerings on page 89 as you can. Be sure to retain the shape of the fingering you have chosen.

Exercise 1: E♭ Lydian mode

Keys to practice: E♭   G♭   F♯   A   C   E   G   B♭   D♭   C♯   F   D   A♭   B

Exercise 2: C Lydian mode in four-note groups

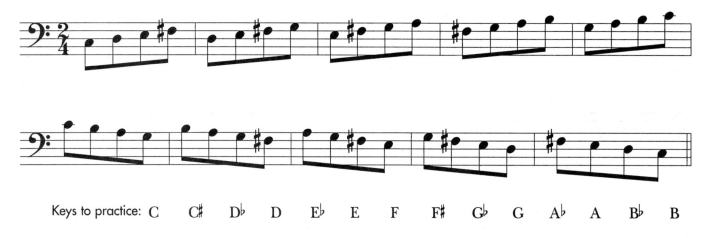

Keys to practice: C   C♯   D♭   D   E♭   E   F   F♯   G♭   G   A♭   A   B♭   B

Exercise 3: B♭ Lydian mode in sixths

Keys to practice: B♭   F   C   G   D   A   E   B   F♯   G♭   D♭   C♯   A♭   E♭

Exercise 4: Fmaj7(♯11)

Keys to practice: F   B♭   E♭   A♭   D♭   C♯   F♯   G♭   B   E   A   D   G   C

Your own Lydian mode and maj7(♯11) ideas:

• Spend some time with this one. The ♯11(♭5) may sound a bit strange to you.

• The more you practice and improvise over the mode and the chord, the more quickly you will be able to hear and to add the ♯11 sound to your lines and solos.

The Aeolian Mode

Aeolian mode facts:

1. Derivation:

The Aeolian mode is built from the sixth scale step of the major scale.

Scale step: 1   2   3   4   5   6

2. Interval construction:

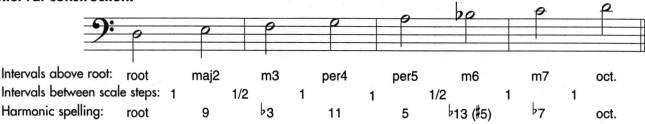

Intervals above root:	root	maj2	m3	per4	per5	m6	m7	oct.
Intervals between scale steps:	1	1/2	1	1	1/2	1	1	
Harmonic spelling:	root	9	♭3	11	5	♭13 (♯5)	♭7	oct.

3. Scale type and tonic chord:

With its minor third above the root, the Aeolian mode is the third minor scale created from the major scale. It is also known as the "natural minor" scale. The m6th (♭13 or ♯5) distinguishes the Aeolian mode from the Dorian mode. Its tonic chord is the m7 or m7(♭13) or m7(♯5) — Gm7, Gm7(♭13) or Gm7(♯5).

4. Intervals above the root that define the Aeolian mode:

- m3rd   • m6th (♭13 or ♯5)   • m7th

5. Most common uses:

- It provides the "6" chord in songs written in major keys.

- It provides the tonic mode and chord for some songs written in a minor key. The Aeolian mode is the "relative minor" of the major key with the same key signature. More about that later.

6. Tetrachord construction:

The Aeolian mode is made up of minor and phrygian tetrachords a whole step apart.

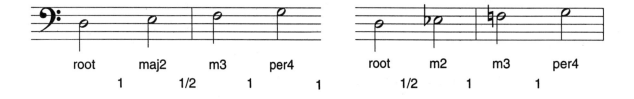

root	maj2	m3	per4		root	m2	m3	per4
1	1/2	1	1		1/2	1	1	

Two important definitions:

Definition 1: Relative minor

Relative minor is the minor mode that starts on the sixth step of the major scale—the Aeolian mode—which is also kown as the natural minor scale. Both the major scale and its relative minor have the same key signature.

To determine the relative minor of any major key, all you have to do is go *up a maj6th or down a m3rd* from the root of the major key with which you are dealing. For example, F major up a maj6th gives you D minor; F major down a m3rd also gives you D minor. So, D minor is the relative minor of F major. The key signature for both F major and D minor is one flat.

Pop quiz #3

Name the relative minor keys of the following major keys:

C major _____	A major_____	D major_____	D♭ major_____
B♭ major_____	G♭ major_____	A♭ major_____	C♯ major_____
G major_____	E♭ major_____	B major_____	E major_____

Give the key signatures for the following minor keys:

E minor_____	C minor_____	G minor_____	B♭ minor_____
A minor_____	F♯ minor_____	E♭ minor_____	F minor_____
B minor_____	D minor_____	C♯ minor_____	G♯ minor_____

Definition 2: Relative major

The term "relative major" means the major key from which a minor key originates.

To determine the relative major key of any minor key, all you have to do is go *up a m3rd or down a maj6th* from the root of the minor key with which you are dealing. This is exactly opposite from determining relative minor keys! For example, E minor up a m3rd produces G major, and E minor down a maj6th also produces G major. G major, then, is the relative major of E minor.

Pop quiz #4

Name the relative major keys of the following minor keys:

C minor_____	E♭ minor_____	A minor_____	F minor_____
B♭ minor_____	G♯ minor_____	E minor_____	C♯ minor_____
G minor_____	B minor_____	F♯ minor_____	D minor_____

Now that you're comfortable with all of this, let's move on to the Aeolian mode exercises.

Aeolian mode exercises in the 1st position:

Play the Aeolian mode in every key using the same plan that has been used for the other modes in the 1st position.

1. Starting from the root of the mode, play up as far as you can in the 1st position;

2. Then, play down the mode as far as you can going below the root for all Aeolian modes except those starting on E and F;

3. Then, play back up to the root;

4. Next, do the same with the tonic chord, in this case the m7(♭13) or m7(♯5). Add the ♭13 (♯5) where you can.

5. Practice B and E♭ Aeolian then move on to the remaining modes and chords.

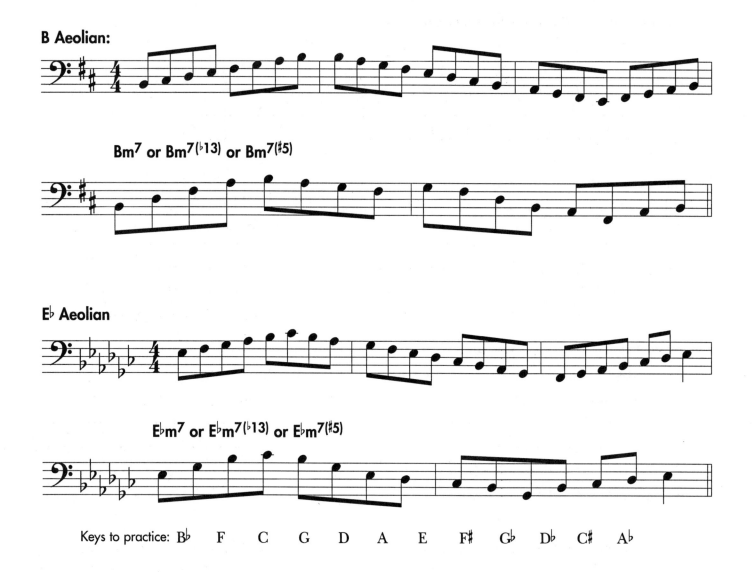

B Aeolian:

Bm⁷ or Bm⁷⁽♭¹³⁾ or Bm⁷⁽♯⁵⁾

E♭ Aeolian

E♭m⁷ or E♭m⁷⁽♭¹³⁾ or E♭m⁷⁽♯⁵⁾

Keys to practice: B♭   F   C   G   D   A   E   F♯   G♭   D♭   C♯   A♭

Do you know what major keys the starting pitches for these Aeolian modes are related to?

Now, make up your own lines using the Aeolian mode in the 1st position. Be sure to include the ♭13 (♯5) in your ideas.

The Aeolian mode outside of the 1st position:

Here are some ideas for playing a one-octave Aeolian mode outside of the 1st position. Practice these, and then come up with some of your own ideas. Play over the entire fingerboard.

1. Up one string – Starting with an open string

0   1   2◄─►1   3   4◄─►1   3

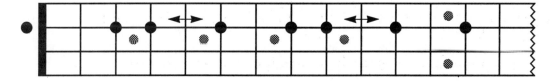

2. Up one string – Starting with a fingered note

1   3   4◄─►1   3   4◄─►1   3

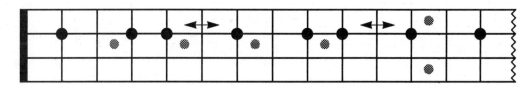

3. Two strings

1◄─►1   2   4   1   2◄─►1   3

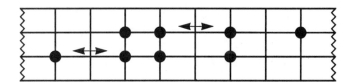

4. Three strings

1   3   4   1   3   4   1   3

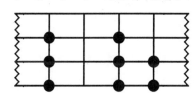

5. Three strings

1   3   4   1◄─►1   2   4   1

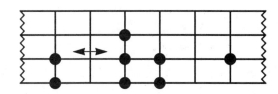

6. Three strings

1◄─►1   2   4   1   2   4   1

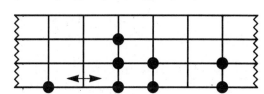

7. Two string pairs – F#, B and E Aeolian

1   3   0◄─►1   3   4   1   3

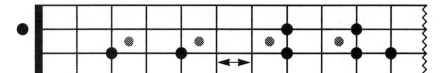

8. Four strings (See #6, p.74 & #8, p.89)

4   1   2   4   1   2   4   1

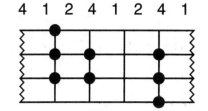

Aeolian mode exercises outside of the 1st position:

Practice these exercises in every key. Use the list of starting pitches following each exercise to keep track of your progress. Play each exercise with as many of the fingerings on page 95 as you can. Be sure to retain the shape of the fingering you have chosen.

Exercise 1: Aeolian mode

Keys to practice: D   A   E   B   F♯   G♭   C♯   D♭   A♭   E♭   B♭   F   C   G

Exercise 2: Aeolian mode – diatonic intervals

Keys to practice: C   D   E   F♯   G♭   A♭   B♭   C♯   D♭   E♭   F   G   A   B

Exercise 3: 3-note groups

Keys to practice: F   B♭   E♭   A♭   D♭   C♯   F♯   G♭   B   E   A   D   G   C

Exercise 4: m7 or m7(♯5) or m7(♭13)

Keys to practice: E   F   F♯   G♭   G   A♭   A   B♭   B   C   C♯   D♭   D   E♭

Your own Aeolian mode (natural minor scale) ideas:

• Come up with Aeolian mode ideas to end all Aeolian mode ideas!

• Pay particular attention to the ♭13 and how it sounds next to the 5th of the mode and the tonic chord.

• Experiment with the sound of the m7(♯5) chord (no regular 5th).

And, Finally, the Locrian Mode

Locrian mode facts:

1. Derivation:

The Locrian mode is built from the seventh scale step of the major scale.

Scale step: 1 2 3 4 5 6 7

2. Interval construction:

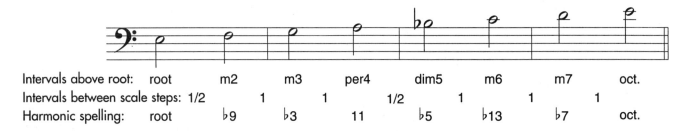

Intervals above root:	root	m2	m3	per4	dim5	m6	m7	oct.
Intervals between scale steps:	1/2	1	1	1/2	1	1	1	
Harmonic spelling:	root	♭9	♭3	11	♭5	♭13	♭7	oct.

3. Scale type and tonic chord:

The Locrian mode is unique among the major scale modes. It's the only major scale mode with *a diminished tonic triad.* In addition to the ♭3 interval that it shares with the Dorian, Phrygian and Aeolian modes, the Locrian mode contains a dim5 (♭5) above its root. The mode, then, is not minor. The most descriptive name for the Locrian mode is the name classical music gave to the tonic 7th chord of the mode—*half-diminished.* The mode is called half-diminished because it has a m7 above it's root rather than a dim7 found in a (full) diminished scale. Many musicians call the Locrian mode the "half-diminished scale."

The tonic chord for the Locrian mode is usually written as a m7(♭5)—**Gm**7(♭5). The "classical" way of writing the same chord, ⌀ (pronounced "half-diminished")—**G**⌀—is often used. Both symbols mean the same thing.

4. Intervals above the root that define the Locrian mode:

- m9th (♭9)   • m3rd   • dim5th (♭5)   • m6th (♭13, ♯5)   • m7th

5. Most common uses:

- as the "2" chord in minor keys   • as a substitute for the "5" chord in major keys

6. Tetrachord construction:

The Locrian mode is made up of phrygian and whole-tone tetrachords a half step apart.

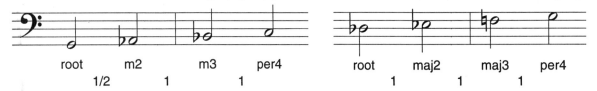

root	m2	m3	per4	root	maj2	maj3	per4
	1/2	1	1		1	1	1

Locrian mode exercises in the 1st position:

Play the Locrian mode in every key in the 1st position with the same plan that was used for the preceding modes .

1. Starting from the root, play up the mode as far as you can in the 1st position;
2. Then, play the mode down as far as you can going below the root for all Locrian modes except E;
3. Then, play back up to the root;
4. Next, do the same with the tonic chord, in this case the m7($\flat$5). Add the $\flat$9 and the $\flat$13.
5. Practice B and E Locrian, then move on to the remaining modes and chords.

B Locrian:

Bm7($\flat$5) or B$^\varnothing$

E Locrian

Em7($\flat$5) or E$^\varnothing$

Keys to practice: A$\sharp$　F　C　G　D　A　D$\sharp$　F$\sharp$　C$\sharp$　G$\sharp$

Do you know what major keys the starting pitches for these Locrian modes are related to?

Now, create your own Locrian mode ideas in the 1st position. Be sure to include the $\flat$9 and the $\flat$13.

The Locrian mode outside of the 1st position:

Here are some ideas for playing a one octave Locrian mode outside of the 1st position. Practice these, and then come up with some of your own. Play over the entire fingerboard.

1. Up one string – Starting with an open string

0 1 3 ◄►1 2 4 ◄►1 3

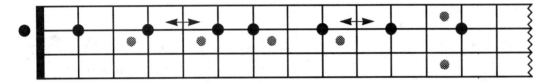

2. Up one string – Starting with a fingered note

1 2 4 ◄►1 2 4 ◄►1 3

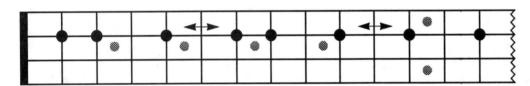

3. Two strings

1 2 4 1 2 4 ◄►1 3

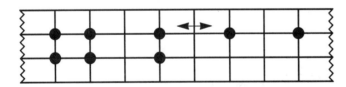

4. Three strings

1 2 4 1 2 ◄►2 4 1

5. Three strings

1 2 ◄►1 3 4 1 ∧ 4 1

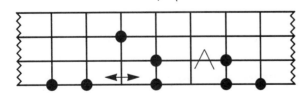

6. Four strings (See #8, p.79 & #8 p.95)

3 4 1 3 4 1 ∧ 4 1

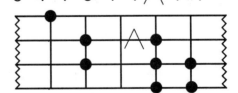

7. Two string pairs – F♯, B and E Locrian

1 2 0 ◄►1 2 4 1 3

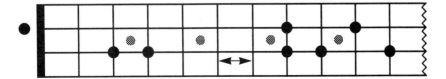

8. Three strings

1 2 4 1 2 4 1 3

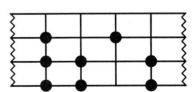

Locrian mode exercises outside of the 1st position:

Practice these exercises in every key. Use the list of starting pitches following each exercise to keep track of your progress. Play each exercise with as many of the fingerings on page 100 as you can.

Be sure to retain the shape of the fingering you have chosen.

Exercise 1: Locrian mode

Keys to practice: C♯ D D♯ E F F♯ G G♯ A A♯ B

Exercise 2: Locrian mode bass line – play with a latin feel

Keys to practice: F♯ A C E G A♯ C♯ F D G♯ B

Exercise 3: m7(♭5) – sixteenth note pattern

Keys to practice: A D G C F A♯ D♯ G♯ C♯ F♯ B

Exercise 4: m7(♭5) or ∅ – triplet pattern

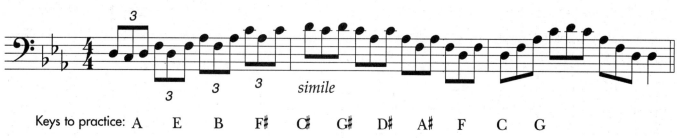

Keys to practice: A E B F♯ C♯ G♯ D♯ A♯ F C G

Your own Locrian mode ideas:

• The Locrian mode or the half-diminished scale; the m7($\flat$5) or $\emptyset$—whatever you choose to call the mode and chord—make them you own.

• Pay particular attention to the diminished triad with its $\flat$5.

7

Major Scale Modes & Chords Part 2: Putting Them All Together

Now that we have studied all of the major scale modes and their 7th chords separately, let's put them back in order to hear how they function within a major key.

Because most of the music you'll be hearing and playing is based on the modes and chords of the major scale, your ability to hear and to play through them is essential to your success as a bass player. Practicing all the modes and chords together in a key will help to develop your sense of *how the modes and chords relate to one another* in that key or any key. All of this business about tonic chords, "5" chords, "2" chords and "4" chords will start to make a lot more sense to you as your ears and hands get a key together. Your skill at hearing and playing through chord changes, both with music in front of you and by ear, can't help but grow.

Playing diatonically through modes and chords is also a great way to build up your technique on the bass. In the examples that follow, you'll notice some mode and chord fingerings that were not covered in Chapter 6. These fingerings allow the modes and chords to flow more smoothly up and down the neck. The feeling of *key* is retained as the last shift with one mode or chord sets up your left hand for playing the next mode or chord. For example, in the second fingering given for diatonic chords on page 116 of Chapter 6, there is a shift in the middle of every chord! Your left hand is moving constantly. As you move through a key diatonically, you'll find that playing each mode or chord with its "regular" fingering creates some amazingly awkward left-hand movement.

In this chapter, there many fingerings are given for the modes and their chords. Be creative with them. Play up one set of fingerings and down another. Mix and match all of them. In the exercises that follow the examples, fingerings are not provided for you. Ugh! Looks like you'll have to come up with some fingerings of your own.

Listen to your playing very carefully. Be certain that the notes you are playing are correct all the time. Make sure that your shifting is smooth and quiet. Being able to play this material accurately at a slow tempo is much better than making a ton of mistakes as you play at the speed of light. Be patient and your ears and your technique will blossom.

Major modes – key of E – starting from the open E string – 4 strings

This set of fingerings stays in the 1st position as long as possible.
If you have a 5-string or a 6-string bass, add the key of B starting from the open B string.

These fingerboard charts will help you with E the major modes.

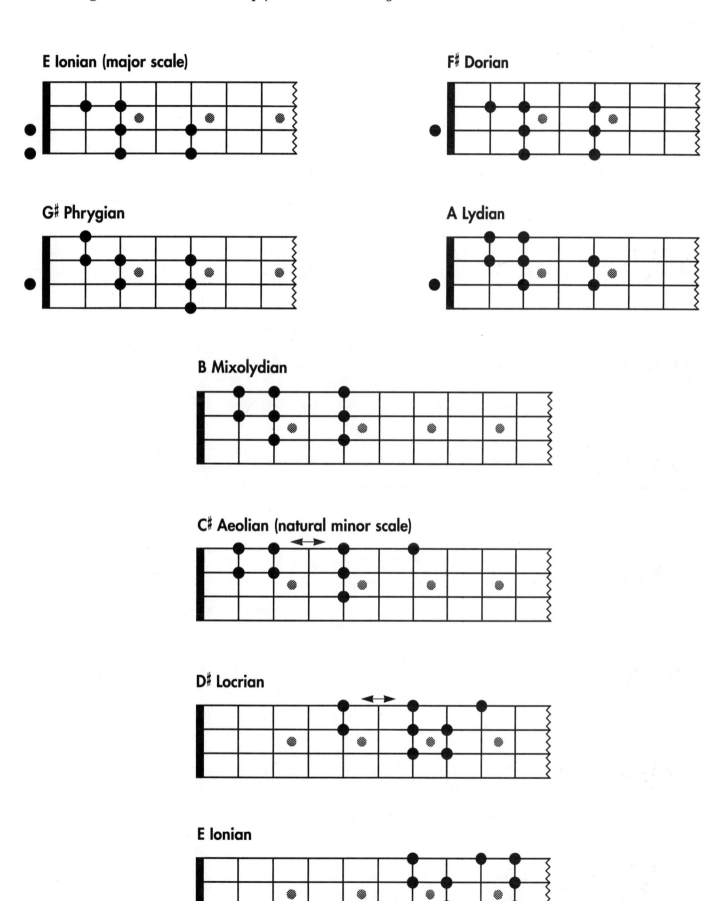

E Ionian (major scale)

F# Dorian

G# Phrygian

A Lydian

B Mixolydian

C# Aeolian (natural minor scale)

D# Locrian

E Ionian

Major modes – keys of E and A – starting from an open string

This set of fingerings uses three strings and leaves the 1st position quickly. Practice both keys.
If you have a 5-string bass, add the key of B starting from the open B string. Those of you with 6-string basses, add the key of B and also the key of D, starting from the open D string.

These fingerboard charts will help you with the major modes played on three strings.

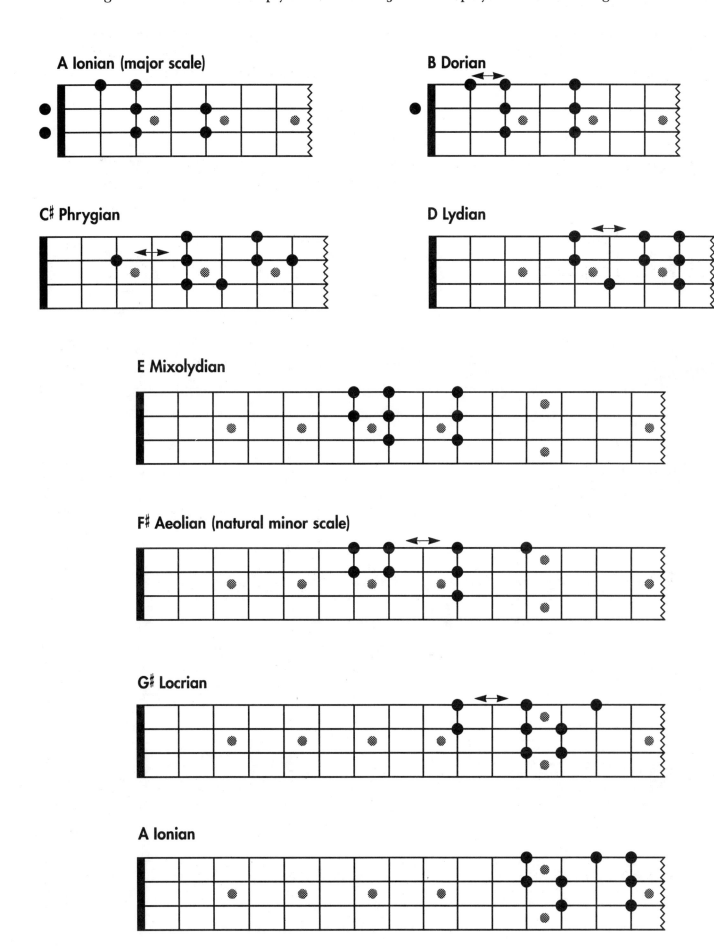

Diatonic 7th chords – starting from the open E string

The **1st set** of fingerings is good for E major only as it **covers four strings.** If you have a 5-string bass, add the key of B. If you have a 6-string bass, you can add the keys of B and A.

The **2nd set** of fingerings works for both E and A major as it **covers three strings.** If you have a 5-string bass, add the key of B. You 6-string players can add the keys of B and D.

```
1st set:  0   4   2   1     2   0   4   2     4   2   1   4     0   4   2   1
2nd set:  0   4   2   1     2   0→3   1     3   1→3   1     2   1→2   1

          2   1→3   1     3   1→3   1     3   1→2   1     2   1   4   3
          2   1→3   1     3   1→3   1     3   1→2   1     2   1   4   3

          3   4   1   2     1   2→1   3     1   3→1   3     1   3→1   2
          3   4   1   2     1   2→1   3     1   3→1   3     1   3→1   2

          1   2   4   0     4   1   2   4     2   4   0   2     1   2   4   0
          1   2→1   2     1   3→1   3     1   3→0   2     1   2   4   0
```

1st set: Key of E major – covers four strings – starts with the open E string

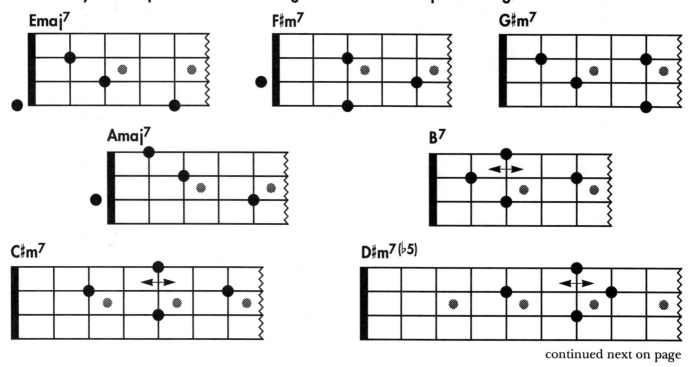

continued next on page

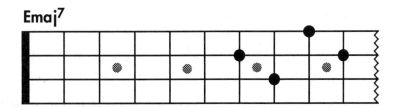

Emaj⁷

2nd set: Keys of A and E major – 3 strings – starts on either the open A or E strings

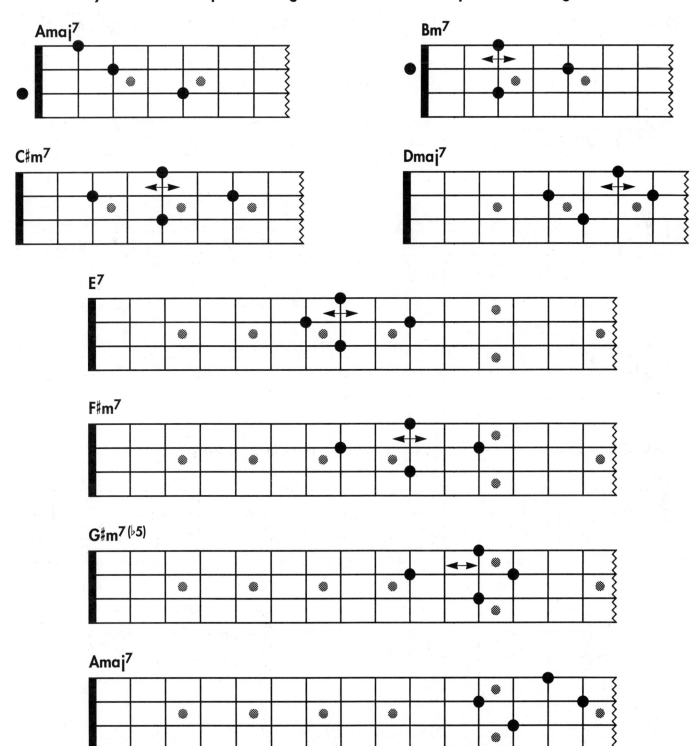

Amaj⁷

Bm⁷

C♯m⁷

Dmaj⁷

E⁷

F♯m⁷

G♯m⁷ (♭5)

Amaj⁷

Check off the keys of the diatonic chords you've practiced: A E
5-string bass - B E A   6-string bass - B E A D

Major modes – all keys – starting with a fingered note – 4 strings – #1

This set of fingerings **stays in the 1st position as long as possible.**

G Ionian (major scale)

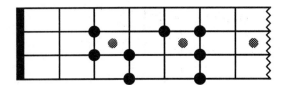

A Dorian

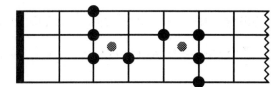

B Phrygian

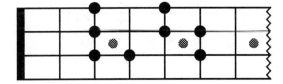

C Lydian

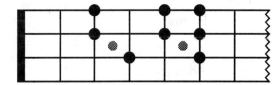

D Mixolydian

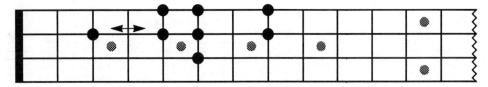

E Aeolian (natural minor scale)

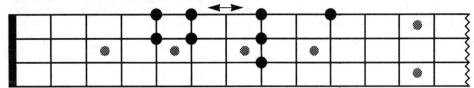

F♯ Locrian

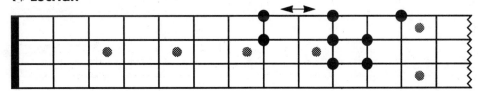

G Ionian

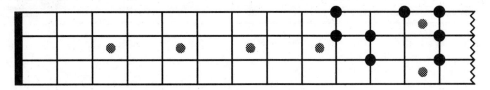

Check off the keys of the diatonic major modes you've practiced:

G   C   F   B♭   E♭   A♭   D♭   C♯   F♯   G♭   B   E   A   D

Major modes – all keys – starting with a fingered note – 4 strings – #2

This set of fingerings **leaves the 1st position quickly.**

G Ionian (major scale)

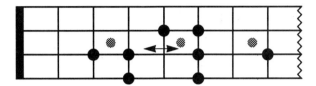

A Dorian

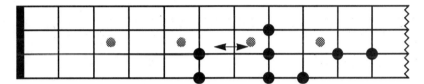

B Phrygian

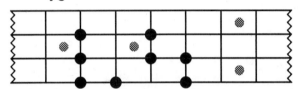

C Lydian

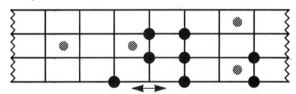

D Mixolydian

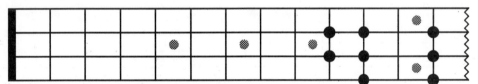

E Aeolian (natural minor scale)

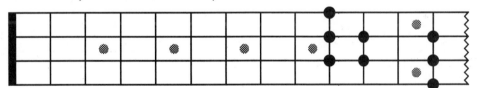

F♯ Locrian

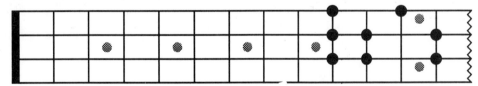

G Ionian

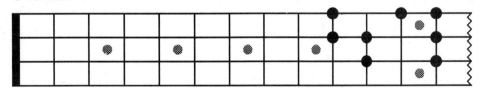

Check off the keys of the diatonic major modes you've practiced:

G   C   F   B♭   E♭   A♭   D♭   C♯   F♯   G♭   B   E   A   D

Major modes – all keys – starting with a fingered note – 3 strings

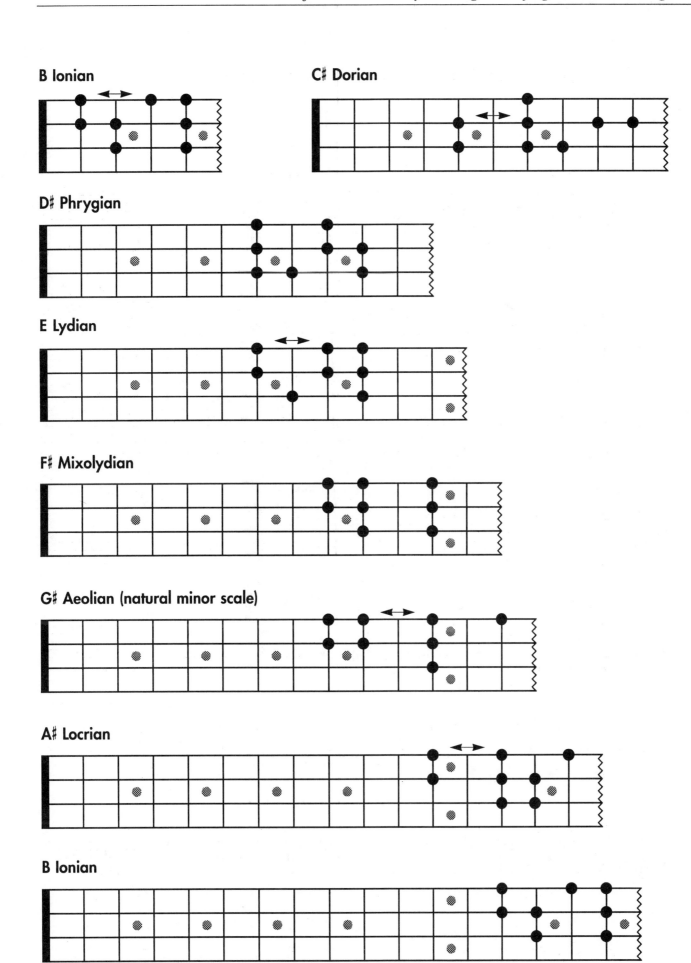

Check off the keys of the diatonic major modes you've practiced:

B   E   A   D   G   C   F   B♭   E♭   A♭   D♭   C♯   F♯   G♭

Diatonic 7th chords – starting with a fingered note

The **1st set** of fingerings **covers four strings.**

The **2nd set** of fingerings **covers three strings.**

Practice both sets of fingerings in *every* key.

1st set: All keys – starting with a fingered note – 4 strings

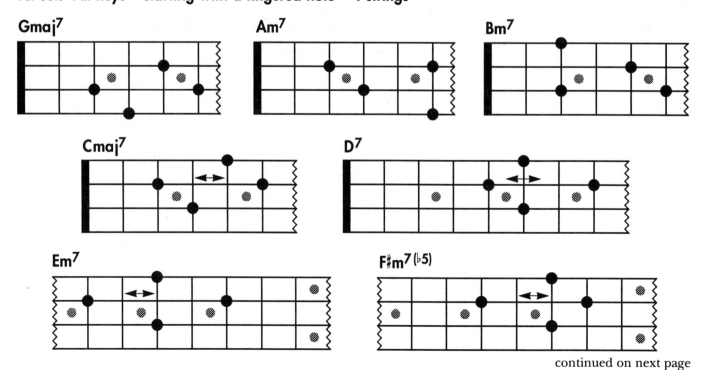

continued on next page

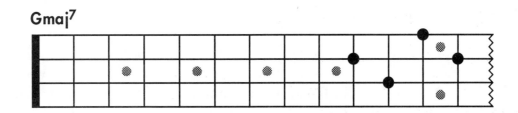

Gmaj7

2nd set : All keys – starting with a fingered note – 3 strings

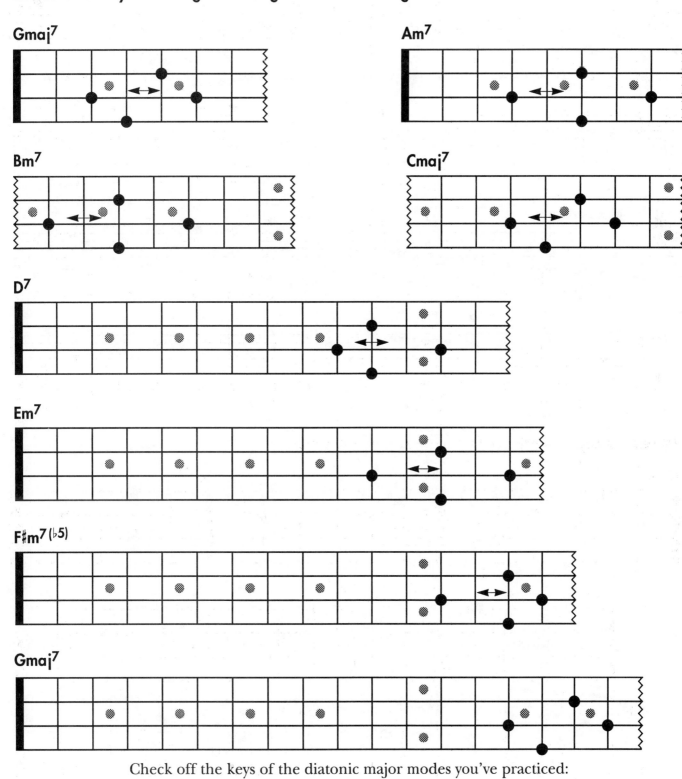

Gmaj7

Am7

Bm7

Cmaj7

D7

Em7

F#m7(b5)

Gmaj7

Check off the keys of the diatonic major modes you've practiced:

G   C   F   Bb   Eb   Ab   Db   C#   F#   Gb   B   E   A   D

Diatonic Mode and Chord Exercises

Take the time to work out each exercise in every key. When you're finished, you will have covered the entire neck of your bass in ways you never thought possible. Remember, only the 1st position is separate from the rest of the neck as its fingerings are unique. You'll never get a bass part with a position number or fingerings on it. You're expected to know where the notes are!

Exercise 1: Diatonic modes

Check off the keys of the diatonic modes you've practiced:

G   C   F   B♭   E♭   A♭   D♭   C♯   F♯   G♭   B   E   A   D

Exercise 2: Diatonic modes played around the cycle of 5ths down or 4ths up

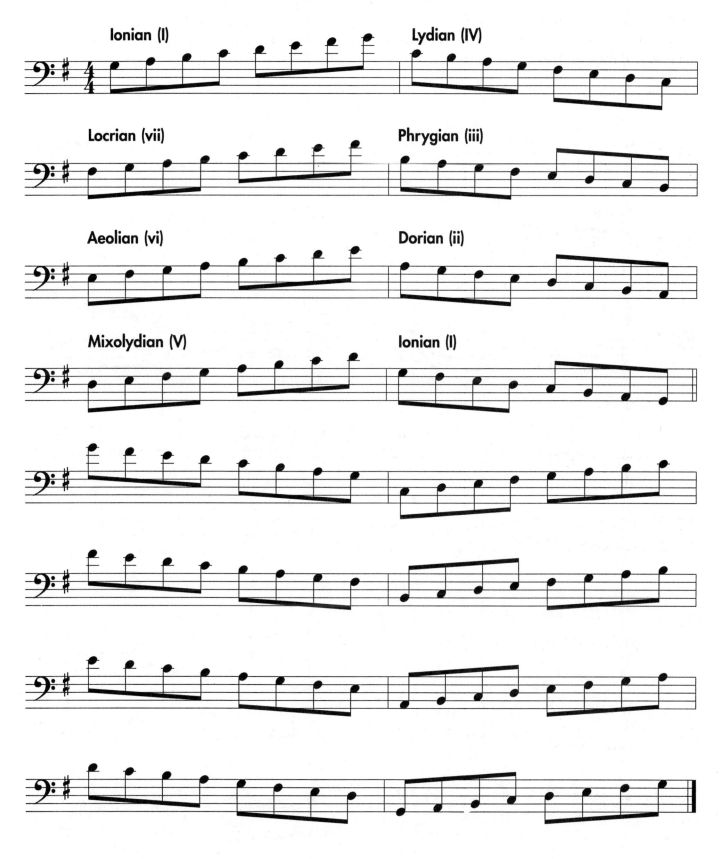

Check off the keys of the diatonic major modes you've practiced:

G   C   F   B♭   E♭   A♭   D♭   C♯   F♯   G♭   B   E   A   D

Exercise 3: Diatonic triads

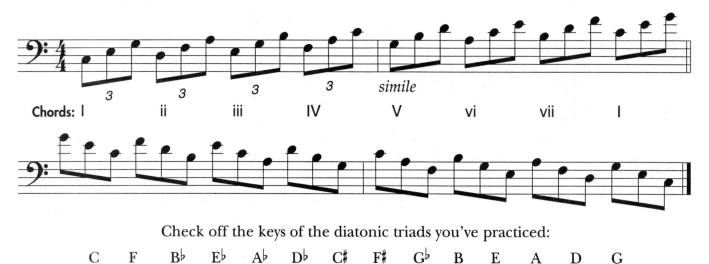

Chords: I   ii   iii   IV   V   vi   vii   I

Check off the keys of the diatonic triads you've practiced:

C   F   B♭   E♭   A♭   D♭   C♯   F♯   G♭   B   E   A   D   G

Exercise 4: Diatonic triads up and down

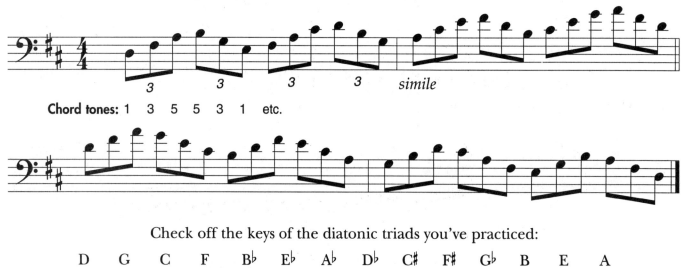

Chord tones: 1   3   5   5   3   1   etc.

Check off the keys of the diatonic triads you've practiced:

D   G   C   F   B♭   E♭   A♭   D♭   C♯   F♯   G♭   B   E   A

Exercise 5: Diatonic triads played around the cycle of 4ths

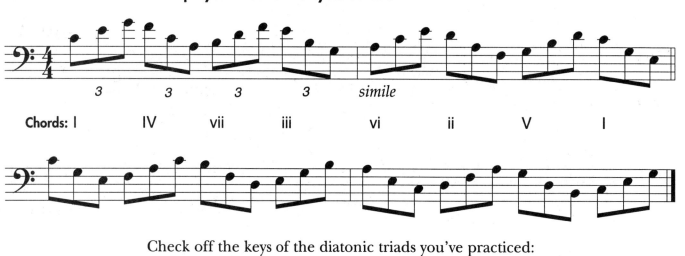

Chords: I   IV   vii   iii   vi   ii   V   I

Check off the keys of the diatonic triads you've practiced:

C   F   B♭   E♭   A♭   D♭   C♯   F♯   G♭   B   E   A   D   G

Exercise 6: Diatonic 7th chords

Chord tones: 1 3 5 7 7 5 3 1 etc.

Check off the keys of the diatonic 7th chords you've practiced:

A   D   G   C   F   B♭   E♭   A♭   D♭   C♯   F♯   G♭   B   E

Exercise 7: Diatonic 7th chords

Chord tones: 1 7 5 3 1 7 5 3 etc.

Check off the keys of the diatonic 7th chords you've practiced:

G   C   F   B♭   E♭   A♭   D♭   C♯   F♯   G♭   B   E   A   D

Exercise 8: Diatonic 7th chords played around the cycle of 4ths

Chord tones: 1 3 5 7 1 3 5 7 etc.

1 7 5 3 1 7 5 3 etc.

Check off the keys of the diatonic 7th chords you've practiced:

G   C   F   B♭   E♭   A♭   D♭   C♯   F♯   G♭   B   E   A   D

Your own diatonic mode and 7th chord ideas:

8

Two-Octave Major Scale Modes
&
Arpeggios

"OK. What am I going to get out of playing two-octave major scale modes and arpeggios…hmm?"

"Plenty!"

1. They are great confidence builders.

Because two-octave major scale modes and arpeggios make you cover large sections of the neck of your bass, you'll lose your fear of staying in one position all of the time. You've probably seen bass players who play for a while in one position, then make a huge shift to some other position on the neck, then play some more of their hot licks, then shift back to the position they came from, then shift back, and so on and so on. What happened to the notes in between those two positions? The study of two-octave scales and arpeggios will teach you how to cover the *entire* neck smoothly and efficiently. You'll be able to handle that "middle-of-the-neck" gray area.

2. They are terrific technique builders.

As you build up your speed practicing the two-octave scales and arpeggios, you'll be amazed at how you've increased your ability to cover the whole neck quickly and accurately.

3. They are great pattern busters.

You probably have a favorite pattern for playing two-octave scales. So, I'm sure that you'll be surprised to find that there are at least ten different ways of playing a two-octave major scale! For the remaining modes, you may write in your own fingerings on the four blank fingerboard diagrams provided. The arpeggio exercises start with four ways to play the same chord. How can you remember them all? Well, I guess you will to have to recall what the notes are in each scale and chord. What a concept!

4. They will help with bass lines and solos.

As you are building up your confidence, building up your technique and busting patterns, you will also be hearing and playing the material all over the neck—perhaps in places and in ways you never thought possible. You'll be able to add many new melodic and harmonic ideas to your arsenal. Plus, you'll be learning, playing and hearing the *whole* bass.

Two-octave Major scales

Here are ten, count 'em, ten ways to play a two-octave major scale. Don't worry! You aren't expected to remember all of them. The ten examples show various ways to accomplish the same thing. The purpose of all these fingerings is to break you out of the habit of playing the same old patterns every time you play a two-octave scale. In fact, you should be thinking about the notes you are playing rather than just about a pattern.

Notice that in fingering **1**, most of the notes are played in the low end of the neck—whereas the opposite is true for fingering **10**. As you progress through each example, one or two notes of the scale are moved up the neck. If you want to, you could probably come up with many more fingerings. In fact, as you play two-octave major scales in every key, why don't you invent some fingerings of your own? For example, if you have a bass with a two-octave neck, play the scale up one string. All the fingerings I've suggested cover four strings. So, invent some that cover three strings—or five or six if you own a 5-string or 6-string bass. Cover the neck of your bass in as many ways as you can and don't forget to play all the fingerings in every key.

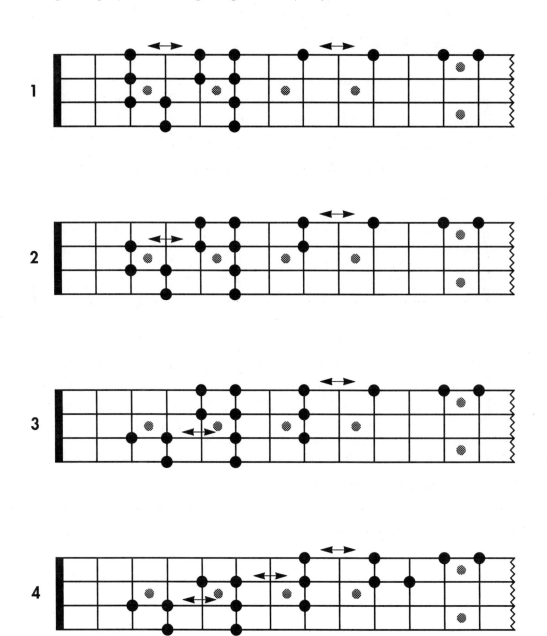

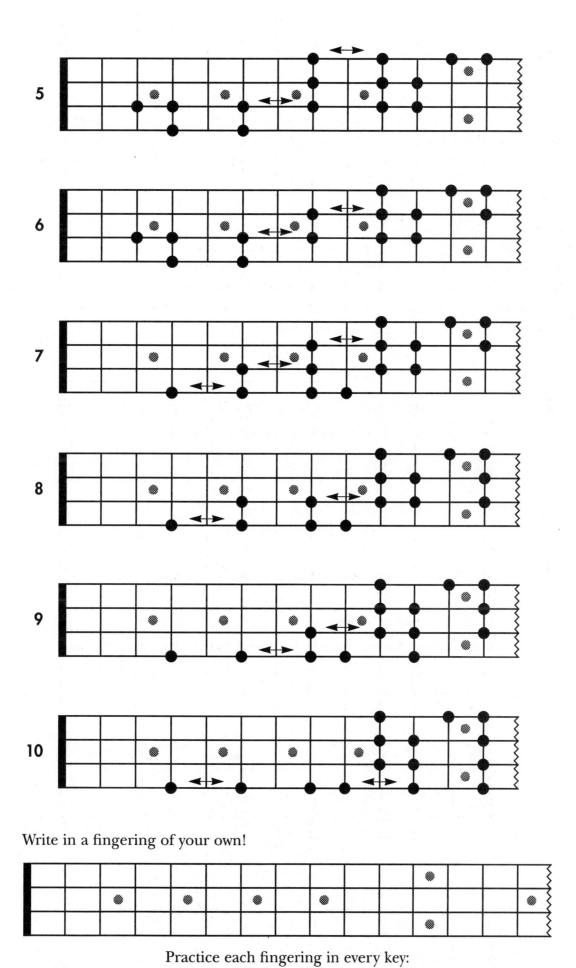

Write in a fingering of your own!

Practice each fingering in every key:

G   C   F   B♭   E♭   A♭   D♭   C♯   F♯   G♭   B   E   A   D

Two-octave Lydian modes

Like the ten two-octave major scales shown on the previous page, the first example stays in the 1st position as long as possible, while the last example gets to the top end of the bass as quickly as possible. Fill in the empty fingerboard charts with your own ideas for the two-octave Lydian mode.

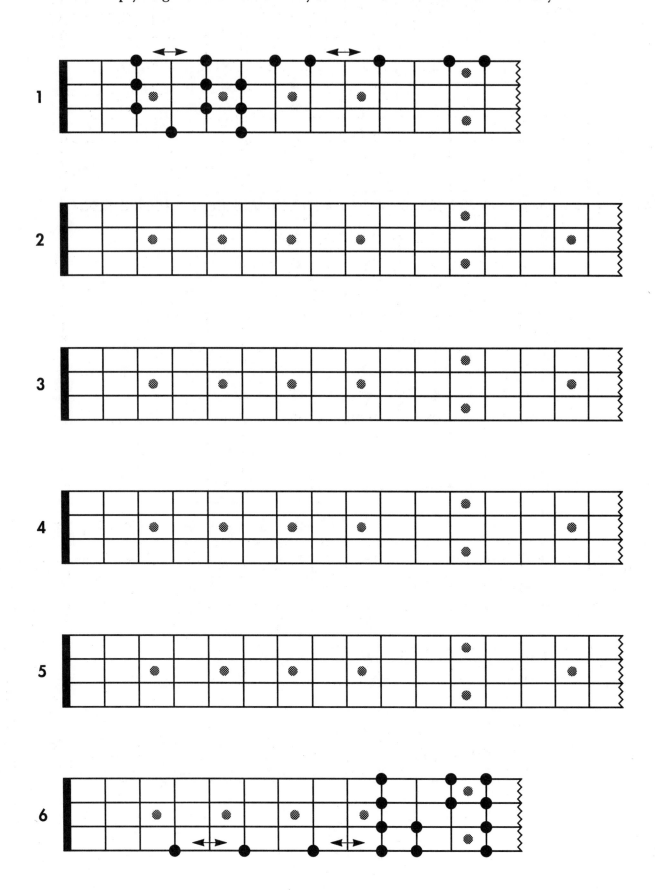

Two-octave maj7th arpeggios: the 1 (tonic) chord in major keys

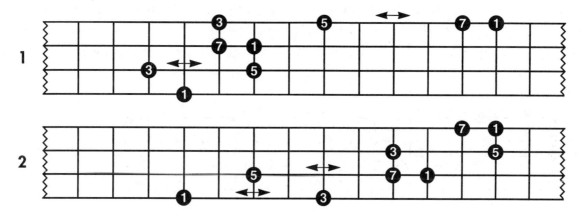

Two-octave maj7(#11) arpeggios: 1 or 4 chord in major keys – Lydian mode

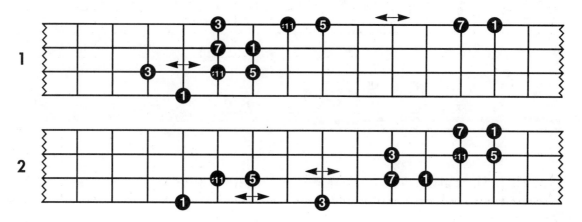

Exercise 1: maj7th chord arpeggio – check out both fingerings

Exercise 2: maj7th chord arpeggio

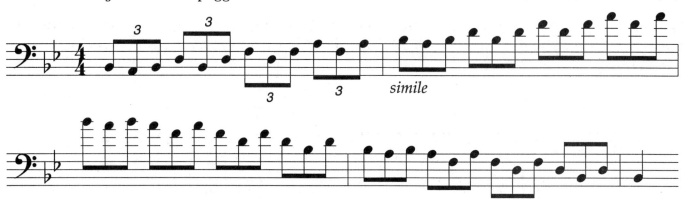

Exercise 3: maj7th chord arpeggio with chromatic lower neighbor tones

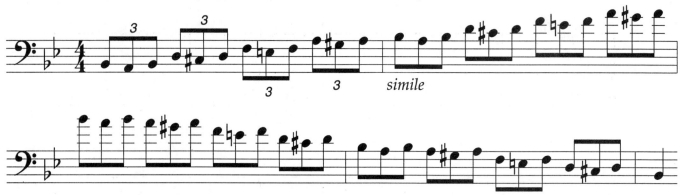

Exercise 4: maj7th chord arpeggio with diatonic upper and chromatic lower neighbor tones

Check off the keys of the maj7th arpeggios you've practiced:

B♭   E♭   A♭   D♭   C♯   F♯   G♭   B   E   A   D   G   C   F

Two-octave Dorian modes

Example 1 stays in the 1st position as long as possible. Example 6 gets to the top end of the bass as quickly as possible. Fill in the empty fingerboard charts with your own ideas for the two-octave Dorian mode.

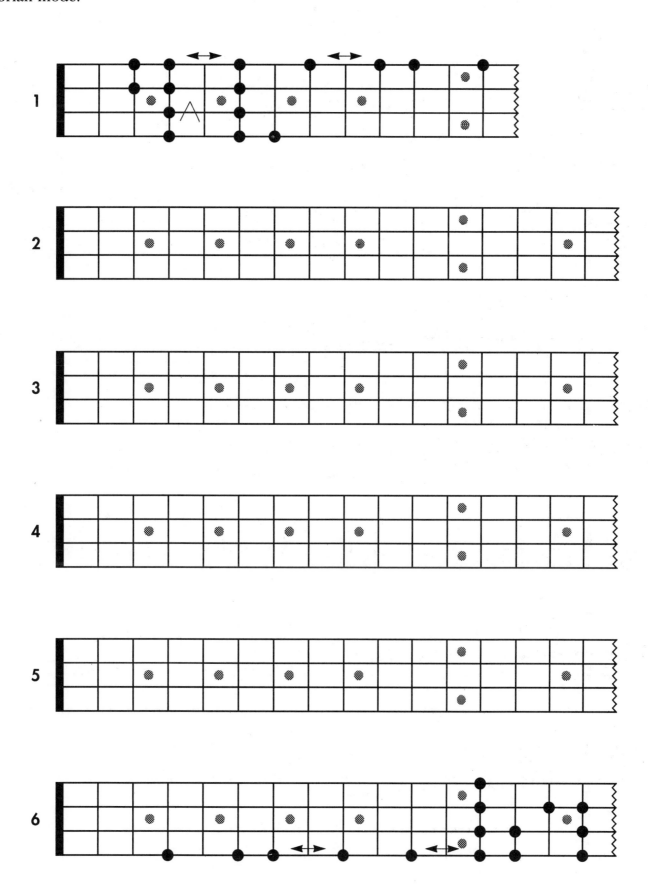

Two-octave Phrygian modes

Example 1 stays in the 1st position as long as possible. Example 6 gets to the top end of the bass as quickly as possible. Fill in the empty fingerboard charts with your own two-octave Phrygian mode ideas.

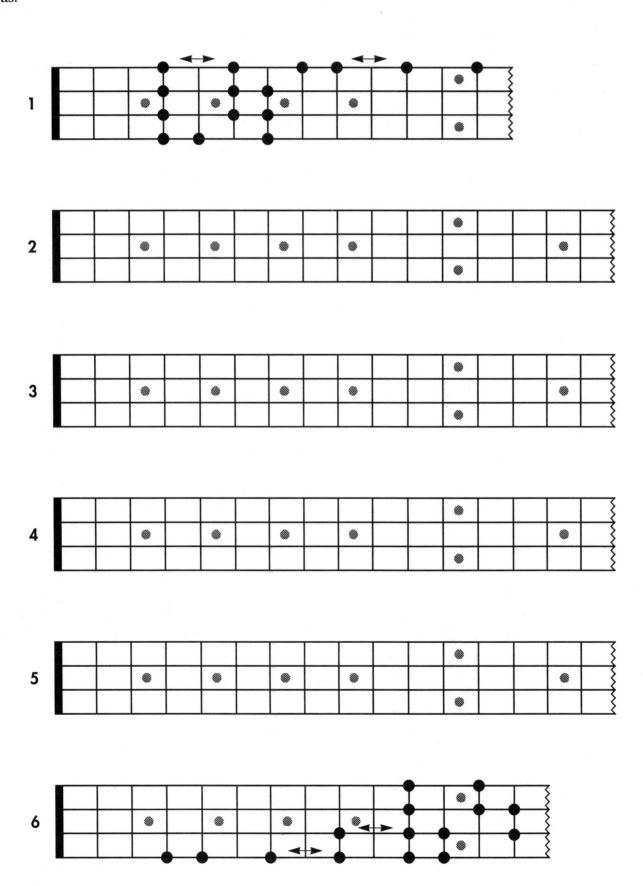

Two-octave Aeolian modes

As usual, Example 1 stays in the 1st position as long as possible. Example 6 gets to the top end of the bass as quickly as possible. Fill in the empty fingerboard charts with your own two-octave Aeolian mode ideas.

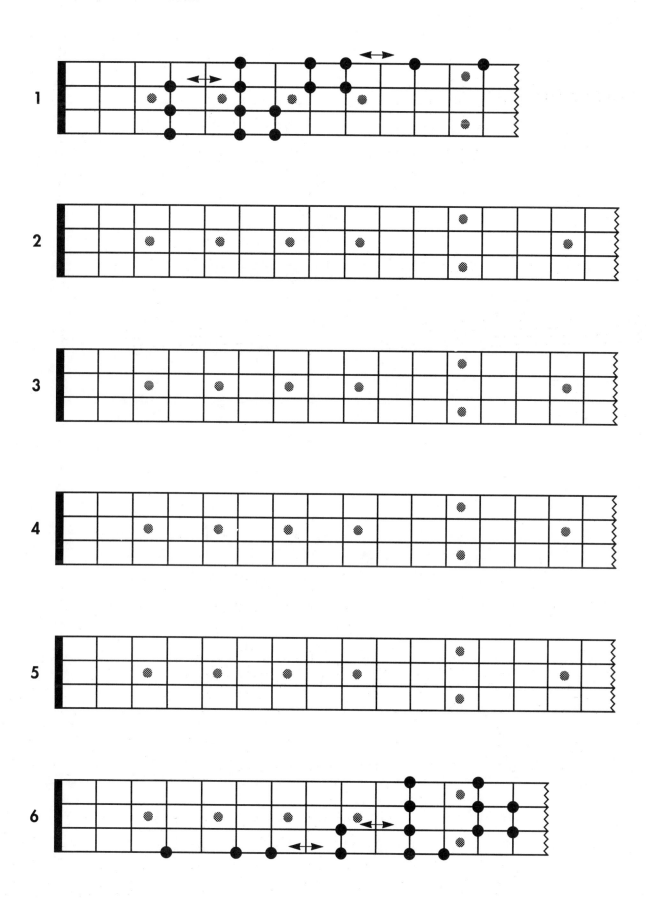

Two-octave m7th arpeggios – 2, 3 or 6 chords in major keys – tonic chord in minor

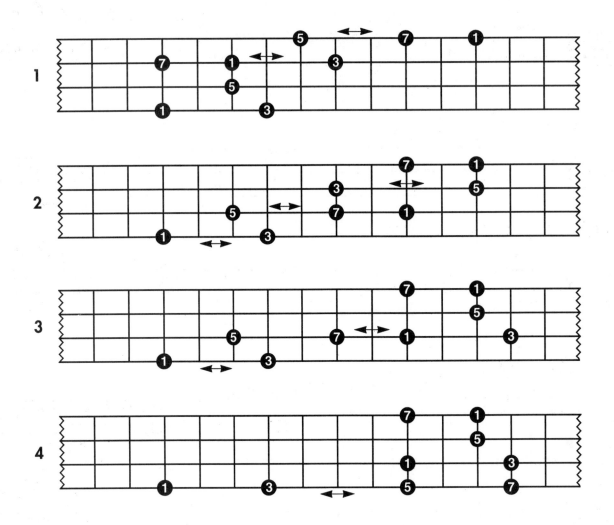

Exercise 5: m7th chord arpeggio – check out both fingerings

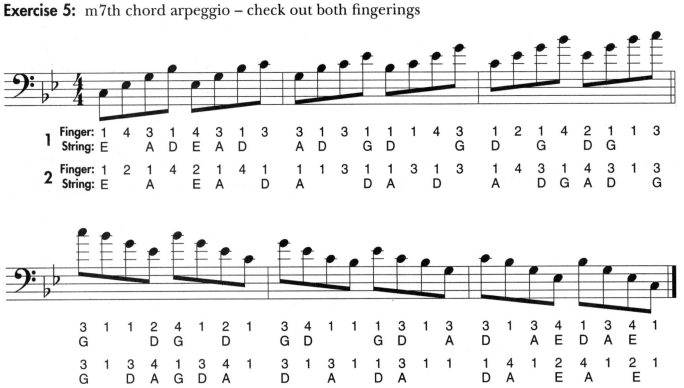

	Finger:	1	4	3	1	4	3	1	3		3	1	3	1	1	1	4	3		1	2	1	4	2	1	1	3
1	String:	E		A	D	E	A	D			A	D		G	D			G			G	D		G		D	G

	Finger:	1	2	1	4	2	1	4	1		1	1	3	1	1	3	1	3		1	4	3	1	4	3	1	3
2	String:	E		A		E	A		D		A			D	A		D			A			D	G	A	D		G

3	1	1	2	4	1	2	1		3	4	1	1	1	3	1	3		3	1	3	4	1	3	4	1
G			D	G		D			G	D			G	D		A		D			A	E	D	A	E

3	1	3	4	1	3	4	1		3	1	3	1	1	3	1	1		1	4	1	2	4	1	2	1
G		D	A	G	D	A			D		A		D	A				D	A		E	A		E	

Exercise 6: m7th chord arpeggio

Exercise 7: m7th chord arpeggio with chromatic lower neighbor tones

Exercise 8: m7th chord arpeggio with diatonic upper and chromatic lower neighbor tones

Check off the keys of the m7th arpeggios you've practiced:

C F B♭ E♭ A♭ D♭ C♯ F♯ G♭ B E A D G

Two-octave Mixolydian modes

You guessed it—Example 1 stays in the 1st position as long as possible. Example 6 gets to the top end of the bass as quickly as possible. Fill in the empty fingerboard charts with your own two octave Mixolydian mode ideas, then practice the arpeggios in every key.

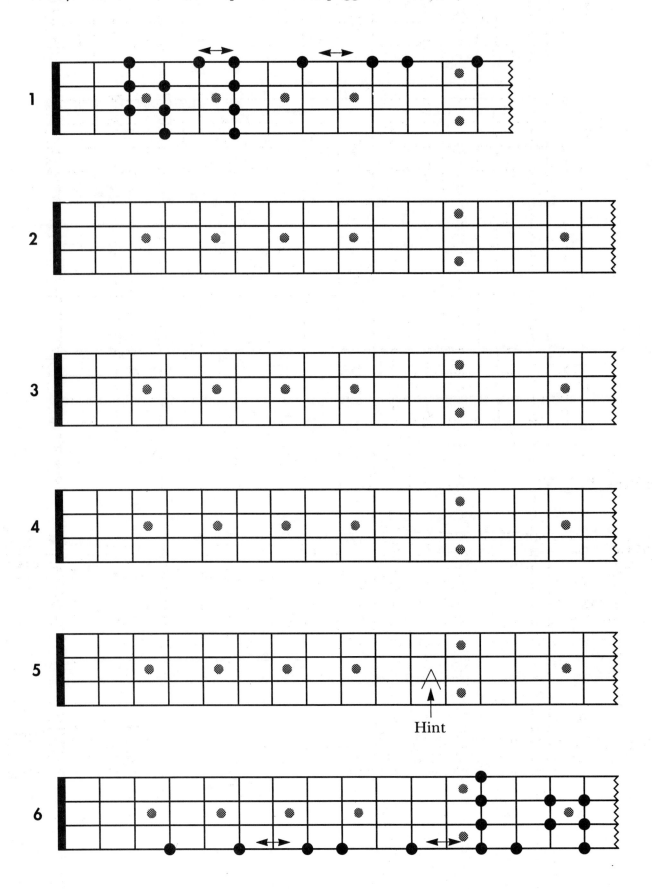

Hint

Two-octave dom7th arpeggios – the 5 chord or tonic chord in major keys

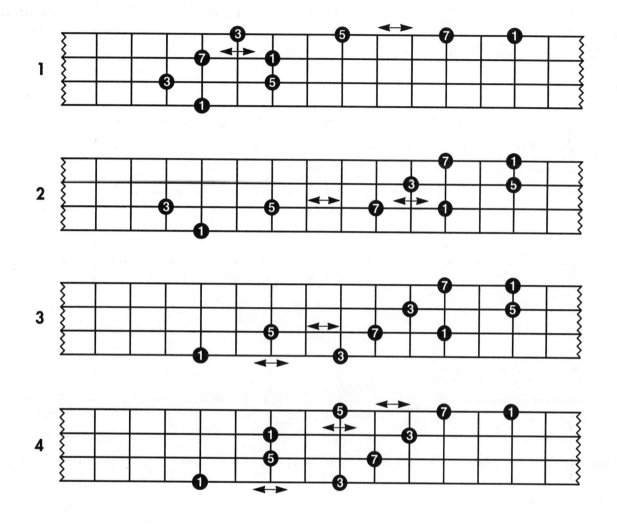

Exercise 9: dom7th chord arpeggio – check out both fingerings

1 Finger: 1 0 3 1 0 3 1 3   3 1 3 2 1 2 1 4   2 3 1 4 3 1 1 3
   String: E A   D A   D   A D   G D   G   D   G   D G

2 Finger: 1 3 1 4 3 1 1 3   3 1 3 2 1 2 1 4   2 1 4 2 1 4 2 4
   String: E   A   E A   E A   D A   D   A D   G D   G

3 1 1 3 4 1 3 2   4 1 2 1 2 3 1 3   3 1 3 0 1 3 0 1
G   D G   D   G   D   G D   A   D   A   D A   E

4 2 4 1 2 4 1 2   4 1 2 1 2 3 1 3   3 1 1 3 4 1 3 1
G   D   G D   A   D   A   D A   E A   E A   E

Exercise 10: dom7th chord arpeggio

Exercise 11: dom7th chord arpeggio with chromatic lower neighbor tones

Exercise 12: dom7th chord arpeggio with diatonic upper and chromatic lower neighbor tones

Check off the keys of the dom7th arpeggios you've practiced:

F   B♭   E♭   A♭   D♭   C♯   F♯   G♭   B   E   A   D   G   C

Two-octave Locrian modes

For the last time, Example 1 stays in the 1st position as long as possible. Example 6 gets to the top end of the bass as quickly as possible. Fill in the empty fingerboard charts with your own two-octave Locrian mode ideas and practice everything in *every* key.

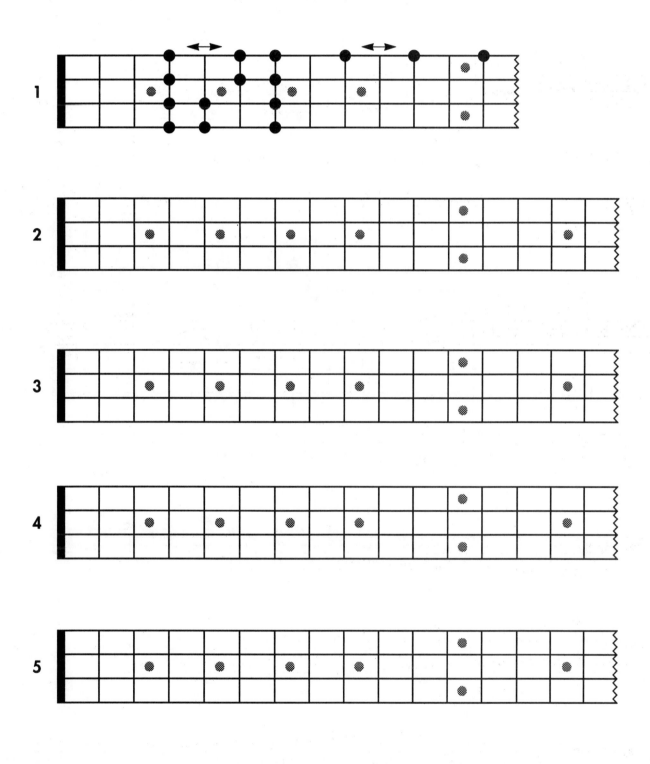

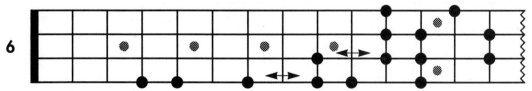

Two-octave m7(♭5) arpeggios – 7 chord in major keys – 2 chord in minor keys

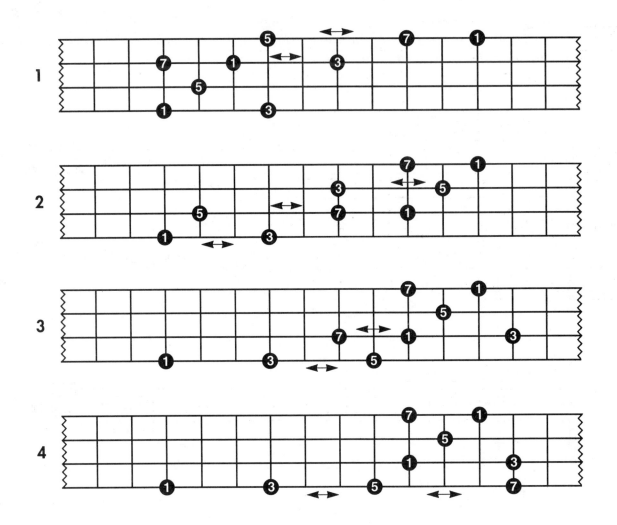

Exercise 13: m7(♭5) arpeggio – check out both fingerings

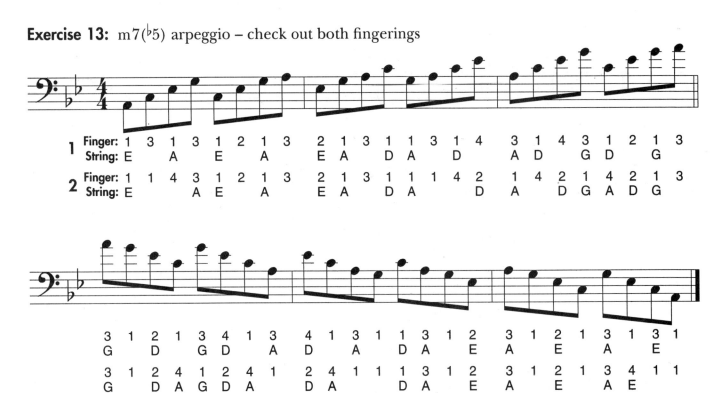

Exercise 14: m7(♭5) chord arpeggio

Exercise 15: m7(♭5) chord arpeggio with chromatic lower neighbor tones

Exercise 16: m7(♭5) chord arpeggio with diatonic upper and chromatic lower neighbor tones

Check off the keys of the m7(♭5) arpeggios you've practiced:

A   D   G   C   F   B♭   E♭   A♭   D♭   C♯   F♯   G♭   B   E

Major Scale Mode and Chord Summary

Scale step and Mode	Scale type	Chord symbol	Alternate chord symbols
1. Ionian (major scale)	major	maj7	ma7, maj6, ma6, 6^9, maj9, ma9, maj11, ma11, maj13, ma13
2. Dorian	minor	m7	mi7, m9, mi9, m9(13), mi9(13), m11, mi11, m13, mi13
3. Phrygian	minor	m7	mi7, m7($\flat$9,$\flat$13), mi7($\flat$9,$\flat$13)
4. Lydian	major	maj7($\sharp$11)	ma7(+11), maj7($\flat$5), ma7($\flat$5), maj9($\sharp$11), ma9(+11), maj6^9($\sharp$11), ma6^9(+11), maj13($\sharp$11), ma13(+11)
5. Mixolydian	dominant	7	9, 11, 13
6. Aeolian (natural minor)	minor	m7	mi7, m9, mi9, m7($\sharp$5), mi7(+5), m7($\flat$13), mi7($\flat$13)
7. Locrian	half-diminished	m7 ($\flat$5)	mi7 ($\flat$5), ø

More ways chord symbols could be written:

It would be very nice if all musicians wrote chord symbols the same way. That is, every major 7th chord would be written "maj7," every minor 7th chord would be written "m7,"and so on—the classical way. But there is no set way of writing chord symbols. More often than not, you will see "maj7" for a major 7th chord and "m7" for a minor 7th chord; however, you should be aware that other ways of writing chord symbols exist. Here are a few examples using G as the root of each chord.

Chord type	Common symbol	Other symbols
1. *Major 7th*	Gmaj7	GM7, GMa7, G$^\triangle$7, G7̵

The number 7 with a line through it is used *only* in the U.S. to designate a maj7 chord. But in most European countries, the number 7 is *always* written with a line through it no matter what the application. For example, in Italy, 7th chords of every type have a line through the 7. So, if you find yourself in an "international" band, make sure that everyone is clear about the meaning of a 7 with a line through it.

2. *Minor 7th*	Gm7	Gmi7, Gmin7, G−7
3. *A chord with a* $\flat$	G7($\flat$9)	G7(-9)

"Flat" and "minus" mean the same thing when used in a chord:
($\flat$5) = (-5); ($\flat$9) = (-9); ($\flat$13) = (-13)

4. *A chord with a* $\sharp$	G7($\sharp$5)	G7(+5)

"Sharp" and "plus" mean the same thing when used in a chord:
($\sharp$4) = (+4); ($\sharp$5) = (+5); ($\sharp$9) = (+9); ($\sharp$11) = (+11)

5. *Augmented 7th*	G7($\sharp$5)	G+7, G7(+5), Gaug7
6. *Diminished 7th*	G^{o}7	Gdim7

9

The Five-Position System

This chapter is very cool.

Now, to complete our study of major scale modes and chords and—equally important—the entire fingerboard, we will study the major scale starting from the lowest note available in a particular key on the bass. Also, we will also play—across all 4 or 5 or 6 strings—all of the notes of the key we are in, resulting in fingering patterns that often encompass more than one octave. This is a departure from previous studies that covered modes root to root and chords root to 7th.

For any major key, five positions will cover all the modes and chords of a key before the cycle starts over again an octave higher. Three of the positions have no shifts, whereas the remaining two have one compression shift each.

In each of these five positions, not only will you find at least four complete diatonic modes—check this out—but you will also find every diatonic 7th chord in the key you happen to be playing either in root position or an inversion. Amazing!!

Consider this #1: Consider that four or five frets, covered by each of these positions—including open strings when playing close to the nut of the bass—now provide you with all the diatonic information needed to create wonderful lines and solos.

Consider this #2: Consider also that by changing one note in a position (say, while in the key of C, you change the note B to B♭), you are able to change keys quickly and easily (in this case, from C to F) without having to make a huge position shift on the neck.

This is *exciting* stuff!

From now on, no matter where you place your hand on the fingerboard you will be in a "key." Scales, chords and key centers are now easily connected. Four or five frets now provide you with a huge block of harmony for making music.

The five-position system creates easy access to all the modes of the major scale. Combined with the simple, elegant layout of the bass fingerboard, this system allows you to gain complete mastery of the component parts of a scale while utilizing a smooth, graceful left-hand technique over the entire length of the fingerboard.

Numbering the five positions:

Here's the numbering system for the set of five positions for any key.

Only complete modes (root to root) are listed.

Position 7–1:

- Starts on the **7th scale step** – first finger
- No shifts
- Contains the complete Locrian, Ionian, Dorian, Phrygian and Lydian modes

Position 2:

- Starts on the **2nd scale step** – first finger
- One compression shift
- Contains the complete Dorian, Phrygian, Lydian and Mixolydian modes

Position 3–4:

- Starts on the **3rd scale step** – first finger
- No shifts
- Contains the complete Phrygian, Lydian, Mixolydian and Aeolian modes

Position 5:

- Starts on the **5th scale step** – second finger
- No shifts
- Contains the complete Mixolydian, Aeolian, Locrian and Ionian modes

Position 6:

- Starts on the **6th scale step** – first finger
- One compression shift
- Contains the complete Aeolian, Locrian, Ionian and Dorian modes

Important things to remember:

1. Because of the open strings that are available, positions that start with either low E or low F contain more notes. In fact, the entire chromatic scale is available. Those positions will contain more modes and chords than the others.

2. Positions away from the low end of the neck that do not have shifts in them (positions 7-1, 3-4 and 5) lack one note of the chromatic scale. The missing note differs from key to key.

For all the major keys, either the open E string or F, first finger on the E string, will be your starting point for this new set of positions. This series of fingerboard charts shows the first available position for all 12 keys. Since none of the positions begin with either the 1st scale step or the 4th scale step, the open E found in the E and B major charts is not highlighted; however, you may use it in scale and chord patterns.

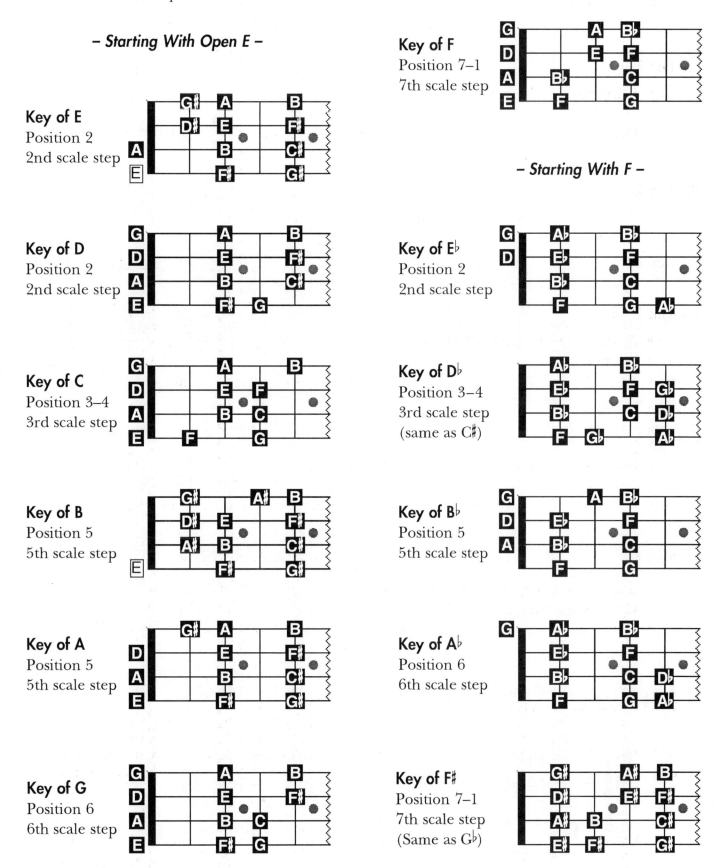

– Starting With Open E –

Key of E
Position 2
2nd scale step

Key of D
Position 2
2nd scale step

Key of C
Position 3–4
3rd scale step

Key of B
Position 5
5th scale step

Key of A
Position 5
5th scale step

Key of G
Position 6
6th scale step

Key of F
Position 7–1
7th scale step

– Starting With F –

Key of E♭
Position 2
2nd scale step

Key of D♭
Position 3–4
3rd scale step
(same as C♯)

Key of B♭
Position 5
5th scale step

Key of A♭
Position 6
6th scale step

Key of F♯
Position 7–1
7th scale step
(Same as G♭)

Here are the five positions in C major:

Position 3–4:
- Starts on the 3rd scale step – open E string
- No shifts
- Contains the complete Phrygian, Lydian, Mixolydian, Aeolian and Locrian modes

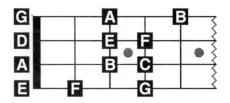

Position 5:
- Starts on the 5th scale step – second finger (3rd fret)
- No shifts
- Contains the complete Mixolydian, Aeolian, Locrian and Ionian modes

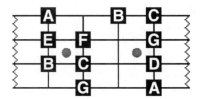

Position 6:
- Starts on the 6th scale step – first finger (5th fret)
- One compression shift
- Contains the complete Aeolian, Locrian, Ionian and Dorian modes

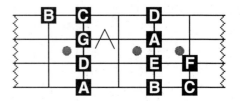

Position 7–1:
- Starts on the 7th scale step – first finger (7th fret)
- No shifts
- Contains the complete Locrian, Ionian, Dorian, Phrygian and Lydian modes

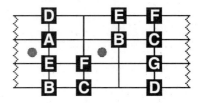

Position 2:
- Starts on the 2nd scale step – first finger (10th fret)
- One compression shift
- Contains the complete Dorian, Phrygian, Lydian and Mixolydian modes

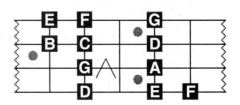

Here are all five C major positions put together on the fingerboard:

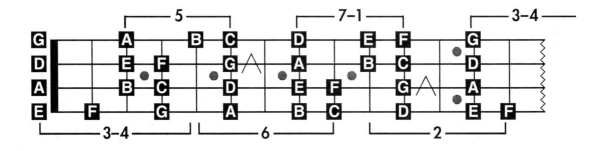

Here are the five positions in B♭ major:

Position 5:

- Starts on the 5th scale step – first finger (1st fret)
- No shifts
- Contains the complete Mixolydian, Aeolian, Locrian and Ionian modes

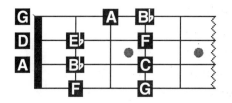

Position 6:

- Starts on the 6th scale step – first finger (3rd fret)
- One compression shift
- Contains the complete Aeolian, Locrian, Ionian, and Dorian modes

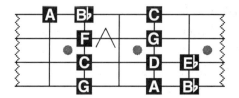

Position 7–1:

- Starts on the 7th scale step – first finger (5th fret)
- No shifts
- Contains the complete Locrian, Ionian, Dorian, Phrygian and Lydian modes

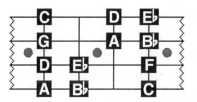

Position 2:

- Starts on the 2nd scale step – first finger (8th fret)
- One compression shift
- Contains the complete Dorian, Phrygian, Lydian and Mixolydian modes

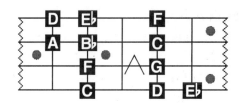

Position 3–4:

- Starts on the 3rd scale step – first finger (10th fret)
- No shifts
- Contains the complete Phrygian, Lydian, Mixolydian and Aeolian modes

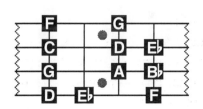

Here are all five B♭ major positions put together on the fingerboard:

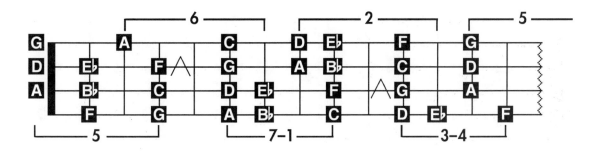

The next two charts both start with open E, but they look rather different.

Compare these charts with the C major chart on page 144.

Key of G:

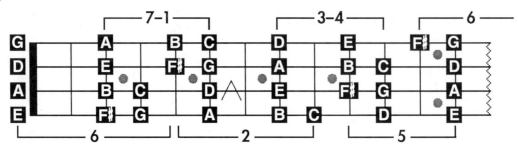

Key of F:

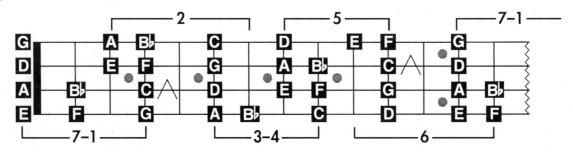

These charts start on F, first finger on the E string.

Compare them with the B♭ major chart on page 145.

Key of E♭:

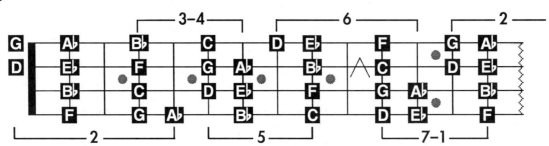

Key of D♭:

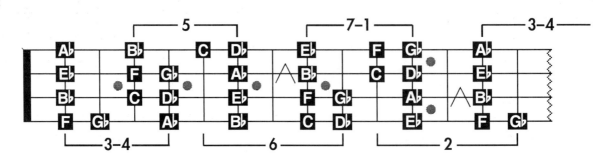

Question 1:

Have you noticed that no matter what key you are in, every note of that key is available in each position and that some notes are repeated?

This means that no matter where you are on the neck, your left hand is covering all the modes and chords of a key all at once! Check out the fingerboard charts on pages 144–146.

Question 2:

Are you aware that each of the five positions has a specific shape and that the positions overlap one another by two frets?

The fingerboard charts below show the specific shape for each of the five positions. The arrangement of the charts shows that the notes played on the last two frets of one position are the same as those played on the first two frets of the next position.

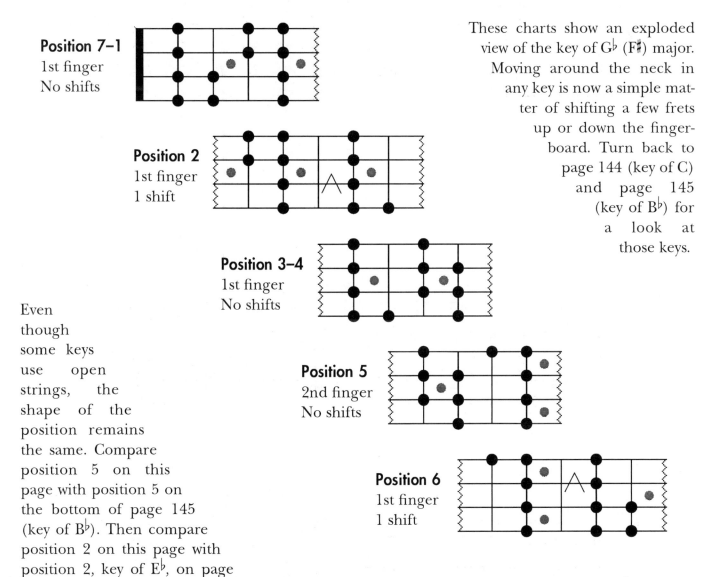

Position 7–1
1st finger
No shifts

Position 2
1st finger
1 shift

Position 3–4
1st finger
No shifts

Position 5
2nd finger
No shifts

Position 6
1st finger
1 shift

These charts show an exploded view of the key of G♭ (F♯) major. Moving around the neck in any key is now a simple matter of shifting a few frets up or down the fingerboard. Turn back to page 144 (key of C) and page 145 (key of B♭) for a look at those keys.

Even though some keys use open strings, the shape of the position remains the same. Compare position 5 on this page with position 5 on the bottom of page 145 (key of B♭). Then compare position 2 on this page with position 2, key of E♭, on page 146. Compare any of the positions that share the same number and you'll see that all the 7–1 positions have the same shape as do all of the 2, 3-4, 5 and 6 positions. Cool, huh?

Suggestions for Scale-and-Mode Practice Using the Five-Position System:

1. Play through each mode contained in the individual fingerboard charts on page 144. The column to the left of each chart will help you to remember which modes are found in each position. After you've learned the positions in the key of C to your satisfaction, move on to page 145, and do it all over again in the key of B♭. Then cover all the other keys.

2. On page 146 you have to play through each of the positions in the four keys given without the help of the individual fingerboard charts. Start at the low end of the fingerboard and, after playing all of the modes in that position, move to the next position nonstop. Be sure to shift from position to position smoothly and accurately.

3. Fingerboard charts are written out for you in only six keys: C, B♭, G, F, E♭ and D♭. Now's your chance to figure out and to play the remaining keys – B, D, E, G♭, A♭ and A.

4. The next exercise covers the neck in the key of F major using all five positions. Run through it in every key. It's a great exercise.

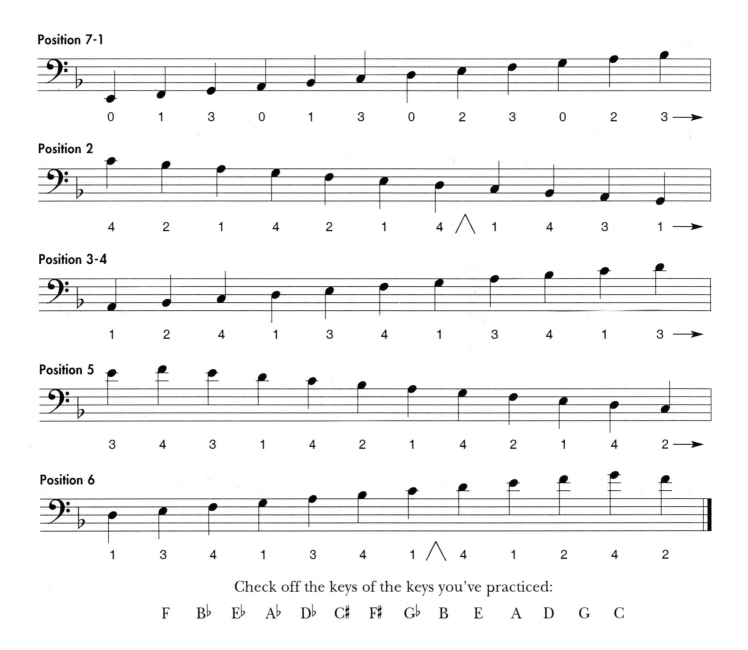

Check off the keys of the keys you've practiced:

F   B♭   E♭   A♭   D♭   C♯   F♯   G♭   B   E   A   D   G   C

Diatonic 7th Chords using the Five-Position System:

This is the big one! Every diatonic chord in any major key is found in each of the five positions for that key. Here's a position-by-position breakdown in the key of C major.

Position 3–4: Starts with the open E string – no shifts

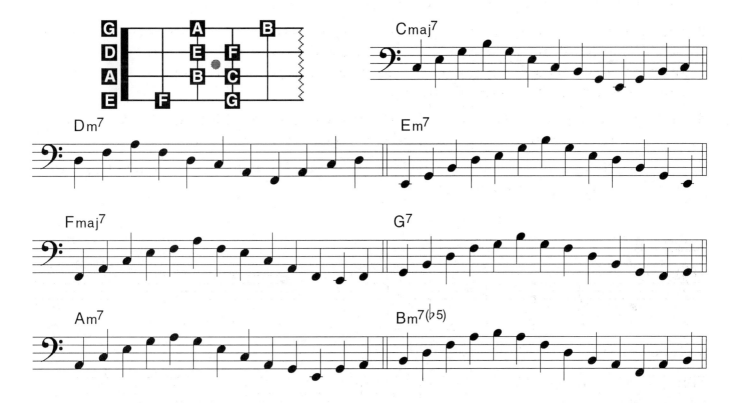

Position 5: Starts with G – second finger – no shifts

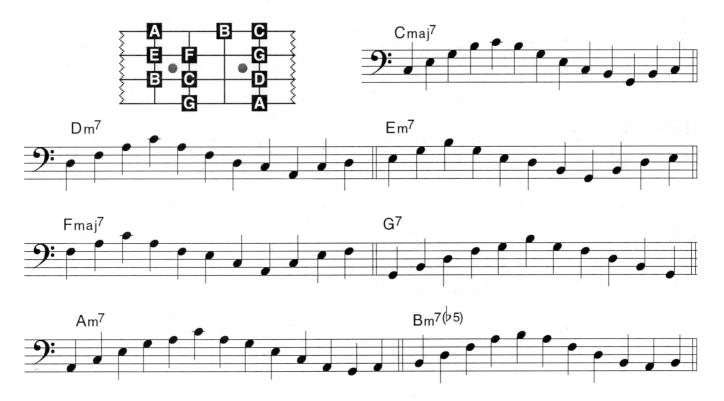

Position 6: Starts with A – first finger – one compression shift

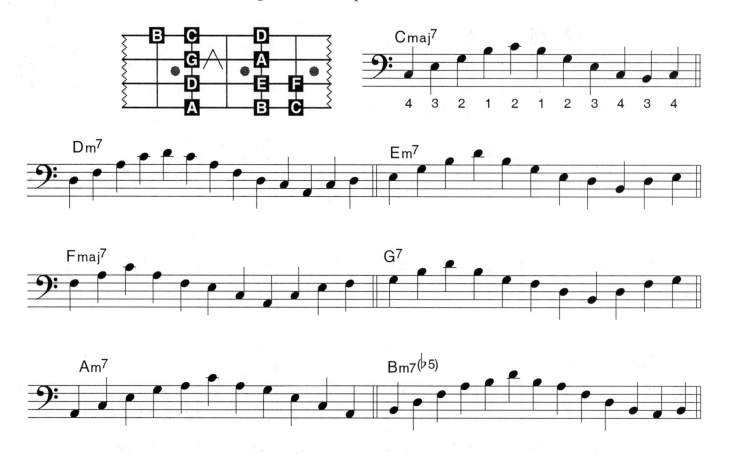

Position 7–1: Starts with B – first finger – no shifts

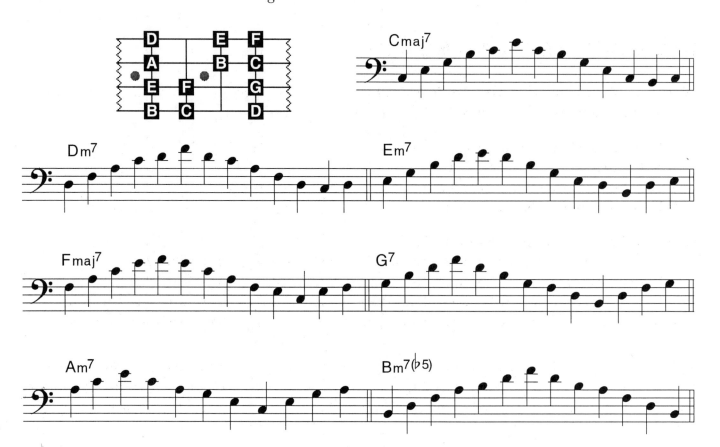

Position 2: Starts with D – first finger – one compression shift

I know it's a lot of work, but you should practice each position in every key.

C   F   B♭   E♭   A♭   D♭   C♯   F♯   G♭   B   E   A   D   G

Diatonic 7th Chords And Their Inversions:

When you play the diatonic 7th chords from any major key, remember that each note of the scale serves four functions within that set of diatonic chords:

1. Root of the chord – root position
2. 3rd of the chord – 1st inversion
3. 5th of the chord – 2nd inversion
4. 7th of the chord – 3rd inversion

Consider the note E in the key of C major:
1. It is the root of the chord built on the third scale step – Em7 (root position).
2. It is the 3rd of the chord built on the first scale step – Cmaj7 (Cmaj7/E – 1st inversion).
3. It is the 5th of the chord built on the sixth scale step – Am7 (Am7/E – 2nd inversion).
4. It is the 7th of the chord built on the fourth scale step – Fmaj7 (Fmaj7/E – 3rd inversion).

This next exercise takes each note of the C major scale as it appears in the five positions and builds root position 7th chords plus the three inversions of the diatonic 7th chords that contain that note. Pay particular attention to chords that start with your third or fourth finger as you may not be too familiar with playing them.

Position 3–4: Starts with the open E string – no shifts

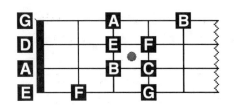

Open E
Root pos - Em7
1st inv - Cmaj7
2nd inv - Am7
3rd inv - Fmaj7

F starting note
Root pos - Fmaj7
1st inv - Dm7
2nd inv - Bm7 (♭5)
3rd inv - G7

G starting note
Root pos - G7
1st inv - Em7
2nd inv - Cmaj7
3rd inv - Am7

A starting note
Root pos - Am7
1st inv - Fmaj7
2nd inv - Dm7
3rd inv - Bm7 (♭5)

B starting note
Root pos - Bm7 (♭5)
1st inv - G7
2nd inv - Em7
3rd inv - Cmaj7

C starting note
Root pos - Cmaj7
1st inv - Am7
2nd inv - Fmaj7
3rd inv - Dm7

D starting note
Root pos - Dm7
1st inv - Bm7 (♭5)
2nd inv - G7
3rd inv - Em7

Position 5: Starts with G – second finger – no shifts

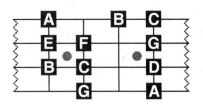

G starting note
Root pos - G7
1st inv - Em7
2nd inv - Cmaj7
3rd inv - Am7

A starting note
Root pos - Am7
1st inv - Fmaj7
2nd inv - Dm7
3rd inv - Bm7 (♭5)

B starting note
Root pos - Bm7 (♭5)
1st inv - G7
2nd inv - Emi7
3rd inv - Cma7

C starting note
Root pos - Cma7
1st inv - Am7
2nd inv - Fmaj7
3rd inv - Dm7

D starting note
Root pos - Dm7
1st inv - Bm7 (♭5)
2nd inv - G7
3rd inv - Em7

E starting note
Root pos - Em7
1st inv - Cmaj7
2nd inv - Am7
3rd inv - Fmaj7

F starting note
Root pos - Fmaj7
1st inv - Dm7
2nd inv - Bm7 (♭5)
3rd inv - G7

Position 6: Starts with A – second finger – 1 compression shift

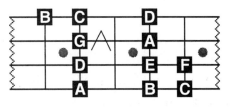

A starting note
Root pos - Am7
1st inv - Fmaj7
2nd inv - Dm7
3rd inv - Bm7 (♭5)

B starting note
Root pos - Bm7♭5
1st inv - G7
2nd inv - Em7
3rd inv - Cmaj7

C starting note
Root pos - Cmaj7
1st inv - Am7
2nd inv - Fmaj7
3rd inv - Dm7

D starting note
Root pos - Dm7
1st inv - Bm7 (♭5)
2nd inv - G7
3rd inv - Em7

E starting note
Root pos - Em7
1st inv - Cmaj7
2nd inv - Am7
3rd inv - Fmaj7

F starting note
Root pos - Fmaj7
1st inv - Dm7
2nd inv - Bm7 (♭5)
3rd inv - G7

G starting note
Root pos - G7
1st inv - Em7
2nd inv - Cmaj7
3rd inv - Am7

Position 7-1: Starts with B – first finger – no shifts

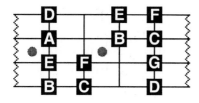

B starting note
Root pos - Bm7(♭5)
1st inv - G7
2nd inv - Em7
3rd inv - Cmaj7

C starting note
Root pos - Cmaj7
1st inv - Am7
2nd inv - Fmaj7
3rd inv - Dm7

D starting note
Root pos - Dm7
1st inv - Bm7(♭5)
2nd inv - G7
3rd inv - Em7

E starting note
Root pos - Em7
1st inv - Cmaj7
2nd inv - Am7
3rd inv - Fmaj7

F starting note
Root pos - Fmaj7
1st inv - Dm7
2nd inv - Bm7(♭5)
3rd inv - G7

G starting note
Root pos - G7
1st inv - Em7
2nd inv - Cmaj7
3rd inv - Am7

A starting note
Root pos - Am7
1st inv - Fmaj7
2nd inv - Dm7
3rd inv - Bm7(♭5)

Position 2: Starts with D – first finger – 1 shift

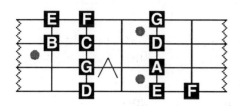

D starting note
Root pos - Dm7
1st inv - Bm7(♭5)
2nd inv - G7
3rd inv - Em7

E starting note
Root pos - Em7
1st inv - Cmaj7
2nd inv - Am7
3rd inv - Fmaj7

F starting note
Root pos - Fmaj7
1st inv - Dm7
2nd inv - Bm7(♭5)
3rd inv - G7

G starting note
Root pos - G7
1st inv - Em7
2nd inv - Cmaj7
3rd inv - Am7

A starting note
Root pos - Am7
1st inv - Fmaj7
2nd inv - Dm7
3rd inv - Bm7(♭5)

B starting note
Root pos - Bm7(♭5)
1st inv - G7
2nd inv - Em7
3rd inv - Cmaj7

C starting note
Root pos - Cmaj7
1st inv - Am7
2nd inv - Fmaj7
3rd inv - Dm7

Practice this material in every key.

C   F   B♭   E♭   A♭   D♭   C♯   F♯   G♭   B   E   A   D   G

ARRGH! Not EVERY key!

Sorry…it's the only way to *really* get the fingerboard together.

Here are a several ways to practice this stuff. You could:

1. Play it as is.
2. Play, in root position, all of the chords in one position. Then, play 1st, 2nd and 3rd inversions (Cmaj7 root position, Dm7 root position…, then Cmaj7 1st inversion, Dm7 1st inversion…).
3. Pick the starting pitch for a chord in a position, and run through the chord from root position to 3rd inversion, eventually covering all the diatonic scale steps found in the position (Cmaj7 root position, 1st, 2nd and 3rd inversions, D root position, 1st, 2nd and 3rd inversions…).
4. Play the chords in a position around the cycle of fourths, the cycle of fifths, or up and down in thirds. (See next page.)
5. Then sit back and realize that you've *really* gotten the fingerboard together. (Cool…)

Playing through each chord in each position in a given key is a great way to both learn the diatonic chords and learn the fingerboard more thoroughly than you ever imagined.

Don't forget that a few notes in each position are repeated. Be sure to include all of them.

Below, you'll find cycles of fourths, fifths and thirds (up and down) written out for you in four keys. Do yourself a favor. Run through this stuff in the four written keys and in the remaining keys given at the bottom the page.

Key of C

Cycle of fourths:	Cmaj7	Fmaj7	Bm7(♭5)	Em7	Am7	Dm7	G7	Cmaj7
Cycle of fifths:	Cmaj7	G7	Dm7	Am7	Em7	Bm7(♭5)	Fmaj7	Cmaj7
Thirds up:	Cmaj7	Em7	G7	Bm7(♭5))	Dm7	Fmaj7	Am7	Cmaj7
Thirds down:	Cmaj7	Am7	Fmaj7	Dm7	Bm7(♭5)	G7	Em7	Cmaj7

Key of G

Cycle of fourths:	Gmaj7	Cmaj7	F♯m7(♭5)	Bm7	Em7	Am7	D7	Gmaj7
Cycle of fifths:	Gmaj7	D7	Am7	Em7	Bm7	F♯m7(♭5)	Cmaj7	Gmaj7
Thirds up:	Gmaj7	Bm7	D7	F♯m7(♭5)	Am7	Cmaj7	Em7	Gmaj7
Thirds down:	Gmaj7	Em7	Cmaj7	Am7	F♯m7(♭5)	D7	Bm7	Gmaj7

Key of B♭

Cycle of fourths:	B♭maj7	E♭maj7	Am7(♭5)	Dm7	Gm7	Cm7	F7	B♭maj7
Cycle of fifths:	B♭maj7	F7	Cm7	Gm7	Dm7	Am7(♭5)	E♭maj7	B♭maj7
Thirds up:	B♭maj7	Dm7	F7	Am7(♭5)	Cm7	E♭maj7	Gm7	B♭maj7
Thirds down:	B♭maj7	Gm7	E♭maj7	Cm7	Am7(♭5)	F7	Dm7	B♭maj7

Key of D♭

Cycle of fourths:	D♭maj7	G♭maj7	Cm7(♭5)	Fm7	B♭m7	Ebm7	A♭7	D♭maj7
Cycle of fifths:	D♭maj7	A♭7	E♭m7	B♭m7	Fm7	Cm7(♭5)	G♭maj7	D♭maj7
Thirds up:	D♭maj7	Fm7	A♭7	Cm7(♭5)	E♭m7	G♭maj7	B♭m7	D♭maj7
Thirds down:	D♭maj7	B♭m7	G♭maj7	E♭m7	Cm7(♭5)	A♭7	Fm7	D♭maj7

More keys to practice:

F   E♭   A♭   C♯   F♯   G♭   B   E   A   D

Five Keys for the Price of One —
Your Choice of Five Keys in One Position

Get this! As you are playing in any position that doesn't have any open strings, in any key, you can play through five keys—more with a 5-string or 6-string bass—without moving your hand! (Don't forget that you are able to play in *every* key in the low end of the neck when you include the open strings. Check out page 142 again.) Each and every position is part of five key centers. Example 1 starts with A, first finger on the E string. Example 2 starts with C, first finger on the E string.

Example 1: Starts with A

Key of B♭
Position 7–1

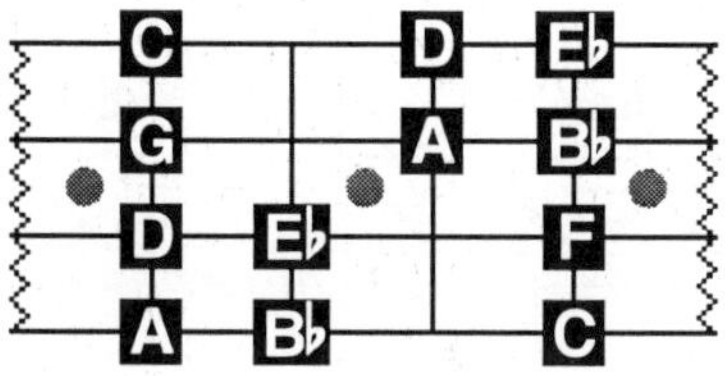

Key of G
Position 2

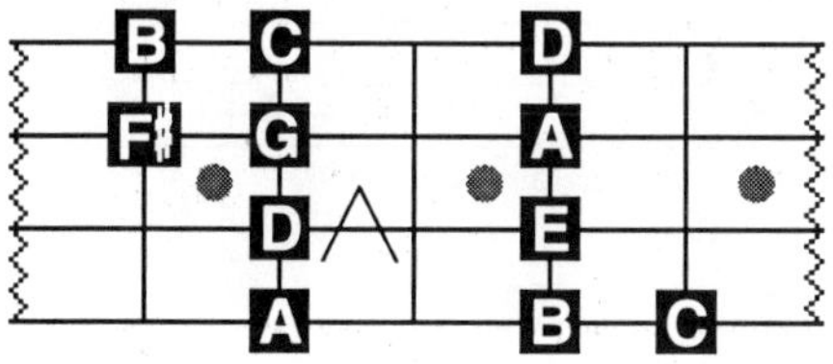

Key of F
Position 3–4

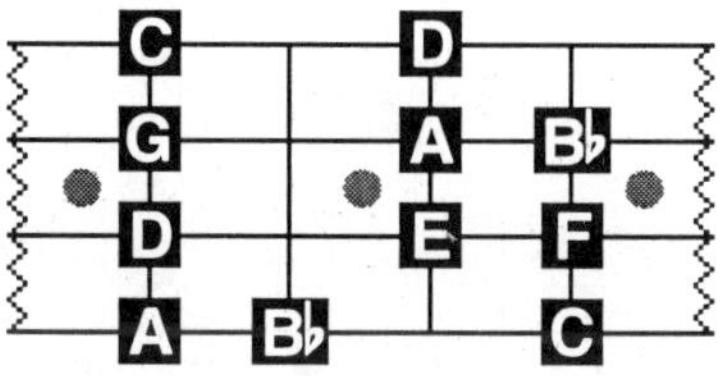

Key of E♭
Position 5

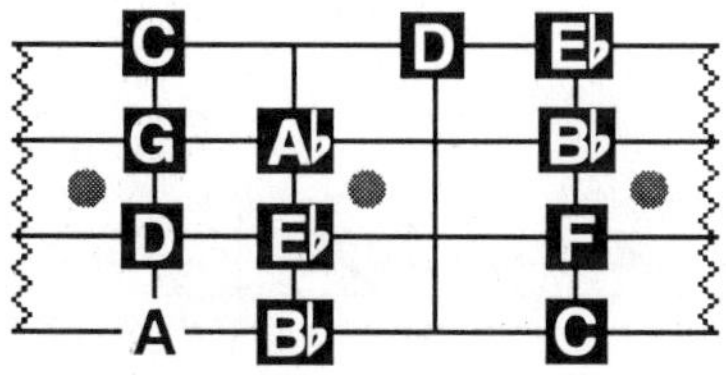

Key of C
Position 6

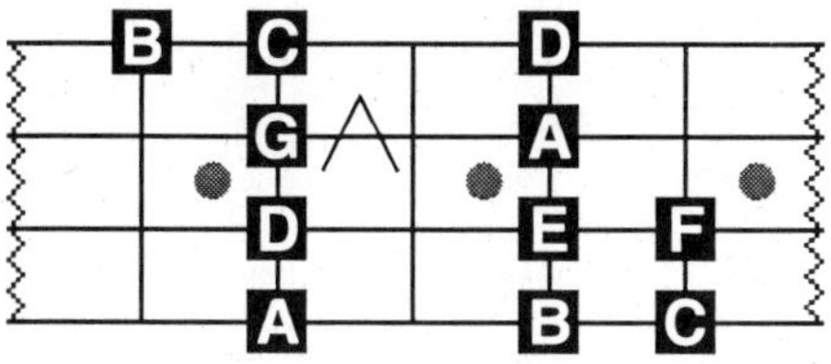

Example 2: Starts with C

Key of D♭
Position 7–1

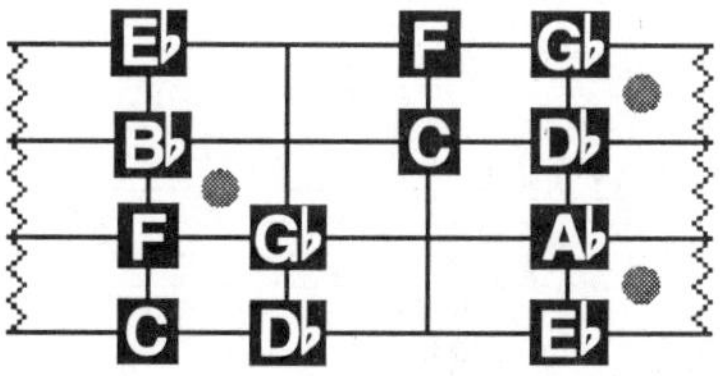

Key of B♭
Position 2

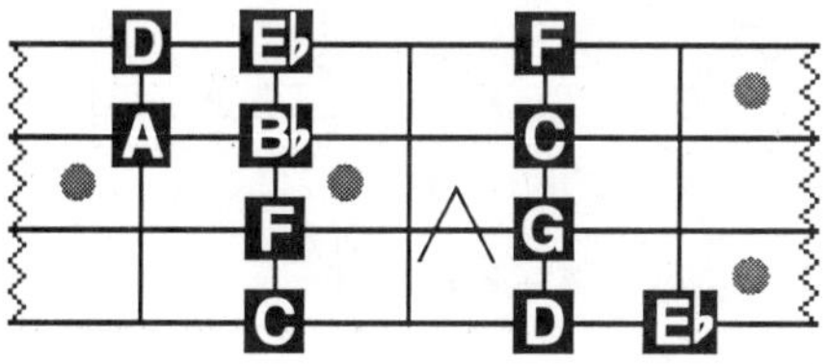

Key of A♭
Position 3–4

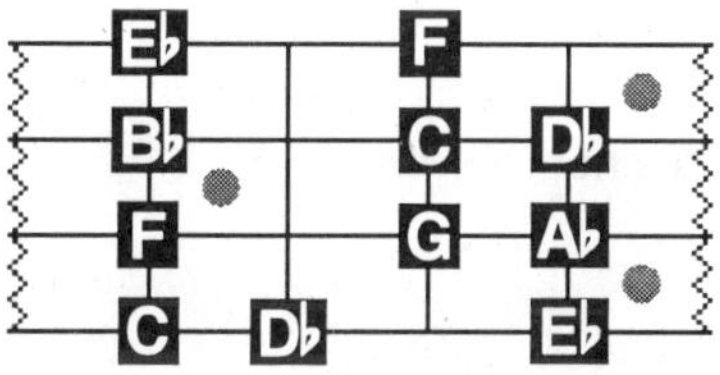

Key of G♭
Position 5

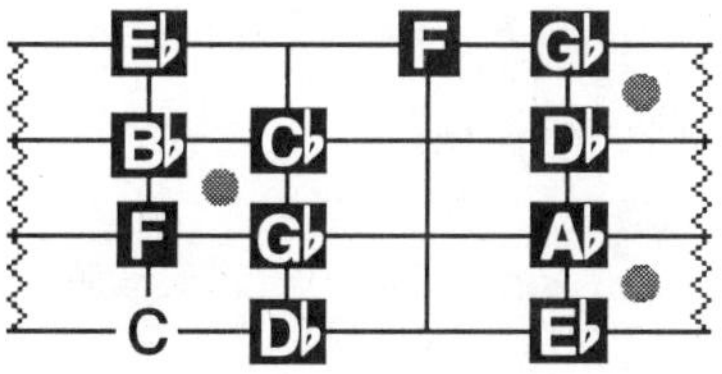

Key of E♭
Position 6

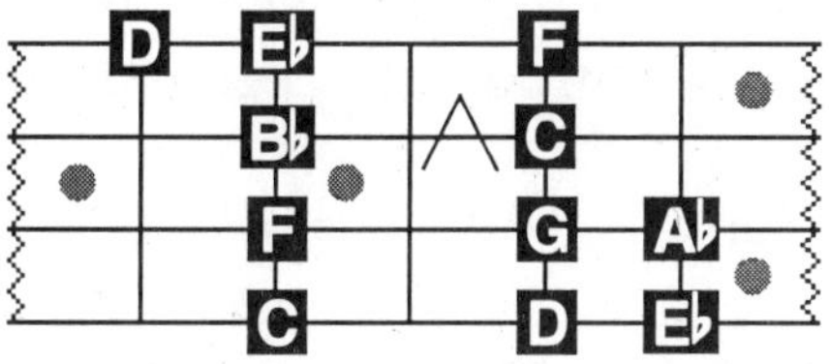

Here are ii–V–I progressions that use the five keys shown in Example 1 on the preceding page. Play through them using as many bass line and solo styles as you can (latin, rock, jazz, pop…).

Don't forget that:
1. *All of the progressions* start with A, first finger, on the E string.
2. You must *stay in the position* for the key you are dealing with.
3. You should *shift only when the position allows*. For this exercise only, the keys of G and C require compression-type shifts.

If you restrict yourself in this manner, it will help—or even *force*—you to develop new ideas for lines and solos. You'll be amazed at how much harmonic territory is covered in the space of four or five frets!

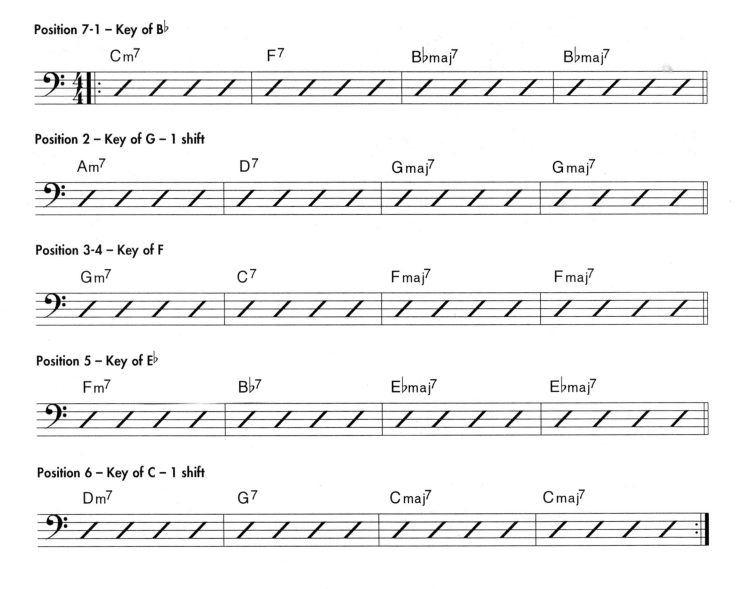

For more practice, play through Examples 1 and 2 on the preceding page in the same way you just played through the exercise above.

Come up with your own ii–V–I ideas.

Find as many one-position, five-key combinations as you can.

Check out this F blues. It uses jazz-style chord changes. Play the chord pattern in all five F major positions. If you can't figure out the five positions in the key of F, here are their starting points on the E string:

1. Open E string – Position 7-1
2. G – 3rd fret – Position 2
3. A – 5th fret – Position 3-4
4. C – 8th fret – Position 5
5. D – 10th fret – Position 6

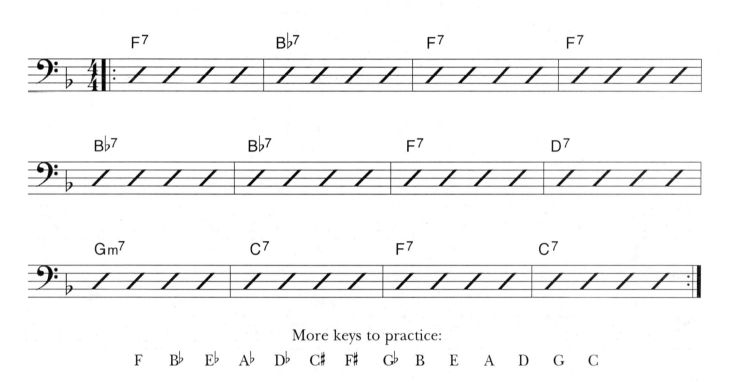

More keys to practice:

F   B♭   E♭   A♭   D♭   C♯   F♯   G♭   B   E   A   D   G   C

The second set of blues changes has two chords per bar in almost every bar. No problem.

It's playable in every position in any key!

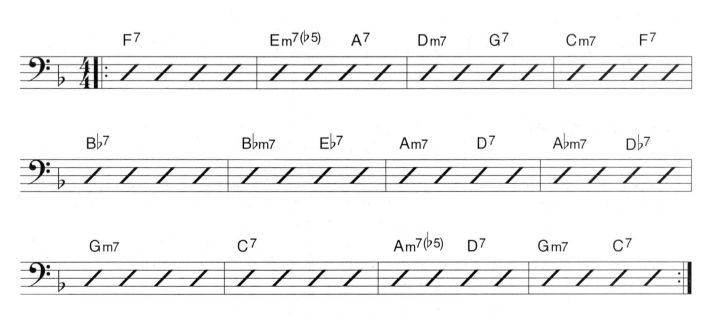

More keys to practice:

F   B♭   E♭   A♭   D♭   C♯   F♯   G♭   B   E   A   D   G   C

This chord chart is the changes to a well known standard song. Like the blues progressions on the preceding page, the entire song is playable in any position in any key.

Remember that if you are playing in a position that has no shifts, namely positions 7-1, 3-4 and 5, that there is always one chromatic pitch missing on a 4-string bass. The missing note differs from key to key and from position to position. For example, if you start the song using position 3-4 in the key of F major (first finger on A on the E string), there is no F♯ available to use in the D7 chords.

Play the song in one position at a time. No cheating! Cover all five positions in the key of F.

Every Key in the Space of Three Frets:

As five keys are found in each position, it follows that if you shift your left hand up or down one fret that you will have picked up five more keys for a total of ten keys within two frets. Move up or down one more fret and you will have covered all 12 keys, with three keys repeated for good measure—all in the space of three frets. Exciting stuff!

Let's check this out using your first finger on A on the E string again. The keys in **bold** type are the five keys found in the starting position. The arrows point to the new keys you will be in as you shift your left hand. When moving from one key to another on a line, the position numbers remain the same. The order for the three groups of keys is 7-1, 2, 3-4, 5 and 6.

1. One fret either side of your starting position:

becomes ← **Key of** → becomes

7-1 -	A ←	**B♭** →	B
2 -	F♯ ←	**G** →	A♭
3-4 -	E ←	**F** →	F♯
5 -	D ←	**E♭** →	E
6 -	B ←	**C** →	D♭

2. Two frets above your starting position:

Key of → becomes → becomes

7-1 -	**B♭** →	B →	C
2 -	**G** →	A♭ →	A
3-4 -	**F** →	G♭ →	G
5 -	**E♭** →	E →	F
6 -	**C** →	C♯ →	D

3. Two frets below your starting position:

becomes ← becomes ← **Key of**

7-1 -	A♭ ←	A ←	**B♭**
2 -	F ←	F♯ ←	**G**
3-4 -	E♭ ←	E ←	**F**
5 -	D♭ ←	D ←	**E♭**
6 -	B♭ ←	B ←	**C**

These two exercises require that you shift between positions.

1. Make up any type of bass line solo you wish.

2. Be sure to shift as follows:
    a. one fret on either side of your starting position; or
    b. two frets above your starting position; or
    c. two frets below your starting position.

Keeping track of where you are in each exercise and on the fingerboard calls for a lot of concentration on your part. But the time and energy you spend will enhance both your knowledge of the fingerboard and your knowledge of harmony.

Exercise 1:   ii–V's around the cycle

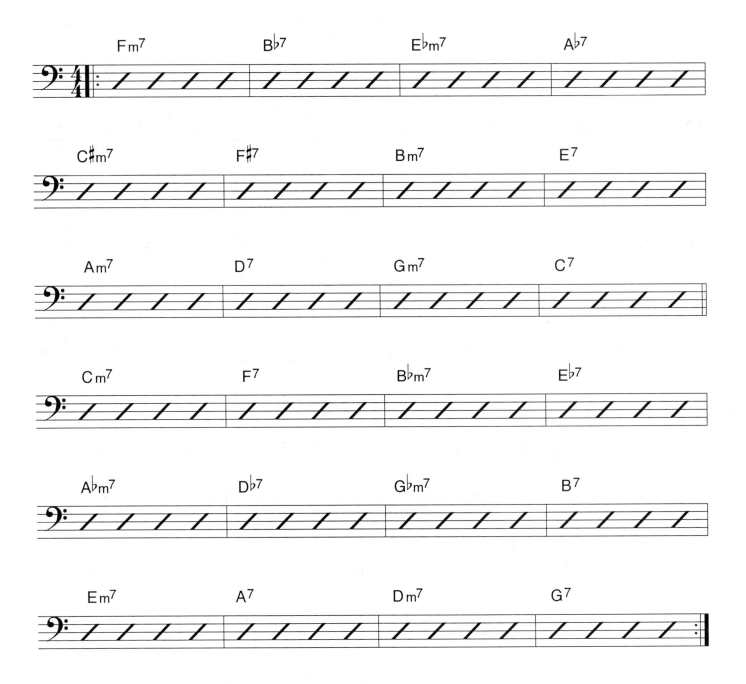

Exercise 2: ii–V's down in half steps

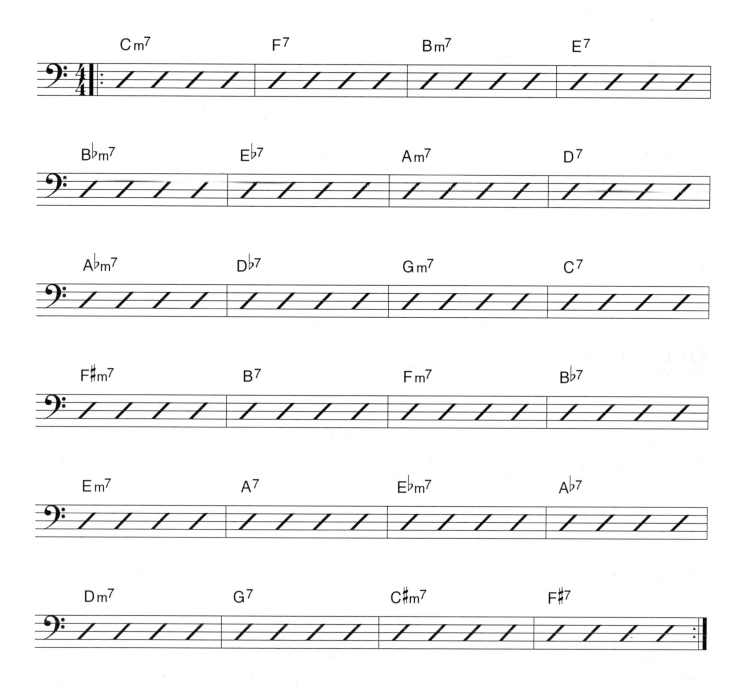

This is an *extremely important* chapter.

Imagine being able to play cohesive, hip lines and solos on your bass without jerking your left hand all over the place.

Imagine being able to look at a bass part or a melody and figuring out a simple way of both reading and playing it smoothly and accurately that avoids huge, scary shifts.

Imagine knowing where every note and chord are on your bass.

Imagine being free of the same old lines and licks that have bored you and everyone else for months, even years.

Imagine practicing this stuff a lot. Integrate the five-position system into your playing and you won't be imagining things anymore.

Your own Five Position System ideas:

10

The Harmonic Minor Scale

Harmonic Minor Scale Facts:

1. Derivation:

There are two easy ways for you to remember how the harmonic minor scale is derived.

a. It could be thought of as a natural minor scale (Aeolian mode) with a major seventh above the root.

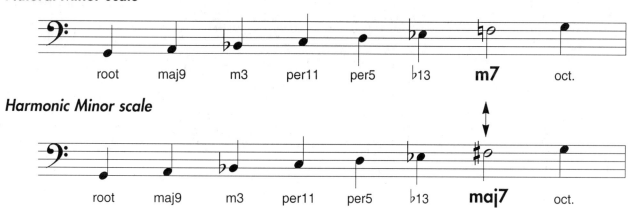

Natural Minor scale

root   maj9   m3   per11   per5   ♭13   **m7**   oct.

Harmonic Minor scale

root   maj9   m3   per11   per5   ♭13   **maj7**   oct.

b. The upper tetrachord of the harmonic minor scale is unique as it has an augmented 2nd between its second and third notes. This "harmonic" tetrachord does not appear in any other scale. The augmented 2nd interval creates a "middle eastern" quality that makes the harmonic minor scale very easy to identify.

aug 2nd

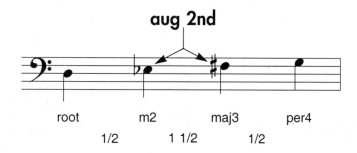

root   m2   maj3   per4
      1/2   1 1/2   1/2

The lower tetrachord of both the harmonic minor scale and the natural minor scale are the same—minor tetrachords. (See page 70 if you forgot what a minor tetrachord is.) With the exceptions of the Phrygian and Locrian modes, every minor scale we'll be studying has a minor tetrachord as its lower tetrachord.

2. Interval construction:

Intervals above root:	root		maj2		m3		per4		per5		m6		maj7		oct.
Intervals between scale steps:	1		1/2		1		1		1/2		11/2		1/2		
Harmonic spelling:	root		9		♭3		11		5		♭13		7		oct.

> **Check this out:** The harmonic minor scale is the first scale we've run into that has *both flats and sharps* in it.

3. Tonic chord:

The tonic seventh chord for the harmonic minor scale is the m(maj7).

"Minor major seventh? Weird. What kind of a name is that?"

A very descriptive one actually. The "minor" in the chord refers to the tonic triad of the scale—a minor triad. The "maj7" in the chord refers to the maj7th interval above the root of the harmonic minor scale. So there you have it—a m(maj7) chord. The tonic chord in the example above is a Gm(maj7).

4. Intervals above the root that define the harmonic minor scale:

- m3rd
- m6 (♭6 or ♭13)
- maj7th

5. Tetrachord construction:

On the bottom of the last page, I mentioned that, with the exception of the Phrygian and Locrian modes, the lower tetrachord of every minor scale is the same. The next example compares the upper tetrachords of the Dorian mode, the natural minor and the harmonic minor scales.

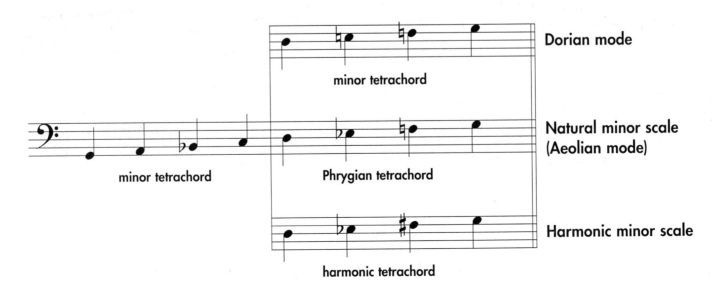

Dorian mode

minor tetrachord

Natural minor scale (Aeolian mode)

minor tetrachord

Phrygian tetrachord

Harmonic minor scale

harmonic tetrachord

The harmonic minor scale in the 1st position:

Remember the world famous 1st position from Chapter 3? Well, here it is again!

These exercises start from the root of the scale, go up as high as possible in the 1st position, down as low as possible, and then spell out the tonic 7th chord in the same way. Improvise.

Exercise 1: E harmonic minor

Exercise 2: D harmonic minor

Exercise 3: B harmonic minor

Practice the harmonic minor scale in every key in the 1st position.

F B♭ E♭ A♭ D♭ C♯ F♯ G♭ A D G

The harmonic minor scale outside of the 1st position:

Here are some ideas for playing a one-octave harmonic minor scales outside the 1st position. Practice these, and then come up with some of your own. Play over the entire fingerboard.

1. Up one string – Starting with an open string

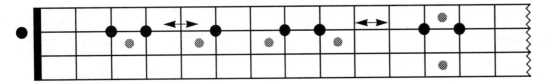

2. Up one string – Starting with a fingered note

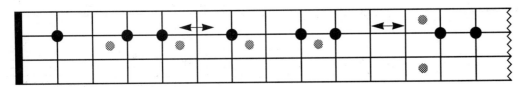

3. Two strings

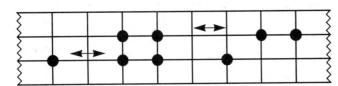

4. Three strings

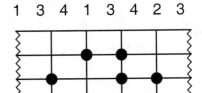

5. Three strings

6. Four strings

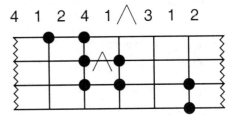

7. Two string pairs – F♯, B and E harmonic minor

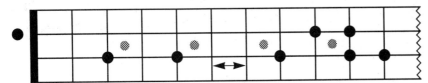

Harmonic minor scale exercises outside of the 1st position:

Practice these exercises in every key. To keep track of your progress, use the list of starting pitches following each exercise. Play each exercise with as many of the fingerings on page 166 as you can. Be sure to retain the shape of the fingering you have chosen.

Exercise 4: Harmonic minor scale

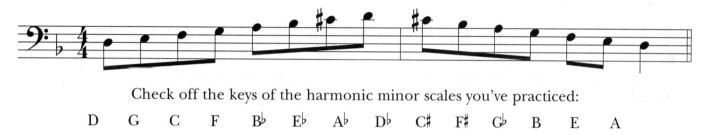

Check off the keys of the harmonic minor scales you've practiced:

D   G   C   F   B♭   E♭   A♭   D♭   C♯   F♯   G♭   B   E   A

Exercise 5: Harmonic minor scale in four-note groups

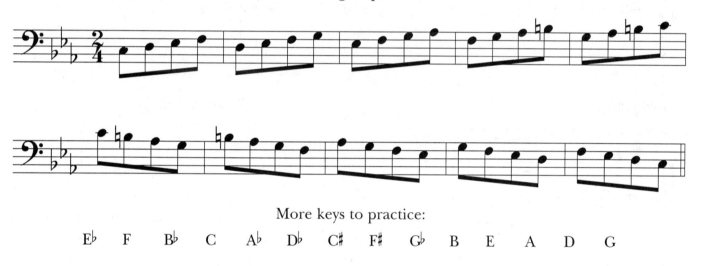

More keys to practice:

E♭   F   B♭   C   A♭   D♭   C♯   F♯   G♭   B   E   A   D   G

Exercise 6: Harmonic minor scale in sixteenths

Still more keys to practice:

D   G   C   F   B♭   E♭   A♭   D♭   C♯   F♯   G♭   B   E   A

Two-octave harmonic minor scales:

Example 1 stays in the 1st position as long as possible. Example 6 gets to the top end of the bass as quickly as possible. Fill in the empty fingerboard charts with your own two-octave harmonic minor scale ideas.

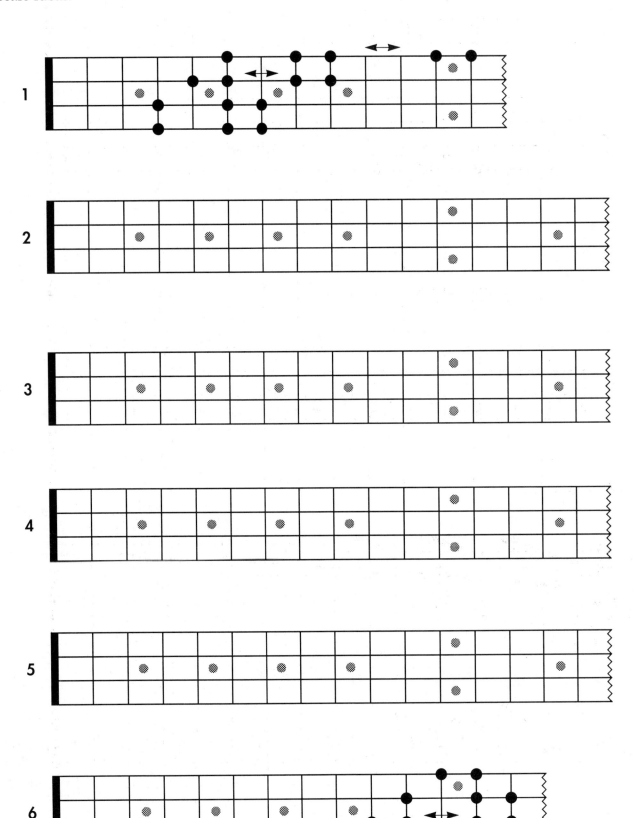

Two-octave m(maj7) arpeggios – tonic chord – harmonic minor

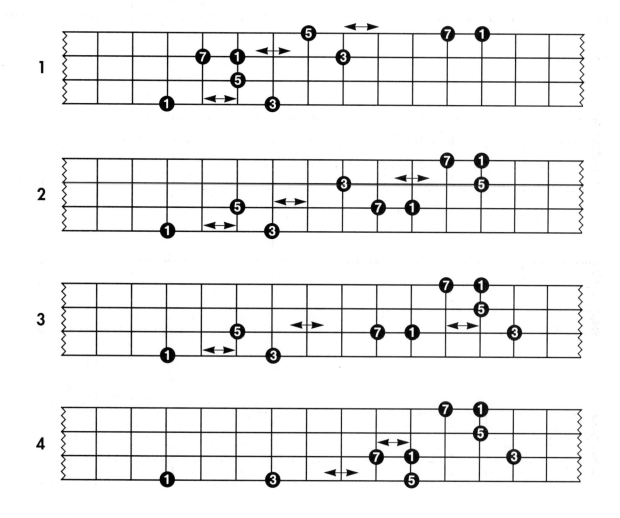

Exercise 7: m (maj7) arpeggio

1	Finger:	1	4	3	2	4	3	2	3	3	2	3	1	2	1	4	3	1	2	1	4	1	4	3	4
	String:	E		A	D	E	A	D		A	D		G	D		G	D	G		D		G			
2	Finger:	1	2	1	4	1	3	2	3	3	2	3	1	2	3	1	3	1	4	3	2	4	3	2	3
	String:	E		A		E		A		E	A		D	A		D		A		D	G	A	D	G	

4	3	4	1	4	1	2	1	3	4	1	2	1	3	2	3	3	2	3	4	2	3	4	1
G	D	G		D		G	D		G	D		G	D	A		D		A	E	D	A	E	
3	2	3	4	2	3	4	1	3	1	3	2	1	3	2	3	3	2	3	1	4	1	2	1
G		D	A	G	D	A		D		A		D	A	E		A		E		A		E	

Your own two-octave harmonic minor scale and m(maj7) chord ideas:

The Fifth Mode of the harmonic minor scale – dom7(♭9, ♭13)

Like the major scale, the harmonic minor scale—or any other scale for that matter—may be divided up into modes. Although only the first (the harmonic minor scale itself) and fifth modes of the harmonic minor scale are commonly used melodically and harmonically in popular music, let's listen to all of them.

Mode 1: Harmonic minor scale – m(maj7)

Mode 2: m7(♭5, ♭9, 13)

Mode 3: maj7(♯5, 11)

Mode 4: m7(♯11)

Mode 5: dom7(♭9, ♭13)

Mode 6: maj7(♯9, ♯11)

Mode 7: dim7(♯9)

Modes 2, 3, 4, 6 and 7 provide some interesting melodic possibilities; but the chords derived from them are rarely, if ever, used. Mode 5, on the other hand, creates a cool sounding "5" chord in minor keys. Let's check it out.

Fifth mode of the harmonic minor scale facts:

1. Derivation:

Starts on the fifth degree of the harmonic minor scale.

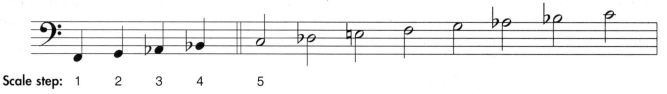

Scale step: 1   2   3   4   5

2. Interval construction:

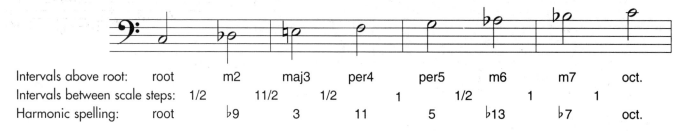

Intervals above root:	root	m2	maj3	per4	per5	m6	m7	oct.
Intervals between scale steps:	1/2	11/2	1/2	1	1/2	1	1	
Harmonic spelling:	root	♭9	3	11	5	♭13	♭7	oct.

3. Scale type and tonic chord:

The fifth mode of the harmonic minor scale is considered a dominant scale as there is a maj3rd and a m7th above the root. The tonic chord is a dom7(♭9, ♭13)—C7(♭9, ♭13).

4. Notes above the root that define the fifth mode of the harmonic minor scale:

- m9th
- maj3rd
- m6th (♭13)
- m7th

5. Most common use:

- "5" chord in minor keys.

6. Tetrachord construction:

The fifth mode of the harmonic minor scale is made up of a harmonic tetrachord and a Phrygian tetrachord a whole step apart.

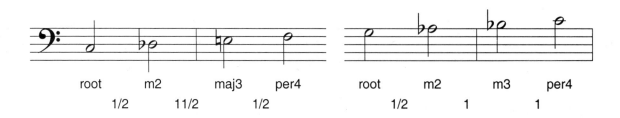

root   m2   maj3   per4   root   m2   m3   per4
    1/2   11/2   1/2   1/2   1   1

The fifth mode of the harmonic minor scale in the 1st position:

These exercises start from the root of the scale, go up as high as possible in the 1st position, down as low as possible and then spell out the dom7(♭9, ♭13) chord.

This is the first scale and chord we've run into that has both a ♭9 and a ♭13 in it. As you play the exercises in the 1st position, and later the exercises that cover the rest of the neck, listen carefully to how these notes resolve— the ♭9 to the root and the ♭13 to the fifth. Improvise!

Exercise 8: E7(♭9, ♭13)

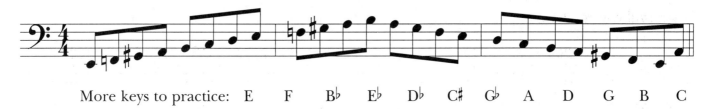

More keys to practice: E   F   B♭   E♭   D♭   C♯   G♭   A   D   G   B   C

Exercise 9: A7(♭9, ♭13)

More keys to practice: A   D   G   B   F   C   B♭   E♭   D♭   C♯   G♭   E

Exercise 10: G7(♭9, ♭13)

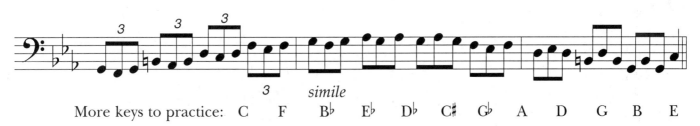

More keys to practice: C   F   B♭   E♭   D♭   C♯   G♭   A   D   G   B   E

Exercise 11: B7(♭9, ♭13)

More keys to practice: D   G   B   E   F   B♭   E♭   D♭   C♯   G♭   A   C

The fifth mode of the harmonic minor scale mode outside of the 1st position:

Here are some ideas for playing the fifth mode of the harmonic minor scale outside of the 1st position. Practice these and then come up with some of your own.

1. Up one string – Starting with an open string

0 1 4 ◄►1 3 4 ◄►1 3

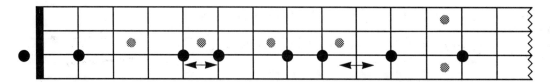

2. Up one string – Starting with a fingered note

1◄►1 4◄►1 3 4 ◄►1 3

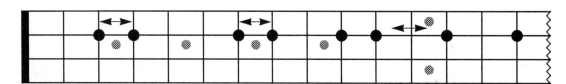

3. Two strings

1 2◄►3 4 1 2◄►1 3

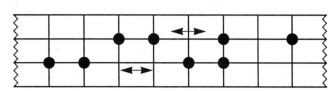

4. Three strings

1 2◄►3 4 1 2 4 1

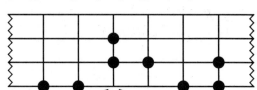

5. Three strings

2 3 1 2◄►1 2 4 1

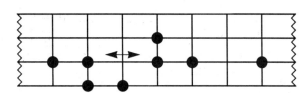

6. Three strings

2 3 1◄►1 3 4 1 3

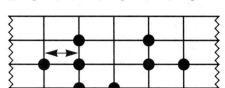

7. Two string pairs – F, B♭ and E♭ 5th mode – harmonic minor

1 2 0◄►1 3 4 1 3

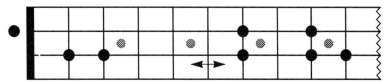

Fifth mode of the harmonic minor scale outside of the 1st position:

Practice these exercises in every key. To keep track of your progress, use the list of starting pitches that follow each exercise . Play each exercise with as many of the fingerings on page 174 as you can. Be sure to retain the shape of the fingering you have chosen.

Exercise 12: Fifth mode of the harmonic minor scale

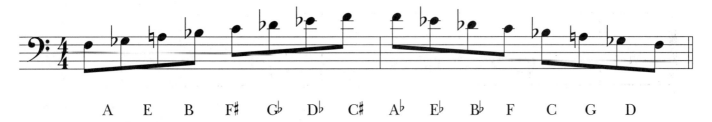

A   E   B   F♯   G♭   D♭   C♯   A♭   E♭   B♭   F   C   G   D

Exercise 13: Fifth mode tetrachords – This exercise covers every key

The last four exercises explore some melodic possibilities of the fifth mode of the harmonic minor scale and the dom7(♭9, ♭13) chord. They are designed to help you hear how the notes of the mode and the chord resolve.

Here's a couple tips for playing these exercises in every key:

- As you play through each exercise in the given key, sing along. If you can sing the exercise, you'll be able to play it in any key.
- Almost every downbeat of each exercise is a chord tone. Use the chord tones as guides as you transpose.

Exercise 14: dom7(♭9, ♭13) in 4-note groups

C   C♯   D♭   D   E♭   E   F   F♯   G♭   G   A♭   A   B♭   B

Exercise 15: dom7(♭9, ♭13) in triplets

A   C   E   G   B♭   D♭   C♯   F   A♭   B   E♭   G♭   F♯

Exercise 16 : dom7(♭9, ♭13) in sixteenths

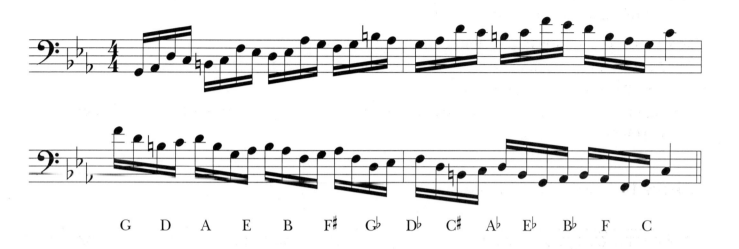

G   D   A   E   B   F♯   G♭   D♭   C♯   A♭   E♭   B♭   F   C

Exercise 17 : Two-octave scale and arpeggio

G   A♭   A   B♭   B   C   C♯   D♭   D   E♭   E   F   F♯   G♭

Your own dom7(♭9, ♭13) ideas:

11

The Melodic Minor Scale

Melodic Minor Scale Facts:

1. Derivation:

Like the harmonic minor scale, there are a couple of easy ways to remember the make-up of the melodic minor scale.

a. It could be thought of as a harmonic minor scale with a major 6th(13th) above the root.

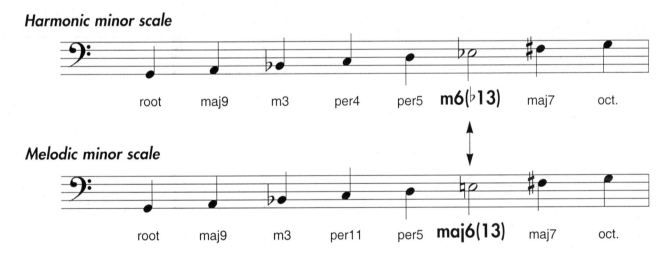

b. The melodic minor scale could also be thought of as an Aeolian mode with a major 6th (13th) and major 7th above the root.

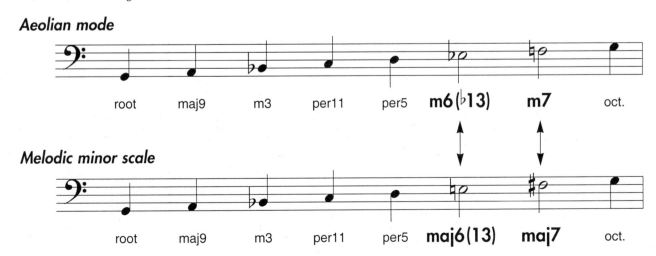

2. Interval construction:

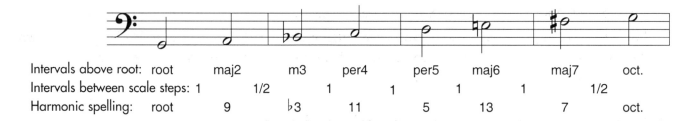

Intervals above root:	root	maj2	m3	per4	per5	maj6	maj7	oct.
Intervals between scale steps: 1		1/2	1	1	1	1	1/2	
Harmonic spelling:	root	9	♭3	11	5	13	7	oct.

3. Tonic chord:

The tonic chord for the melodic minor scale is the m(maj7)—a minor triad with a maj7th above the root. Gm(maj7) or Gmi(+7) for example.

4. Why is this scale called "melodic" minor?

According to *The New Harvard Dictionary Of Music:*

> Compositions [in minor keys] often approach the tonic from below by a semitone [a half-step], thus raising the seventh scale degree of the natural minor scale [Aeolian mode] by a semitone to produce what is termed the harmonic minor scale. This produces an interval of three semitones between the sixth and seventh scale degrees—an interval called an augmented second that is regarded as melodically awkward. Hence, in approaching the tonic from below, compositions [in minor keys] often raise both the sixth and seventh scale degrees by a semitone. This results in what is termed the melodic minor scale...[1986, p.729]

We can assume from this definition that when the musical line *descends* from the tonic that *the sixth and seventh scale degrees are lowered one half step* in order to retain the minor quality of the music. This form of the melodic minor scale with its raised sixth and seventh scale degrees going up and lowered sixth and seventh scale degrees—a natural minor scale or Aeolian mode—going down, is taught in traditional theory classes.

Ascending: melodic minor   **Descending: Aeolian mode (natural minor)**

5. The melodic minor scale in popular music:

Musicians who play popular music—pop, latin or jazz—use the melodic minor scale *and its modes* not only as sources of melody, but also as sources of new and great sounding chords that go way beyond the chords derived from the modes of the major scale in complexity. Classical musicians are limited to playing the notes on the page exactly as written with no concern for chord changes and no thought of improvising. On the other hand, the musicians playing any form of popular music, pay attention to both the melody *and* the chord changes. They are expected to improvise using the very things that the Classical musicians ignore—the chord.

If, for example, a jazz musician is playing a tune whose changes call for the melodic minor scale, namely the m(maj7), you can bet that those raised sixth and seventh scale steps will be coming out up, down and in any other way you can imagine.

We'll be studying the melodic minor scale with the notes played the same both up and down. This will also enable us to learn the modes of the melodic minor scale more easily.

6. Intervals above the root that define the melodic minor scale:

- m3rd
- maj6th (13)
- maj7th

7. Tetrachord construction:

The melodic minor scale is made up of a minor tetrachord and a major tetrachord a whole step apart.

8. Minor scales compared:

The lower tetrachord of these scales is the same. Check out the upper tetrachords.

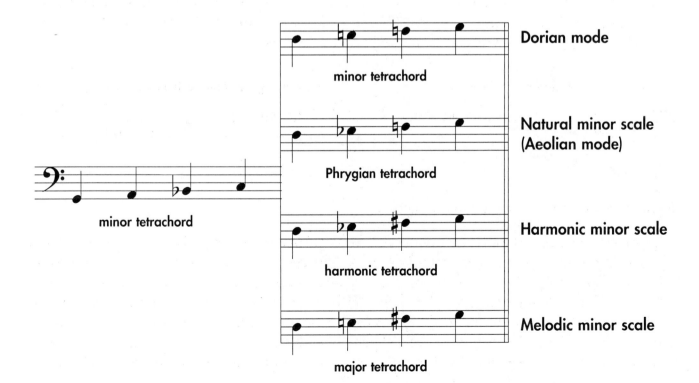

The melodic minor scale in the 1st position:

As usual, these exercises start from the root of the scale, go up as high as possible in the 1st position, down as low as possible and then spell out the tonic 7th chord in the same way. Improvise. Since the scale has a maj6th above the root, run through m6 chords, too.

Exercise 1: E melodic minor – Em(maj7) Em6

Exercise 2: E♭ melodic minor – E♭m(maj7) E♭m6

Exercise 3: B melodic minor – Bm(maj7) Bm6

Practice the melodic minor scale and its tonic chord in every key in the 1st position.

F   B♭   E   A   D   G   C   F♯   G♭   C♯   A♭

The melodic minor scale outside of the 1st position:

Here are some ideas for playing one-octave melodic minor scales outside the 1st position. Practice these and then come up with some ideas of your own. Play over the entire fingerboard.

1. Up one string – Starting with an open string

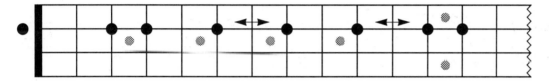

2. Up one string – Starting with a fingered note

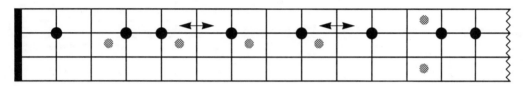

3. Two strings

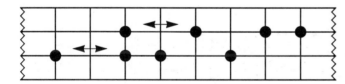

4. Three strings

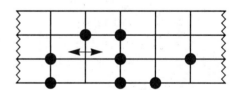

5. Three strings

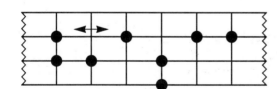

6. Three strings

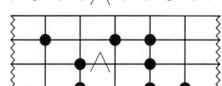

7. Two string pairs – F♯, B and E melodic minor

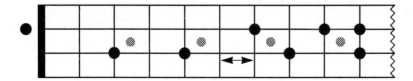

8. Four strings (See #6, p. 100)

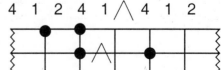

Melodic minor scale exercises outside of the 1st position:

Practice these exercises in every key. To keep track of your progress, use the list of starting pitches following each exercise. Play each exercise with as many of the fingerings on page 183 as you can. Be sure to retain the shape of the fingering you have chosen.

Exercise 4: Four minor scales . This exercise repeats the upper tetrachord of four minor scales. Start each scale with the same finger – 1st or 4th.

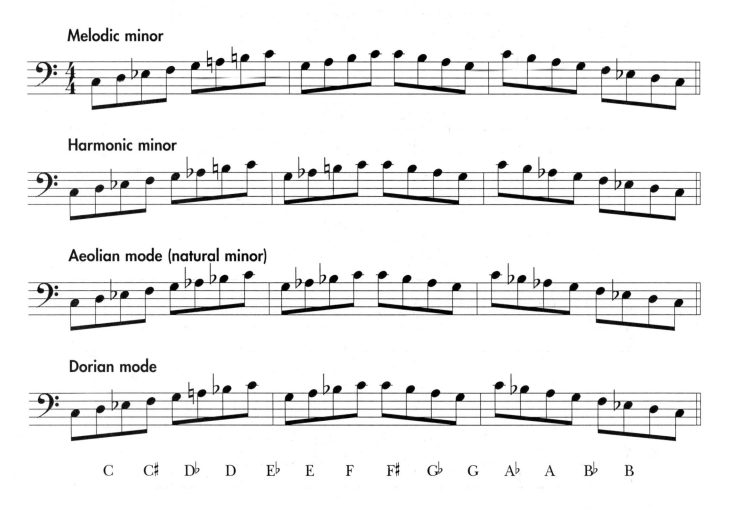

Melodic minor

Harmonic minor

Aeolian mode (natural minor)

Dorian mode

C   C#   Db   D   Eb   E   F   F#   Gb   G   Ab   A   Bb   B

Exercise 5: m(maj7) and m6 chords

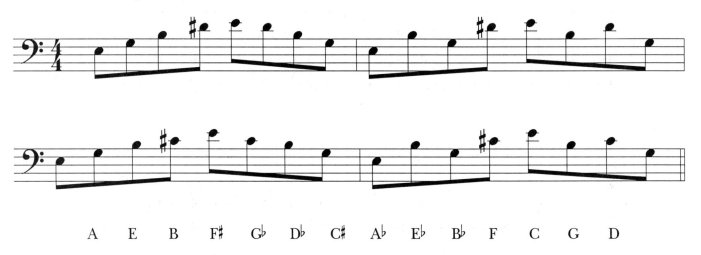

A   E   B   F#   Gb   Db   C#   Ab   Eb   Bb   F   C   G   D

Two-octave melodic minor scales:

Example 1 stays in the low end of the neck as long as possible. Example 6 gets to the top end of the bass as quickly as possible. Fill in the empty fingerboard charts with your own ideas for the two-octave melodic minor scale. For the two-octave m(maj7) arpeggio, see page 169.

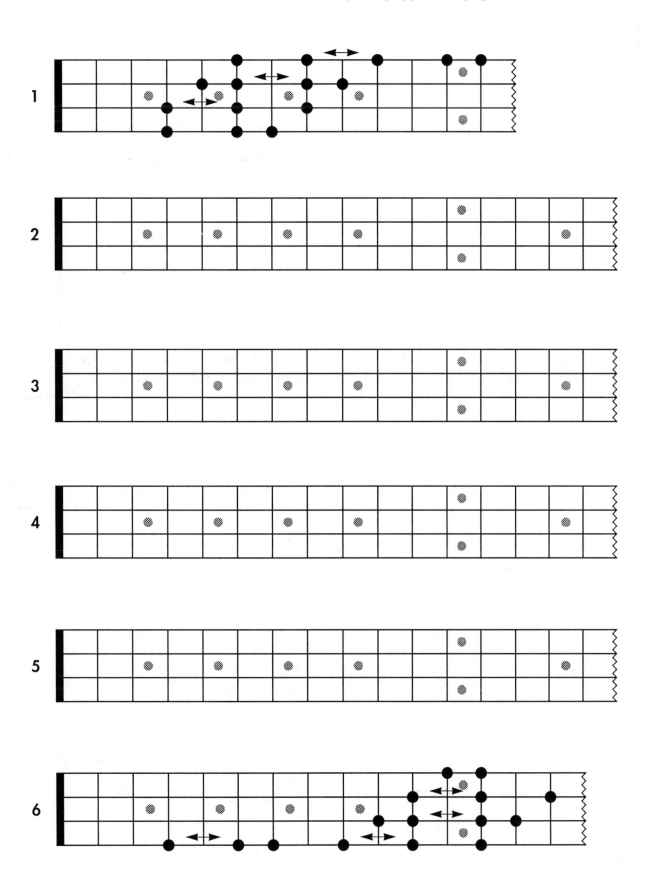

Your own melodic minor scale, m(maj7) and m6 chord ideas:

Melodic minor scale modes and chords

Like the major and harmonic minor scales, the melodic minor scale may be divided up into modes. In contrast to the harmonic minor scale, where only the first and fifth modes are used, *all* the modes of the melodic minor scale—except the second—are commonly used melodically and harmonically in popular music. Let's give a listen to all of them.

Mode 1: Melodic minor scale – m(maj^7)

Mode 2: Dorian ♭9 – m$^{7(♭9,13)}$ (rarely used because of the ♭9)

Mode 3: Lydian augmented scale – maj$^{7(♯5, ♯11)}$

Mode 4: Lydian dominant scale – dom$^{7(♯11)}$

Mode 5: dom$^{7(♭13)}$

Mode 6: Locrian ♯2 – m$^{9(♭5)}$

Mode 7: Altered scale – dom$^{7(♯5, ♯9)}$

Mode 7: Enharmonic spelling

Comparing major scale and melodic minor scale modes:

The major scale and the melodic minor scale differ by only one note—the lowered third scale degree of the melodic minor scale. Placing these two scales and the modes they generate side by side is a great aid in hearing, playing and learning the functions of the new, often exotic sounding modes (scales) and chords that come from the melodic minor scale.

The major scale has only one dominant scale and chord in it—the Mixolydian mode (dom7). The melodic minor scale has three dominant scale/chord combinations—mode 4 (lydian dominant – 7(♯11), mode 5 (dominant ♭13 – 7(♭13) and mode 7 (the altered scale – 7(♯5, ♯9). Together with the remaining modes of the melodic minor scale, the harmonic minor scale from Chapter 10 and the symmetric scales to be discussed in Chapter 12, your ears are in for a sonic treat.

The Third mode of the Melodic Minor scale:
The Lydian augmented scale – maj7(♯4, ♯5)

1. Derivation:

Starts
on
the
third

Scale step: 1   2   3

2. Interval construction:

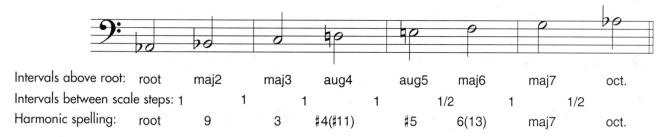

Intervals above root:	root	maj2	maj3	aug4	aug5	maj6	maj7	oct.
Intervals between scale steps: 1		1	1	1	1/2	1	1/2	
Harmonic spelling:	root	9	3	♯4(♯11)	♯5	6(13)	maj7	oct.

Did you notice that there are no minor intervals above the root in this scale? Also, don't forget that a sharp (♯) sign is the same as a plus (+) sign (♯4 = +4).

3. Scale type and tonic chord:

This scale is called Lydian augmented because it contains ♯4(♯11) and maj7 intervals (like the Lydian mode), and a ♯5 interval above the root (augmented). It is used as both an altered major scale and as a dominant scale. Dominant? What? Hold on until item 5 below. Its tonic chord is written in a number of ways. Among them:

a. maj7(+5) or maj7(♯5)

b. maj7(+4, +5) or maj7(♯4, ♯5)

c. maj7(+5, +11) or maj7(♯5, ♯11)

d. Special case. When you come across a polychord in which the upper note (the triad—which in this chord implies the major scale) is a maj3rd above the lower note (the bass note), for example C/A♭, you've got a maj7(♯5) chord on your hands. Check it out.

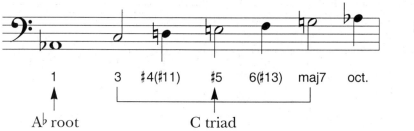

1   3 ♯4(♯11)   ♯5   6(♯13) maj7 oct.

A♭ root   C triad

So...C/A♭ = A♭maj7(♯5)
      E/C = Cmaj7(♯4, ♯5)
      G/E♭ = E♭maj7(♯5, ♯11)
and so on.
Cool, huh?

4. Notes above the root that define the third mode of the melodic minor scale—Lydian augmented:

- maj3rd
- ♯4 or ♯11 (+4 or +11)
- ♯5 (+5)
- maj7th

5. Most common uses:

a. Melodically: a great scale and chord to solo over a m(maj7) chord. It gets you away from starting your line with the root. For example, you can use an A♭maj7(♯5) chord and scale to solo over an Fm(maj7) chord. Or, to put it another way, use the third mode of the melodic minor—lydian augmented—scale to solo over the melodic minor scale it came from. Same notes—much hipper sound.

b. Harmonically: as a dominant chord or as the 1st inversion of an altered dominant chord. In the chord progression A♭maj7(♯5) to Am, the A♭ chord (third mode of the F melodic minor scale) shares the same notes as an E7(♯5, ♯9) (seventh mode of the F melodic minor scale)—a more common choice to resolve to Am. Using the A♭ bass note creates a half-step resolution. The chord may be written as E^alt/G♯.

6. Tetrachord construction:

The third mode of the melodic minor scale, the lydian augmented scale, is comprised of whole-tone and diminished tetrachords a whole step apart.

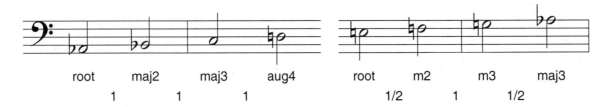

root	maj2	maj3	aug4		root	m2	m3	maj3
	1	1	1			1/2	1	1/2

7. A tetrachord drama.

"What's this? A new tetrachord?"

"Yes, the diminished tetrachord. It covers the interval of a major third."

"Well, then, if it covers the interval of a major third, why is it called 'diminished?'"

"Good question. Because every other tetrachord we've talked about with the exception the whole tone tetrachord covers a perfect fourth, this tetrachord is called 'diminished' as it covers an interval one half step less than a perfect fourth. Don't forget that when a perfect interval is lowered one half step it becomes diminished." (See page 26 if you forgot.)

"Oh."

"In fact, the third mode of the melodic minor scale—the lydian augmented scale—is unique in that neither of its tetrachords, whole-tone and diminished, cover a perfect fourth. Cool, huh?"

"Yeah, sure."

"Well, there you have it."

The third mode of the melodic minor scale in the 1st position:

As usual, these exercises start from the root of the scale, go up as high and as low as possible in the 1st position and then outline the tonic chord. This is a rather exotic sounding scale and chord so listen hard and concentrate as you play. Improvise!

Exercise 7: F Lydian augmented – Fmaj7(♯5)

Exercise 8: E♭ Lydian augmented – E♭maj7(♯4, ♯5)

Exercise 9: G Lydian augmented – Gmaj7(♯5, ♯11)

Be sure to use 1st position fingerings! No cheating!

Come up with your own ideas.

Here's the famous list of keys for you to practice:

A   E   B   F♯   G♭   D♭   C♯   A♭   E♭   B♭   C   D

The Lydian augmented scale outside of the 1st position:

Here are some ideas for playing a one-octave Lydian augmented scale outside of the 1st position. Practice these and then come up with some of your own. Cover the entire bass.

1. Up one string – Starting with an open string
0   1   3◄─►1   3◄─►1   3   4

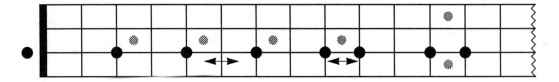

2. Up one string – Starting with a fingered note
1◄─►2   4◄─►1   3◄─►1   3   4

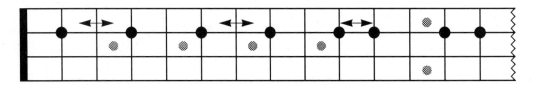

3. Two strings
1◄─►2   4   1   3◄─►1   3   4

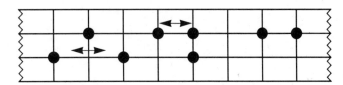

4. Three strings
1◄─►2   4   1   3   4   1   2

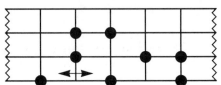

5. Three strings
2   4   1 /\ 4   1◄─►1   3   4

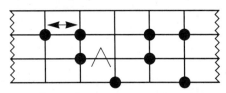

6. Three strings
4   1◄─►2   4   1◄─►1   3   4

7. Two string pairs – F, B♭ and E♭ Lydian augmented
1   3   0◄─►4   1◄─►1   3   4

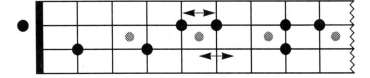

8. Four strings (See #8, page 183)
4   1 /\ 4   1   3   4   1   2

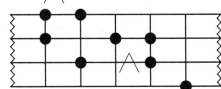

The third mode of the melodic minor scale outside of the 1st position:

Practice these exercises in every key. To keep track of your progress, use the list of starting pitches that follows each exercise. Play each exercise with as many of the fingerings on page 192 as you can. Be sure to retain the shape of the fingering you have chosen.

Exercise 10: Lydian augmented scale

C C♯ D♭ D E♭ E F F♯ G♭ G A♭ A B♭ B

Exercise 11: Lydian augmented scale in triplets

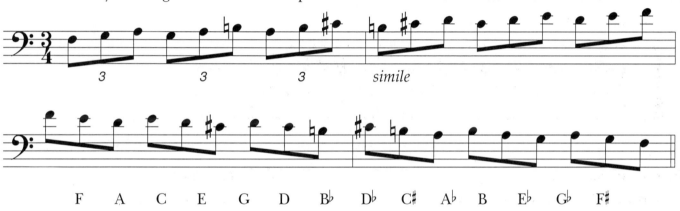

F A C E G D B♭ D♭ C♯ A♭ B E♭ G♭ F♯

Exercise 12: Lydian augmented scale in four-note groups

G D A E B F♯ G♭ C♯ D♭ A♭ B♭ E♭ F C

Exercise 13: maj7(♯5, ♯11) aka maj7(♯4, ♯5)

A E B F♯ G♭ D♭ C♯ A♭ E♭ B♭ F C D G

Two-octave Lydian augmented scales:

The first example stays in the 1st position as long as possible while the last example gets to the top end of the bass as quickly as possible. Fill in the empty fingerboard charts with your own two octave Lydian augmented ideas.

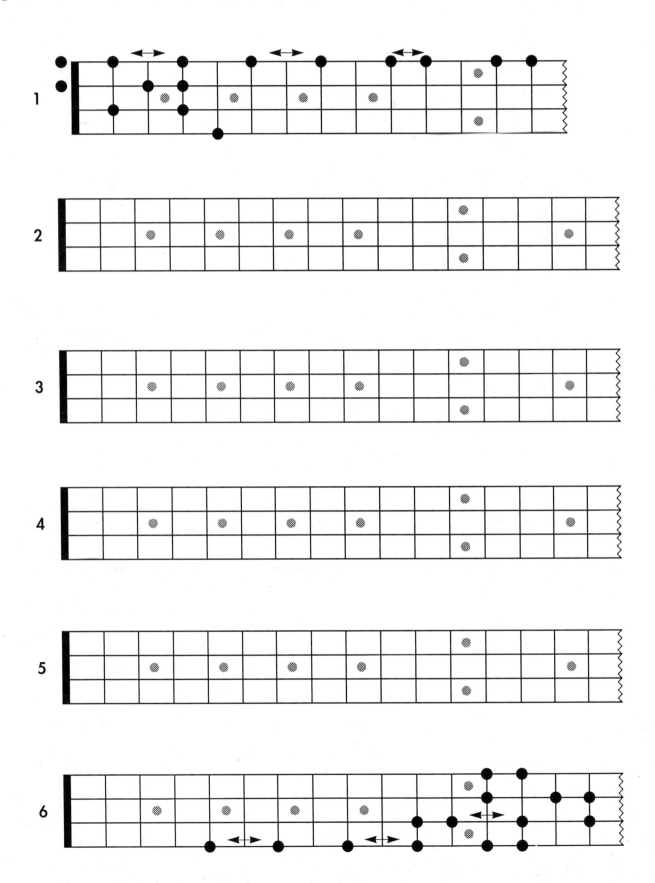

Two-octave maj7(♯5) arpeggios – Tonic chord – Lydian augmented scale:

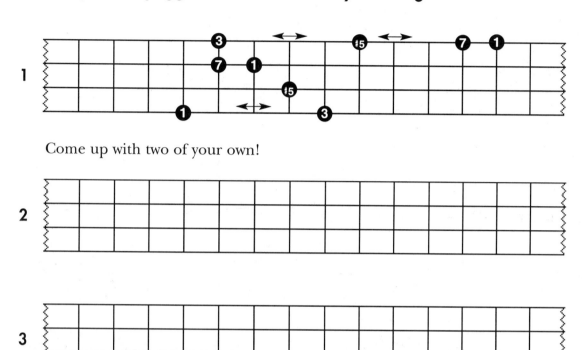

Come up with two of your own!

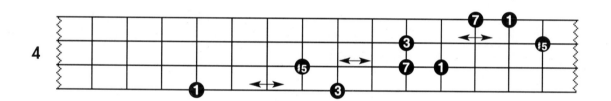

Exercise 14: maj7(♯4, ♯5) arpeggio   Check out both fingerings.

Your own Lydian augmented scale, maj7(#4, #5) chord ideas:

The Fourth mode of the Melodic Minor scale:
The Lydian dominant scale – dom7(♯11)
(aka Lydian ♭7 or Mixolydian ♯4)

1. Derivation:
Starts on the fourth degree of melodic minor scale.

Scale step: 1   2   3   4

2. Interval construction:

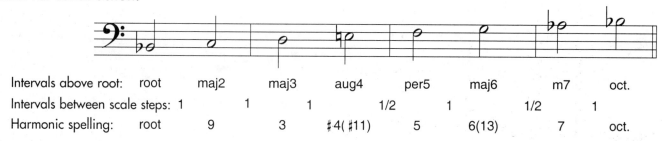

Intervals above root:	root	maj2	maj3	aug4	per5	maj6	m7	oct.
Intervals between scale steps:	1	1	1	1/2	1	1/2	1	
Harmonic spelling:	root	9	3	♯4(♯11)	5	6(13)	7	oct.

3. Scale type, use and tonic chord:

This scale is called Lydian dominant because it contains maj3 and ♯4(♯11) intervals (just like the Lydian mode) and a m7 interval above the root (dominant 7th, just like the Mixolydian mode). It is used as a dominant scale in major keys.

Its tonic chord is usually written dom7(♯11). The chord symbol dom7(♭5) sometimes calls for the same scale. You should know that dom7(♭5) is used occasionally to mean the whole-tone scale which we will be covering later.

4. Notes above the root that define the fourth mode of the melodic minor scale—Lydian dominant:
- maj3   • +4(+11) or ♯4(♯11)   • m7 (dom7)

5. Tetrachord construction:

The Lydian dominant scale, the fourth mode of the melodic minor scale, is made up of whole-tone and minor tetrachords a half step apart.

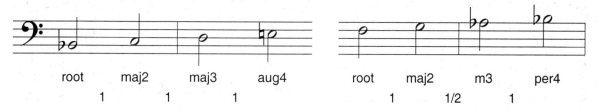

root	maj2	maj3	aug4		root	maj2	m3	per4
1	1	1			1	1/2	1	

The fourth mode of the melodic minor scale in the 1st position:

The first two Lydian dominant exercises start from the root of the scale, go up as high and as low as possible in the 1st position and then outline the tonic chord. This scale and chord are used quite a lot in popular music. Learn it well. Improvise!

Exercise 15: E7(♯11)

Exercise 16: C7(♯11)

More keys to practice: G   D   A   B   F♯   G♭   C♯   D♭   A♭   B♭   F

Exercise 17: dom7(♯11) This exercise covers every key.

The Lydian dominant scale outside of the 1st position:

Here are some ideas for playing a one octave Lydian dominant scales outside of the 1st position. Practice these and then come up with some of your own. Cover the entire bass.

1. Up one string – Starting with an open string
0 1◄►1 3 4◄►1 2 4

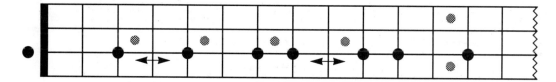

2. Up one string – Starting with a fingered note
1 3◄►1 3 4◄►1 2 4

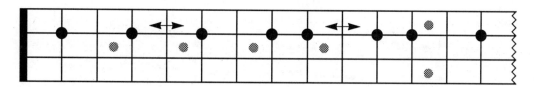

3. Two strings
1◄►2 4 1 2◄►1 2 4

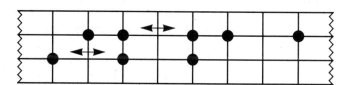

4. Three strings
1◄►2 4 1◄►1 3 4 1

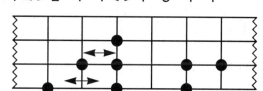

5. Three strings
2 4 1 3 4 1 2 4

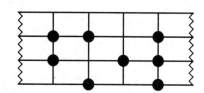

6. Three strings
4 1◄►1 3 4 1 2 4

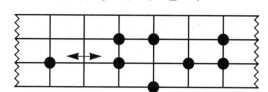

7. Two string pairs – F, B♭ and E♭ Lydian dominant
1 3 0◄►3 4 1 2 4

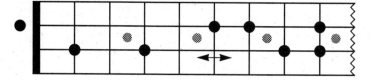

8. Four strings (See #8, page 192)
4 1 ∧ 4 1◄►1 3 4 1

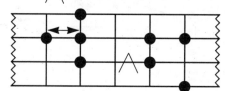

Lydian dominant – dom7(♯11) – exercises outside of the 1st position:

Practice these exercises in every key. Use the list of starting pitches following each exercise to keep track of your progress. Play each exercise with as many of the fingerings on page 199 as you can. Be sure to retain the shape of the fingering you have chosen.

Exercise 18: E♭ Lydian dominant scale

E♭   G♭   F♯   A   C   E   G   B♭   D♭   C♯   F   D   A♭   B

Exercise 19: C Lydian dominant scale in four-note groups

C   C♯   D♭   D   E♭   E   F   F♯   G♭   G   A♭   A   B♭   B

Exercise 20: B♭ Lydian dominant scale in sixths

B♭   F   C   G   D   A   E   B   F♯   G♭   D♭   C♯   A♭   E♭

Exercise 21: F7(♯11)

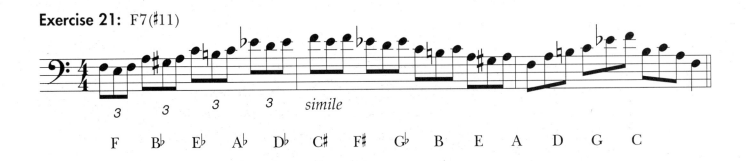

F   B♭   E♭   A♭   D♭   C♯   F♯   G♭   B   E   A   D   G   C

Two-octave Lydian dominant scales:

The first example stays in the 1st position as long as possible whereas the last example gets to the top end of the bass as quickly as possible. Fill in the empty fingerboard charts with your own ideas for two-octave Lydian dominant scales.

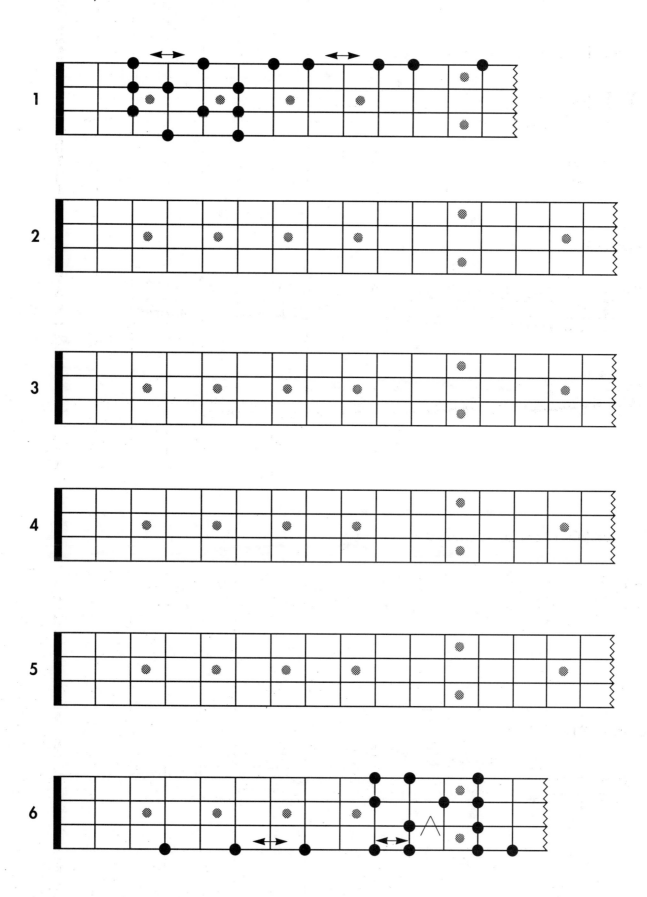

Two-octave dom7(♯11) arpeggios – Tonic chord – Lydian dominant scale

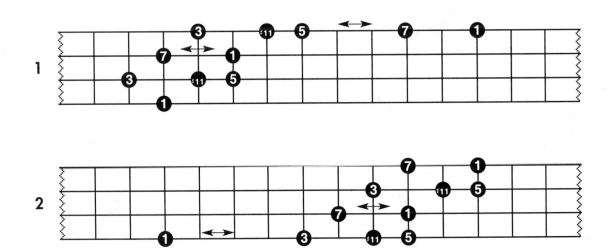

Exercise 22: dom7(♯11) arpeggio

1 Finger:	2	1	3	4	2	1	2	3	1	3	2	3	1	3	2	3	1	3	2	4	1	2	1	3	4
String:	E	A		D	A			D			A		D		G	A	D		G		D		G		

2 Finger:	1	1	3	4	2	1	2	3	1	3	2	3	1	3	2	3	1	3	2	4	1	2	1	3	4
String:	E				A	E			A		E		A		D	E	A		D		A		D		

2	1	3	1	4	3	2	3	1	3	3	1	3	2	3	4	1	3	1	2
D	G				D		G			G	D				G				D

2	1	3	4	2	1	3	4	2	4	4	2	4	3	1	2	4	3	1	2
A	D		G	D			G			G		D			G	D			A

4	3	1	2	1	4	2	3	1	3	2	3	1	3	2	3	1	3	2	1	2	4	3	1	2
G		D			G	D	A	G	D		A		D		A					D	A			E

4	3	1	2	1	4	2	3	1	3	2	3	1	3	2	3	1	3	2	1	2	4	3	1	1
D		A			D	A		E	D	A		E		A		E				A	E			

Your own Lydian dominant scale, dom7(♯11) chord ideas:

The Fifth mode of the Melodic Minor scale:
Dominant ♭13 scale – dom7(♭13)

1. Derivation:

Starts on the fifth degree of the melodic minor scale.

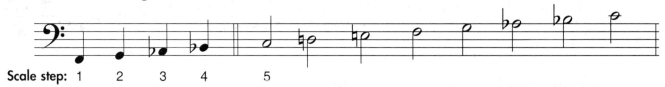

Scale step: 1   2   3   4   5

2. Interval construction:

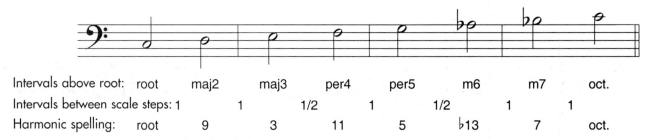

Intervals above root:	root	maj2	maj3	per4	per5	m6	m7	oct.
Intervals between scale steps: 1		1		1/2		1		1/2		1		1	
Harmonic spelling:	root	9	3	11	5	♭13	7	oct.

3. Scale type, use and tonic chord:

The dominant ♭13 scale is the second dominant scale that comes from the melodic minor scale. Except for the ♭13, it it identical to the Mixolydian mode. The dominant ♭13 scale is typically used for the "5" chord in minor progressions.

Its tonic chord is written dom7(♭13)—G7(♭13).

4. Notes above the root that define the fifth mode of the melodic minor scale—dominant ♭13:

- maj3
- m6 (♭6) or m13 (♭13)
- m7 (dom7)

5. Tetrachord construction:

The dominant ♭13 scale, the fifth mode of the melodic minor scale, is made up of major and Phrygian tetrachords a whole step apart.

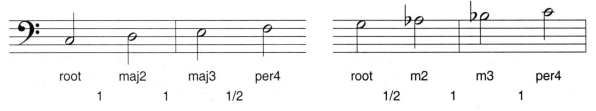

root	maj2	maj3	per4	root	m2	m3	per4
	1	1	1/2		1/2	1	1

The fifth mode of the melodic minor scale in the 1st position:

Exercise 23 starts on the root of the scale, goes up as high and as low as possible in the 1st position and then outlines the tonic chord. Exercise 24 covers the tetrachords in every key. Improvise!

Exercise 23: dom7(♭13)

Keys to practice: G   D   A   B   F♯   G♭   C♯   D♭   A♭   B♭   F

Exercise 24: dom7(♭13) tetrachords in every key

The dominant ♭13 scale outside of the 1st position:

Here are some ideas for playing a one octave dominant ♭13 scales outside of the 1st position. Practice these and then come up with some of your own. Cover the entire bass.

1. Up one string – Starting with an open string

0 1 3 ◄►1 3 4 ◄►1 3

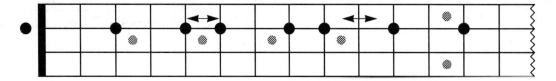

2. Up one string – Starting with a fingered note

1◄►1 3◄►1 3 4 ◄►1 3

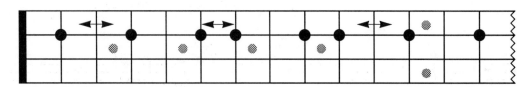

3. Two strings

1◄►1 3 4 1 2◄►1 3

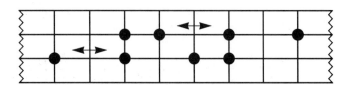

4. Three strings

1◄►1 3 4 1 2 4 1

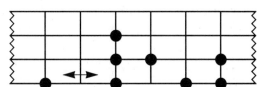

5. Three strings

4 1 3 4◄►3 4 1 3

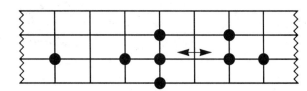

6. Three strings

2 4 1 2◄►3 4 1 3

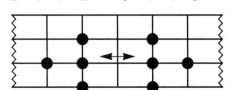

7. Two string pairs – F, B♭ and E♭ dominant ♭13

1 3 0◄►1 3 4 1 3

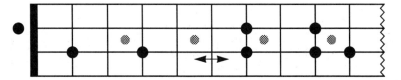

8. Four strings

4 1 3 4 1 2 4 1

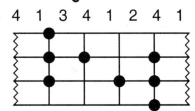

Dominant ♭13 scale – dom7(♭13) exercises outside of the 1st position:

Practice these exercises in every key. Use the list of starting pitches following each exercise to keep track of your progress. Play each exercise with as many of the fingerings on page 206 as you can.

Exercise 25: dom7(♭13) scale

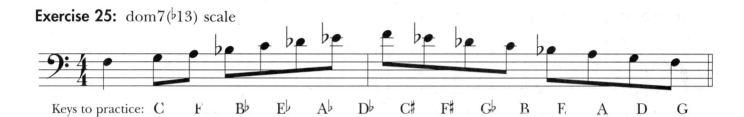

Keys to practice: C   F   B♭   E♭   A♭   D♭   C♯   F♯   G♭   B   E   A   D   G

Exercise 26: dom7(♭13) scale in triplets

More keys to practice: A   D   G   C   F   B♭   E♭   A♭   D♭   C♯   F♯   G♭   B   E

Exercise 27: Dominant ♭13 in every key. Listen for the ♭13 and the maj3 in each four note group.

Two-octave dominant ♭13 scales:

The first example stays in the low end of the bass as long as possible while the last example gets to the top end of the bass as quickly as possible. Fill in the empty fingerboard charts with your own two-octave dominant ♭13 ideas.

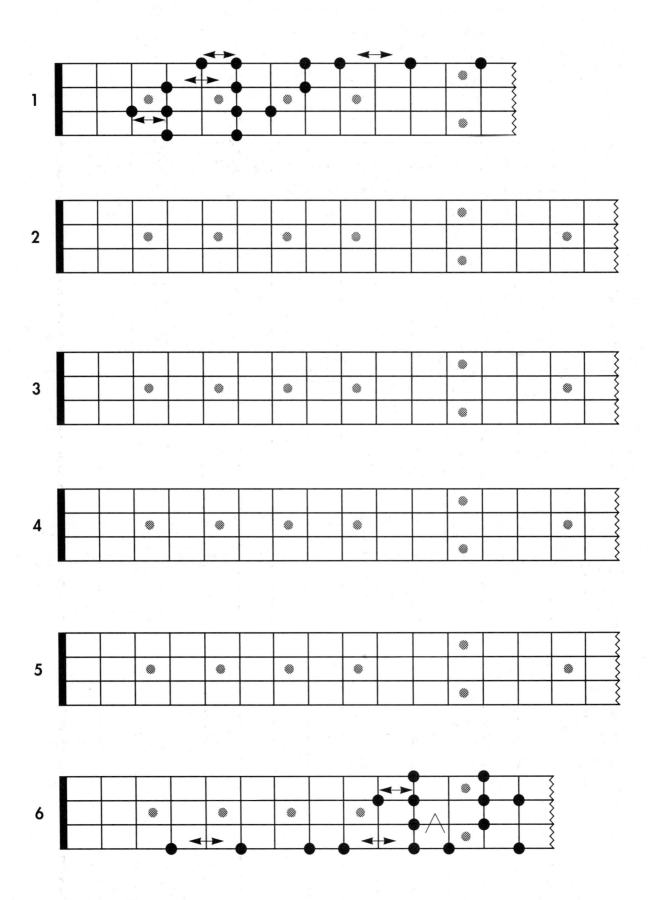

Two-octave dom7(♭13) arpeggios – Tonic chord – dominant ♭13 scale

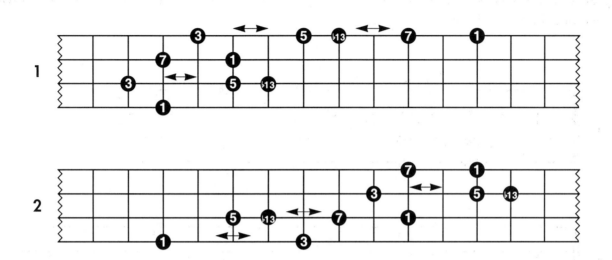

Exercise 28: dom7(♭13) arpeggio

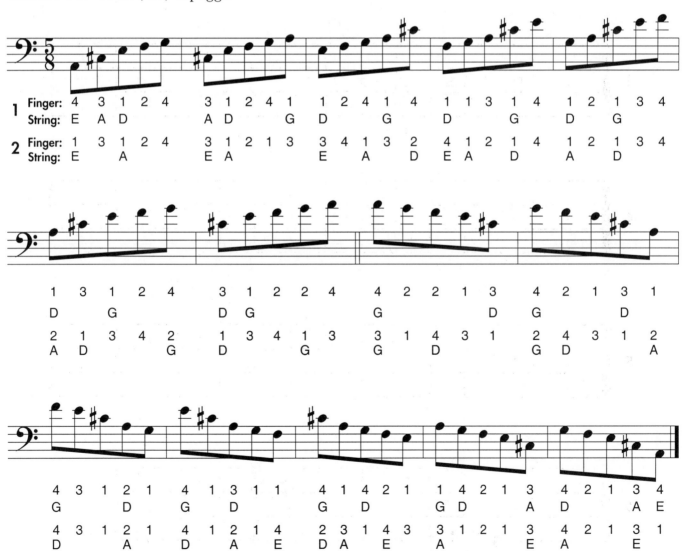

Your own dominant ♭13 scale, dom7(♭13) chord ideas:

The Sixth mode of the Melodic Minor scale:

Locrian ♯2 scale – m9(♭5) (aka Locrian ♮9 or Locrian ♮2)

1. Derivation:

Starts on the sixth degree of the melodic minor scale.

Scale step: 1   2   3   4   5   6

2. Interval construction:

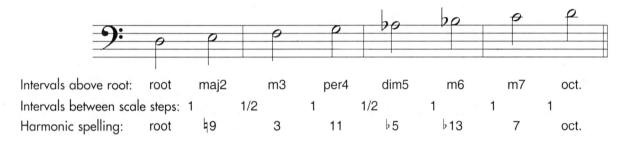

Intervals above root:	root	maj2	m3	per4	dim5	m6	m7	oct.
Intervals between scale steps:	1	1/2	1	1/2	1	1	1	
Harmonic spelling:	root	♮9	3	11	♭5	♭13	7	oct.

3. Scale type, use and tonic chord:

The Locrian ♯2 scale (Locrian ♮9) is the second minor scale that comes from the melodic minor scale. It gains its name from the fact that it has a ♯2 (♮2 or ♮9) above its root when compared to the Locrian mode from the major scale which has a ♭2 (♭9) above its root. The Locrian ♯2 scale is typically used as a "2" chord in minor progressions. Its tonic chord is m7(♭5) or m9(♭5).

4. Notes above the root that define the sixth mode of the melodic minor scale—Locrian ♯2:

- maj2 (maj9)
- m3
- ♭5
- m6 (♭6) or m13 (♭13)
- m7 (dom7)

5. Tetrachord construction:

The Locrian ♯2 scale, the sixth mode of the melodic minor scale, is made up of minor and whole-tone tetrachords a half step apart.

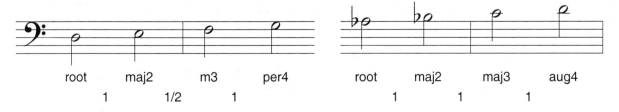

root	maj2	m3	per4	root	maj2	maj3	aug4
	1	1/2	1		1	1	1

The sixth mode of the melodic minor scale in the 1st position:

Exercise 29 starts on the root of the scale, goes up as high and as low as possible in the 1st position and then outlines the tonic chord. Exercise 30 covers the tetrachords in every key.

Exercise 29: Listen for the maj2(9), the ♭5 and the ♭13.

Keys to practice: G   D   A   B   F#   G♭   C#   D♭   A♭   B♭   F

Exercise 30: Locrian ♯2 tetrachords in every key.

The Locrian ♯2 scale outside of the 1st position:

Here are some ideas for playing the sixth mode of the melodic minor scale outside of the 1st position. Practice these and then come up with some of your own. Play over the entire fingerboard in every key.

1. Up one string – Starting with an open string

0   1   2◄►1   2   4◄►1   3

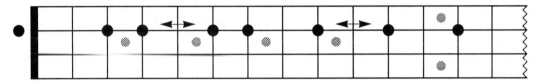

2. Up one string – Starting with a fingered note

1   3   4◄►1   2   4◄►1   3

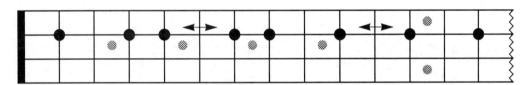

3. Two strings

1   3   4   1   2   4◄►1   3

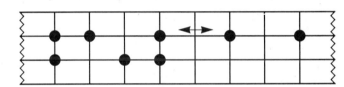

4. Three strings

1   3   4   1   2◄►2   4   1

5. Three strings

1   3◄►1   3   4   1 /\ 4   1

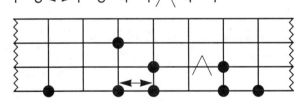

6. Four strings

4   1◄►1   3   4   1 /\ 4   1

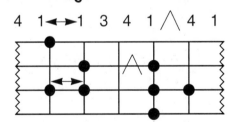

7. Two string pairs – F♯, B and E Locrian ♯2

1   3   0◄►1   2   4   1   3

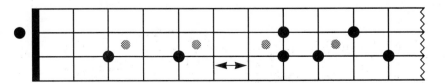

8. Three strings

1   3   4   1   2   4   1   3

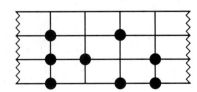

Locrian ♯2 exercises outside of the 1st position:

Practice these exercises in every key. To keep track of your progress, use the list of starting pitches following each exercise. Play each exercise with as many of the fingerings on page 213 as you can. Be sure to retain the shape of the fingering you have chosen.

Compare these exercises with those on page 101 – the Locrian mode from the major scale.

Exercise 31: Locrian ♯2 scale

Keys to practice: C   C♯   D   D♯   E   F   F♯   G   G♯   A   A♯   B

Exercise 32: Locrian ♯2 scale bass line – play with a latin feel

Keys to practice: D♯   F♯   A   C   E   G   A♯   C♯   F   D   G♯   B

Exercise 33: m9(♭5) – dotted-eighth, sixteenth-note pattern – play with a shuffle feel

Keys to practice: E   A   D   G   C   F   A♯   D♯   G♯   C♯   F♯   B

Exercise 34: m9(♭5) – triplet pattern

Keys to practice: D   A   E   B   F♯   C♯   G♯   D♯   A♯   F   C   G

Two-octave Locrian ♯2 scales:

As usual, Example 1 stays in the 1st position as long as possible. Example 6 gets to the top end of the bass as quickly as possible. Fill in the fingerboard charts with your own two-octave ideas for the sixth mode of the melodic minor scale, and practice them in *every* key.

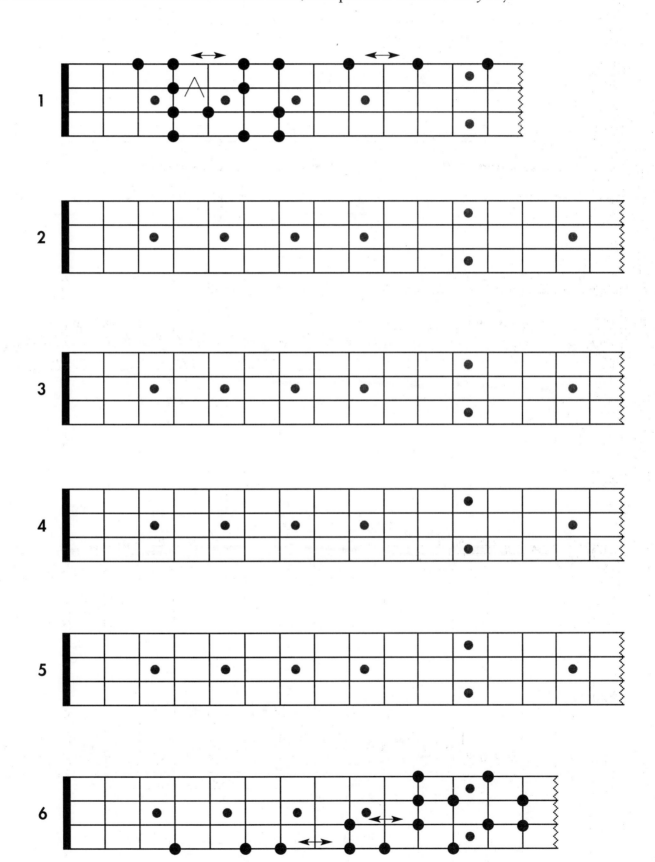

Two-octave m9(♭5) arpeggios – "2" chord in minor

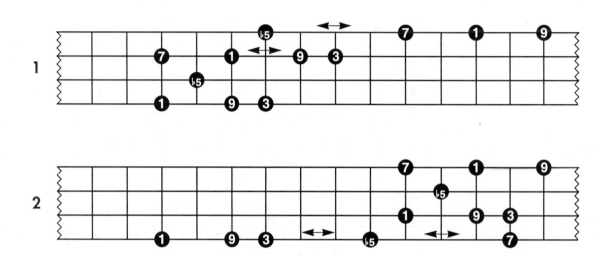

Exercise 35: m9(♭5) arpeggio

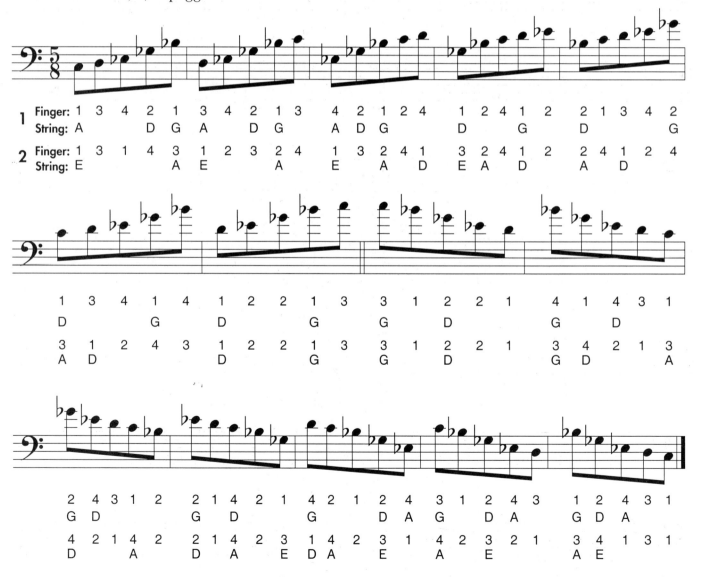

1	Finger:	1	3	4	2	1	3	4	2	1	3	4	2	1	2	4	1	2	4	1	2	2	1	3	4	2
	String:	A			D	G	A			D	G		A	D	G			D		G			D			G

2	Finger:	1	3	1	4	3	1	2	3	2	4	1	3	2	4	1	3	2	4	1	2	2	4	1	2	4
	String:	E		A	E		A			E		A	D	E	A	D			A			D				

1	3	4	1	4	1	2	2	1	3	3	1	2	2	1	4	1	4	3	1
D		G		D		G			G		D			G		D			

3	1	2	4	3	1	2	2	1	3	3	1	2	2	1	3	4	2	1	3
A	D				D		G			G		D			G	D			A

2	4	3	1	2	2	1	4	2	1	4	2	1	2	4	3	1	2	4	3	1	2	4	3	1
G	D				G	D			G				D	A	G		D	A		G	D	A		

4	2	1	4	2	2	1	4	2	"3	1	4	2	3	1	4	2	3	2	1	3	4	1	3	1
D		A			D	A		E	D	A			E		A		E			A	E			

Your own Locrian ♯2 ideas:

Pay particular attention to the ♭5 and the natural 9.

The Seventh mode of the Melodic Minor scale:

The Altered scale – dom7(♯5, ♯9)

1. Derivation:

Starts on the seventh degree of the melodic minor scale.

Scale step: 1   2   3   4   5   6   7

2. Interval construction:

Confusion Alert!!

How should this scale be spelled?

This scale is supposed to produce a dom7(♯5, ♯9) chord. Looking at the half notes above, it seems that the tonic chord is a m7(♭5, ♭9, ♭13) with a ♭11 (♭11??) thrown in for good measure. In order for the scale to give us the tonic chord we are looking for, a number of enharmonic changes need to be made.

By changing
- the G (above) to an F× – the ♯9 (+9) (below),
- the A♭ to a G♯ – the maj3,
- the B♭ to an A♯ – the ♯11 (+11), and
- the C to a B♯ – the ♯5 (+5),

you arrive at the correct spelling and, as a result, the correct interval construction for the E altered scale. Pay particular attention to the harmonic spelling of the scale – the third line.

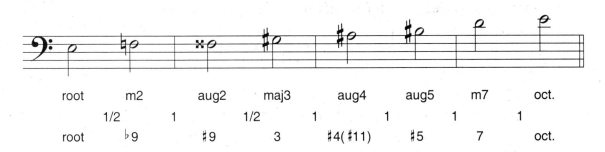

root	m2		aug2	maj3	aug4	aug5	m7	oct.
	1/2	1		1/2	1	1	1	1
root	♭9		♯9	3	♯4(♯11)	♯5	7	oct.

3. A few firsts:

a. This is the first scale we've run into that has two, count 'em, two 9ths in it—the ♭9 and the + or ♯9. Do you remember that when there are altered 9ths in a scale that there is no regular 9th?

b. This is the first dominant scale we've encountered that has a + or ♯5 in it. Do you remember that when a + or ♯5 is found in a scale that there is no regular 5th and that there is usually a ♯11 present, too?

c. This is the first dominant scale we've run into that has no 6th or 13th in it.

d. Finally, this is the first scale we've run into that has two notes with the same letter name in it. Check out the E altered scale in item 2 and you'll notice that there are two F's— an F♯ and an F✕—the two altered 9ths. Although the note F is technically the ninth above the E root in this example, most musicians use the enharmonic equivalent for F✕, G♮. It's easier for them to deal with. For that matter, the A♯ (the ♯11) and the B♯ (the ♯5) cause problems for some people and are often changed to their enharmonic equivalents B♭ and C♮, respectively. (Turn back to page 24 and reread **N.B.1** for more on enharmonic changes.)

Here's how the E altered scale is spelled adding these new enharmonic notes:

| root | ♭9 | ♯9 | 3 | ♯11 | ♯5 | 7 | oct. |

Wait a minute! Now the scale is spelled like the scale in item 1 on page 218 with the A♭ changed to a G♯. Why go through all of that double sharp business? Why bother with all those enharmonic changes?

By using the double sharps and making the enharmonic changes to the scale as it comes from the melodic minor scale, we are able to determine *exactly* how each note of the scale functions above the root. In item 2 on the pervious page, the F✕ is really the ♯9 above the E root, while the A♯ and the B♯ are the actual ♯11 and ♯5.

Changing those double sharps and those pesky A♯'s and B♯'s to more commonly used notes makes life easier for a lot of players. In the above example, G replaces F✕, B♭ replaces A♯ and C replaces B♯. Although the G seems to be a minor third above the root, it functions as the ♯9 in the scale and the resulting chord. The B♭ functions as the ♯11, not a ♭5; and the C functions as the ♯5, not a ♭13.

Although some notes are changed enharmonically to make reading and writing them a bit easier, their function in the altered scale remains the same.

4. Scale type and tonic chord:

With a maj3 and a m7 above the root, the altered scale is a dominant scale. The scale is also known as the diminished whole-tone scale because of its tetrachord make-up and as the Super Locrian scale from Classical music theory.

The basic 7th chord derived from the altered scale is the dom7(♯5). Hold on...that's the same tonic chord found in the whole-tone scale (as we'll discover later). How do you tell them apart?

As we already know, the altered scale has altered nines in it. The whole-tone scale (discussed in Chapter 12) has a regular, unaltered nine in it just like the Mixolydian mode. So, to be sure that your chord symbol is calling for an altered scale, not a whole-tone scale, you must include the altered nine in addition to the ♯5 in the chord symbol, or use the abbreviation "alt."

Here are some examples of chord symbols that call for the altered scale:

dom7(♯5, ♯9), dom7(♯5, ♭9) and dom7^{alt}

5. Why is this scale called the "altered scale?"

I'm sure you are aware by now that "altered scale" refers to a specific succession of intervals as shown in item 2 on page 218. Also, you should be aware that the term "altered" is often used to describe dominant scales that contain chromatic changes to notes above the root that aren't found in the Mixolydian mode. When compared to the Mixolydian mode (dom7), the Lydian dominant scale (dom7, ♯11), the third mode of the melodic minor scale, has an altered 11 in it, whereas the fifth mode of the harmonic minor scale (dom7[♭9, ♭13]) has an altered 9 and an altered 13 in it.

The altered scale has in it every note of a dominant scale that can be changed while still retaining a dominant function.

Its maj3 and m7 above the root are the same as in any other dominant seventh chord. Using the E altered scale as an example, its root, E, its third, G♯, and its seventh, D, are found in every E dominant chord no matter what the scale source. Its nines, its fifth and its eleventh (remember, there is no 13th in the scale) are all changed chromatically by half steps. *Every note that can be altered is altered.* One more time—in the altered scale and its chord, both nines, the eleventh and, most importantly, the fifth are changed chromatically while still retaining the basic dominant 7th chord sound: root, maj3, m7. Totally altered, totally awesome!

6. Altered scale tetrachords:

The altered scale, the seventh mode of the melodic minor scale (aka the diminished whole-tone scale), is made up of diminished and whole-tone tetrachords one whole step apart. "Diminished whole-tone." Get it?

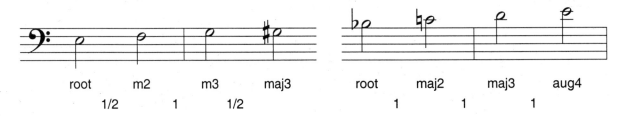

root	m2	m3	maj3	root	maj2	maj3	aug4
1/2		1	1/2		1	1	1

The seventh mode of the melodic minor scale in the 1st position:

The first two altered scale exercises start from the root of the scale and go up as high and as low as possible in the 1st position. Many enharmonic changes have been made in each exercise to get you comfortable with seeing the scale spelled in various ways. Be able to identify how each note functions in the scale and the chord. The third exercise, which also contains many enharmonic notes, outlines the tetrachords in every key. Improvise!

Exercise 36: The altered scale in the 1st position

Keys to practice: C   C♯   D   D♯   E   F   F♯   G   G♯   A   A♯   B

Exercise 37: Altered scale - dom7(♯5, ♯9)

More keys to practice: E   A   D   G   C   F   A♯   D♯   G♯   C♯   F♯   B

Exercise 38: Altered scale tetrachords in the 1st position

The altered scale outside of the 1st position:

Here are some ideas for playing the seventh mode of the melodic minor scale outside of the 1st position. Practice these and then come up with some of your own—many other fingerings are possible. Play over the entire fingerboard in every key.

1. Up one string – Starting with an open string

0   1   3   4◄─►1   3◄─►1   3

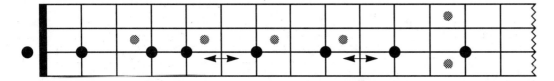

2. Up one string – Starting with a fingered note

1◄─►1   3   4◄─►1   3◄─►1   3

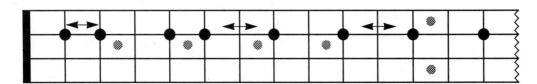

3. Two strings

1   2◄─►3   4◄─►1   3◄─►2   4

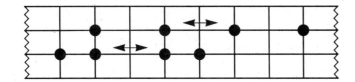

4. Three strings

1   2◄─►3   4   1   4 ∧ 1   3

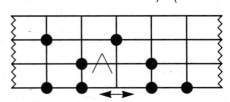

5. Three strings

1   2◄─►1   2   4   1 ∧ 4   1

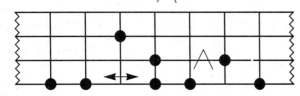

6. Three strings

3   4   1   2◄─►2   4   1   3

7. Two string pairs – F, B♭ and E♭ altered scale

1   2   4   0◄─►2   4   1   3

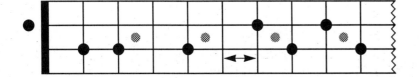

8. Four strings

3   4   1   2   4   1 ∧ 4   1

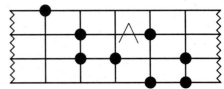

Altered scale exercises outside of the 1st position:

Practice these exercises in every key. Use the list of starting pitches following each exercise to keep track of your progress. Play each exercise with as many of the fingerings on page 222 as you can. Be sure to retain the shape of the fingering you have chosen.

Exercise 39: Altered scale - dom7(♯5, ♯9)

Keys to practice: E   A   D   G   C   F   B♭   E♭   G♯   C♯   F♯   B

Exercise 40: Altered scale in four note groups

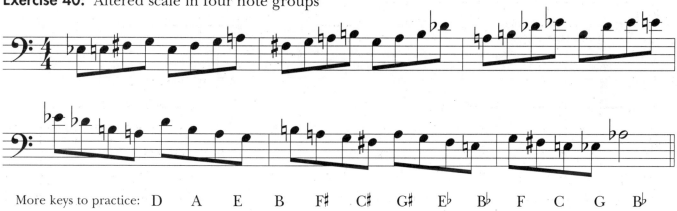

More keys to practice: D   A   E   B   F♯   C♯   G♯   E♭   B♭   F   C   G   B♭

Exercise 41: Altered scales covering the entire neck

Two-octave altered scales:

Example 1 stays in the 1st position as long as possible. Example 6 gets to the top end of the bass as quickly as possible. Fill in the fingerboard charts with your own two octave ideas for the seventh mode of the melodic minor scale, and practice them in *every* key.

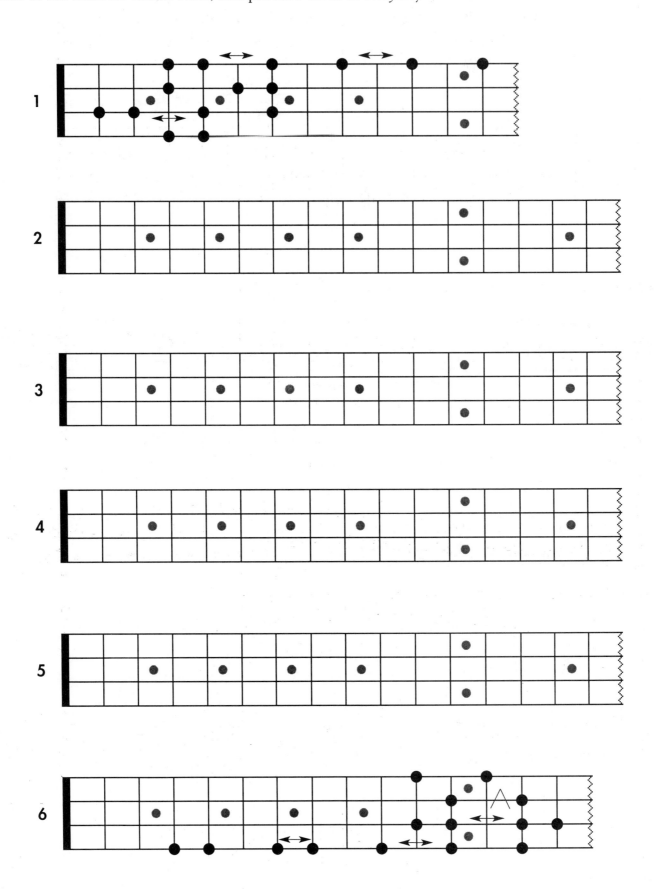

Two-octave dom7(♯5, ♯9) arpeggios – Tonic chord – The altered scale

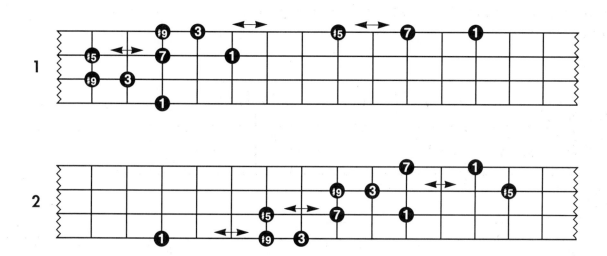

Exercise 42: dom7(♯5, ♯9) arpeggio Check out both fingerings.

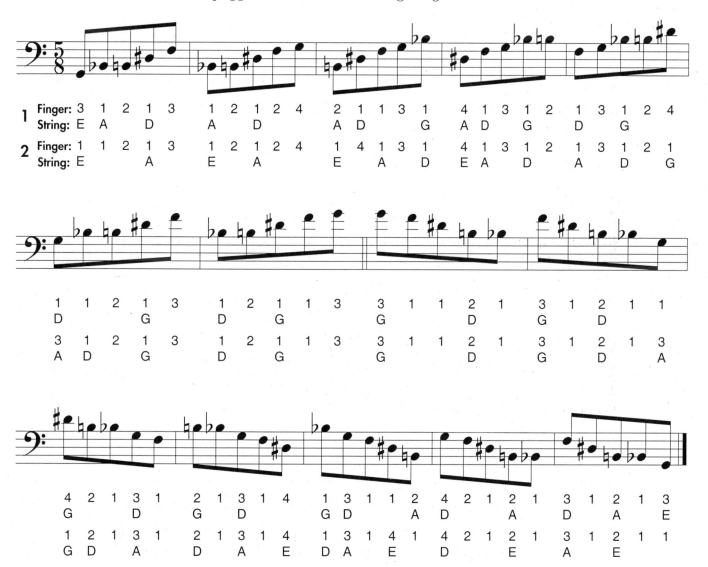

Your own altered scale ideas:

Pay particular attention to the ♯5, the ♯9 and the ♭9.

Melodic Minor Scale, Mode and Chord Summary

Scale step and mode	Scale type	Chord symbol	Alternate chord symbols
1. Melodic minor scale	minor	m(maj7)	mi(ma7); m(#7) or mi(#7); m(+7) or mi(+7); m(Δ7) or mi(Δ7); m(Δ7) or mi(Δ7) m(maj9) or m(maj9); m(ma9) or mi(ma9) – "maj9" or "ma9" in any chord symbol implies that a maj7th is also in the chord; m9(+7) or mi9(+7); a minus sign is often used for "m" or "mi" in a chord symbol – G–(maj7)
2. Mode 2, Dorian ♭9	minor	m7(♭9, 13)	mi7(♭9, 13) rarely used

3. Lydian augmented	major	maj7(#5, #11)	ma7(+5, +11);
			maj7(#4,#5) or maj7(+4, +5);
			maj7(♭5, +5) or ma7(♭5, +5);
			maj9(#5, #11) etc.;
			
			a polychord in which the top triad is a maj3rd above the bass note – for example E/C or D/B♭ (see page 189);
			
			a triangle "Δ" is used sometimes in place of the "maj" or "ma" symbol

4. Lydian dominant	dominant	7(#11)	7(+11); 7(♭5); 9(♭5); 9(#11); 13(#11); a polychord in which the top triad is a whole step above the dom7 chord – for example G/F7
5. Dominant ♭13	dominant	7(♭13)	9(♭13)
6. Locrian (♮2)	minor	m7(♭5)	ø7; m7(♭5, 9); m11(♭5, 9); m9(♭5); ø9
7. Altered scale	dominant	7(#5, #9)	7alt; 7(#5, ♭9); 7(+5, ♭9); +7(#9); +7(♭9); a polychord in which the top triad is a minor 6th above the dom7 chord – for example E♭/G7

Turn back to page 140 for more chord symbol information.

Here are some chord progressions that use chords and modes taken from the melodic minor scale. These are very basic progressions and by no means represent all of the combinations of chords and modes of the melodic minor scale that you might run into.

Exercise 43: This exercise covers the Locrian ♯2 (mode 6), the altered scale (mode 7) and the melodic minor scale (mode 1) in a ii - V - I progression.

Come up with bass line and solo ideas.

If you are having difficulty with a particular chord, mode or key, practice each one individually; and then play the entire progression. Playing them at a piano will help.

Check out the variety of chord symbols that are used to describe only three melodic minor modes. As mentioned on page 140, there is, unfortunately, no uniformly accepted way of writing chord changes. The ability to decipher the meaning of hundreds of chord changes is a big part of your job as a bass player.

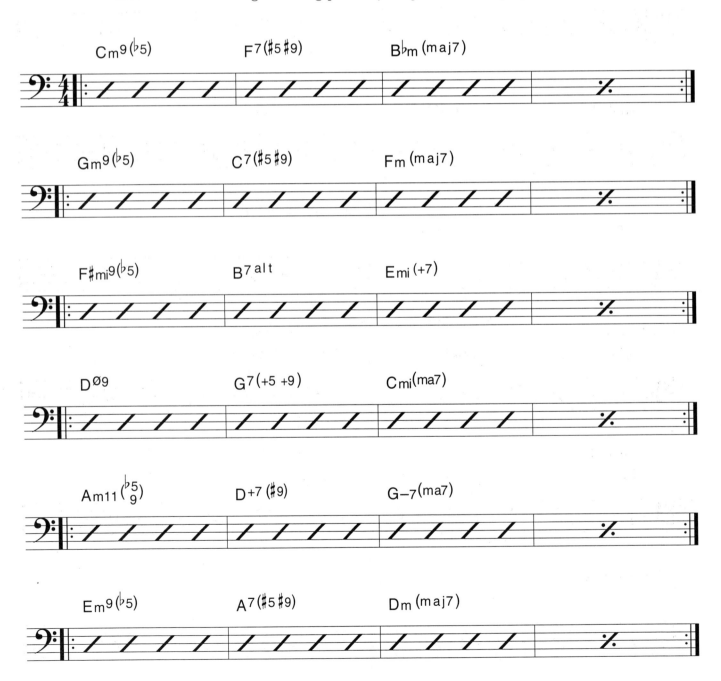

Exercise 44: This exercise contains a combintion of melodic minor, harmonic minor and major scale modes and chords producing ii – V – I progressions that reflect more common types of chord movement that you will encounter in daily playing.

Because we haven't studied harmonic minor modes and chords and major scale modes and chords for a while, I've included the harmonic minor and major mode names that go along with their chords. You will have to know them is a real-life playing situation.

The mode choices for the melodic minor scale modes are left put as we just got finished studying them!

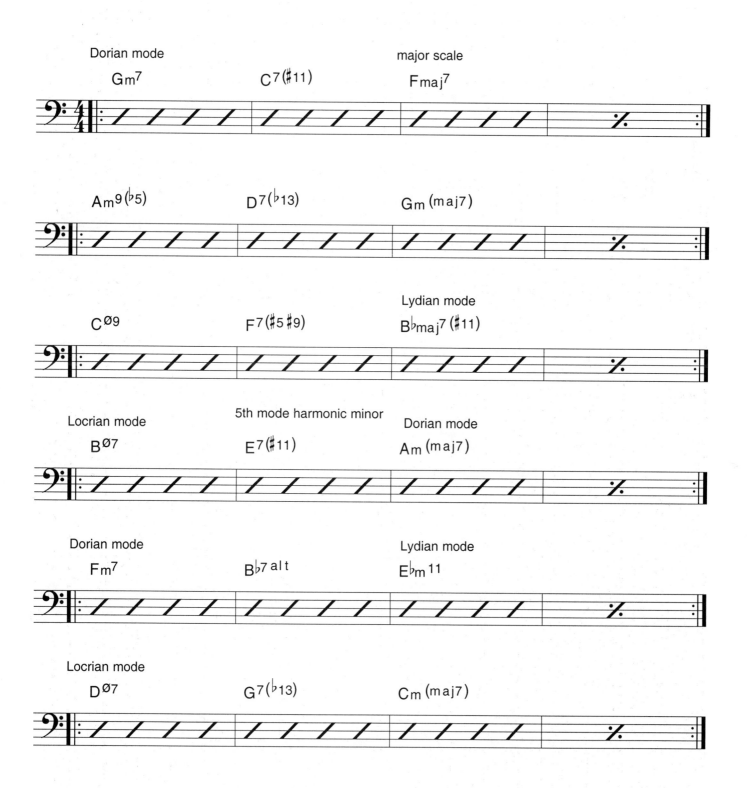

Your own melodic minor scale, mode and chord ideas:

12

Symmetric Scales

What are symmetric scales?

Symmetric scales are scales in which the pattern of whole steps and half steps that make them up repeats over and over within the space of an octave. The three most common symmetric scales are constructed using alternating whole steps and half steps, alternating half steps and whole steps and all whole steps—no half steps at all.

Up to this point, none of the scales and modes we've studied contains these unique, alternating whole-step and half-step patterns. To see for yourself, turn back to Chapter 3 (major scale), Chapter 6 (major scale modes), Chapter 10 (harmonic minor scale modes), or Chapter 11 (melodic minor scale modes) and check out the interval construction of those scales and modes.

The first symmetric scale we will examine is made up of alternating whole steps and half steps. It produces a scale containing eight different notes—all the scales we've studied so far have seven—in which tonic chord is a dim7th. We'll call it the "8-note diminished scale." It is also known as both the "whole-half diminished scale" and the "whole-step diminished scale."

The second symmetric scale is made up of alternating half steps and whole steps. It produces another eight-note scale in which tonic chord is a dom7(♭9). We'll call it the "8-note dominant scale." Other names for this scale are the "half-whole diminished scale" and the "half-step diminished scale." According to *The New Harvard Dictionary of Music*, the definitive book of Classical music definitions, this same scale is called the "octatonic scale." (Wow!)

N.B. While the names "8-note diminished" and "8-note dominant" are not the most commonly used names for these scales, I like to use them because they very clearly describe the function of each scale, leaving no doubt as to their use. Credit for these names goes to Dick Grove who, at one time, ran a wonderful music school in Los Angeles.

The third symmetric scale is made up entirely of whole steps. It produces a six-note scale whose tonic chord is the dom7(♯5). It's known everywhere as the "whole-tone scale."

The 8-Note Diminished Scale:

1. Interval construction:

The 8-note diminished scale is made up of alternating whole steps and half steps.

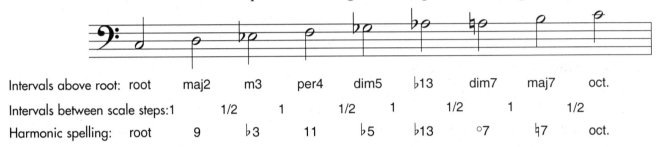

Intervals above root:	root	maj2	m3	per4	dim5	♭13	dim7	maj7	oct.
Intervals between scale steps:	1	1/2	1	1/2	1	1/2	1	1/2	
Harmonic spelling:	root	9	♭3	11	♭5	♭13	°7	♮7	oct.

2. Scale type and tonic chord:

This scale is considered a diminished scale as its tonic chord is a dim7. This is the first scale we have run into that has a *full diminished* 7th chord in it—a diminished triad with a diminished 7th on top. The two other scales which have diminished triads in them, namely the Locrian mode from the major scale and the Locrian ♯2 from the melodic minor scale, both have minor 7th intervals above their roots—*half diminished* 7th chords.

In the 8-note diminished scale in item 1, the note A is the dim7. Although the note A is normally a maj6th above the root C, in this case it is the enharmonic equivalent for the technically correct note, B♭♭—the diminished 7th. Enough ♭♭'s already!

Common chord symbols are:

a. dim7

b. °7

c. °(♯7) or dim(♯7) or °(+7) or dim(+7)– the scale has a major 7th in it.

d. A polychord in which the root of a major triad is a half step below the bass note, for example, B/C. The root of the B chord is the maj7 above the C bass note, while the D♯ (same as E♭), the F♯ (same as G♭) form a diminished triad above the C root—C – E♭– G♭– B—Cdim(+7).

3. More cool symmetrical things about the 8-note diminished scale:

In addition to the whole step, half step symmetry, this scale is symmetrical in a number of other ways, among them: (Refer to item 1 for examples.)

a. The four notes in the tonic chord are a minor third apart from each other—three half steps. The tonic chord is C – E♭ – G♭ – A (B♭♭) – C, all minor thirds.

b. These four minor thirds divide the scale into four equal parts, each three half steps.

c. All the diatonic thirds, either ascending or descending, are minor. All the diatonic fifths, either ascending or descending, are diminished.

d. As a result of item 3, all the triads are diminished!

4. Tetrachord construction:

The 8-note diminished scale is also symmetrical in that it is made up of two minor tetrachords a half step apart—an easy way to remember how to both play and use the scale.

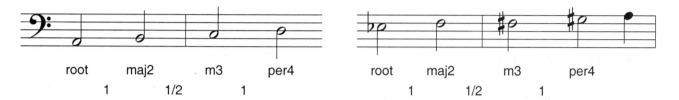

5. Four scales for the price of one!

Because of this interval symmetry, you can start an 8-note diminished scale and a dim7 chord from each of the four notes of the tonic chord. All four scales share the same notes and the same symmetric characteristics.

Here are all four scales and chords contained in the A 8-note diminished scale:

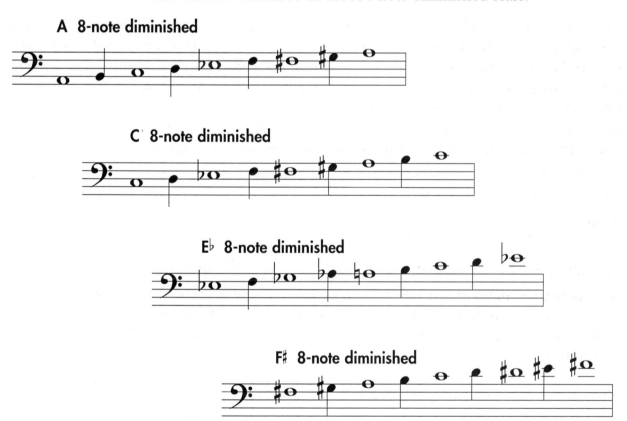

As one 8-note diminished scale produces a total of four like scales and chords, it follows that only three 8-note diminished scales, starting a half step apart, supply 8-note diminished scales and dim7 chords covering all 12 semitones—actually 15 when adding enharmonic starting pitches. Here's the list:

     Group 1 – Starting with A: A, C, E♭ and F♯ (G♭) – as above

     Group 2 – Starting with B♭: B♭, D♭ (C♯), E and G – shown on next page

     Group 3 – Starting with B: B, D, F and A♭ (G♯) – shown on next page

Group 2 – 8-note diminished scales:

Group 3 – 8-note diminished scales:

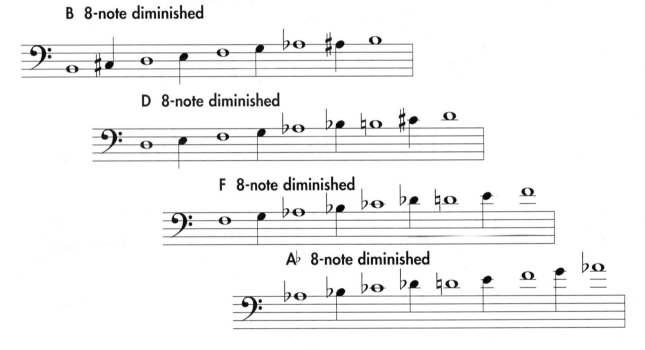

6. How do you spell this scale?

If you thought that spelling the altered scale was confusing (pages 218-219), spelling the 8-note diminished scale can be even more confusing. The A 8-note diminished scale on the previous page looks like it has two 6ths above the root—F♮ and F♯—minor and major. The F♮ functions as the ♭13; the F♯ as the °7. The D♭ 8-note diminished scale above seems to have two 4ths in it—G♭ and G♮—per and aug. The G♭ is the 11; the G♮ is the ♭5. The B 8-note diminished scale looks like it has two 7ths in it—A♭ and A♯—dim and maj. The A♭ is the °7; the A♯ is the maj7. This is done to avoid using ♭♭'s and 𝄪's. While enharmonic changes make the scales easier to read, remember that *no matter how the scale is spelled, the function of each note remains the same.*

The 8-note diminished scale in the 1st position:

This symmetric structure of the 8-note diminished scale is very different from any of the scales we have studied so far. In Exercises 1-3, I've written two scales from each of the three groups. Please figure out the rest. The spelling of each scale changes as the exercises progress, so be careful.

Exercise 1: Group 1 – A and E♭ 8-note diminished. Don't forget C and F♯ (G♭).

Exercise 2: Group 2 – B♭ and E 8-note diminished. Don't forget D♭ (C♯) and G.

Exercise 3: Group 3 – B and A♭ 8-note diminished. Don't forget D and F.

Exercise 4: 8-note diminished tetrachords in the 1st position

The 8-note diminished scale outside of the 1st position:

Here are some ideas for playing the 8-note diminished scale outside of the 1st position. Practice these and then come up with some of your own. Play over the entire fingerboard in every key.

1. Up one string – Starting with an open string

0 1 2◄►1 2 4◄►1 3 4

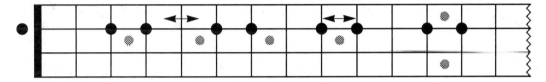

2. Up one string – Starting with a fingered note

1 3 4◄►1 2 4◄►1 3 4

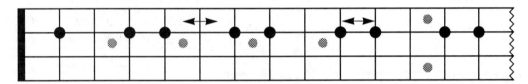

3. Two strings

1 3 4 1 2 4◄►1 3 4

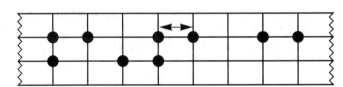

4. Three strings

1 3 4 1 2◄►3 4 1 2   or
1 3 4 1◄►1 3 4 1 2

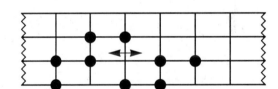

5. Two strings

1 3◄►1 3 4 1◄►1 3 4

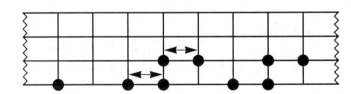

6. Three strings

4 1◄►1 3 4 1◄►1 3 4

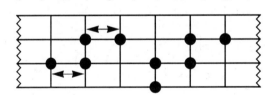

7. Two string pairs – F♯, B and E 8-note diminished

1 3 0◄►1 2◄►3 4 1 2   or   1 3 0◄►1◄►1 3 4 1 2

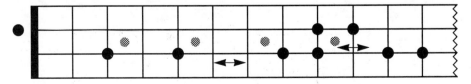

8-note diminished exercises outside of the 1st position:

Practice these exercises in every key. Use the list of starting pitches following each exercise to keep track of your progress. Play each exercise with as many of the fingerings on page 237 as you can. Be sure to retain the shape of the fingering you have chosen.

Exercise 5: 8-note diminished scale

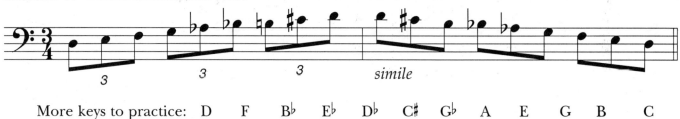

More keys to practice: D   F   B♭   E♭   D♭   C#   G♭   A   E   G   B   C

Exercise 6: 8-note diminished scale

C   C#   D   E♭   E   F   F#   G   A♭   A   B♭   B

Exercise 7: diminished triad arpeggio

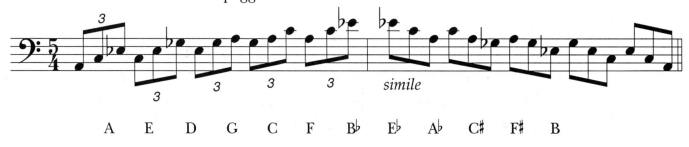

A   E   D   G   C   F   B♭   E♭   A♭   C#   F#   B

Two-octave 8-note diminished scales:

As usual, Example 1 stays in the 1st position as long as possible. Example 6 gets to the top end of the bass as quickly as possible. Fill in the fingerboard charts with your own two octave ideas for the 8-note diminished scale, and practice them in *every* key.

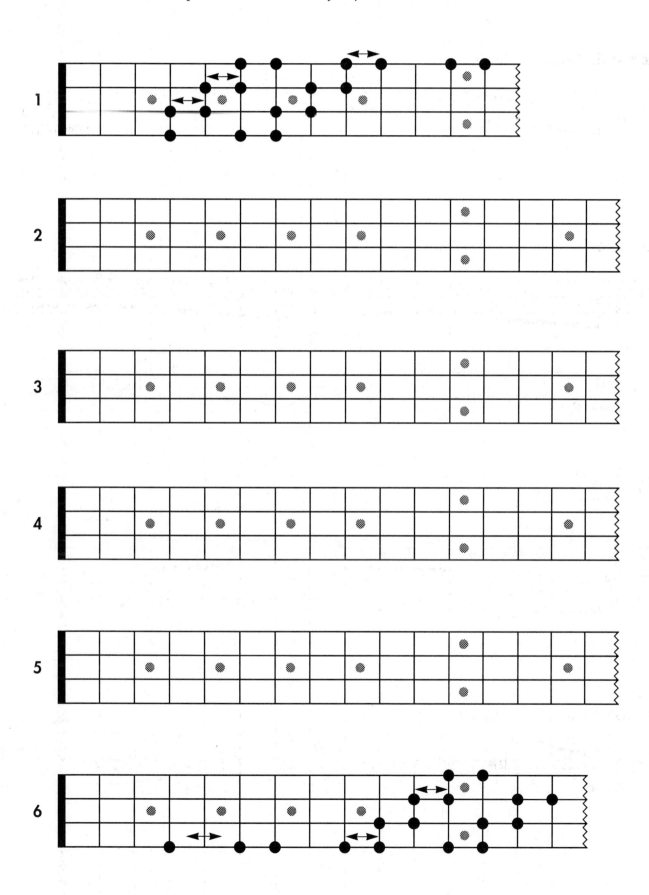

Two-octave dim7 arpeggios:

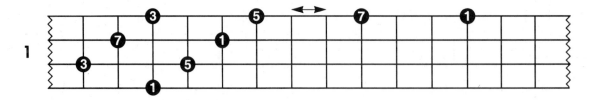

Come up with two of your own.

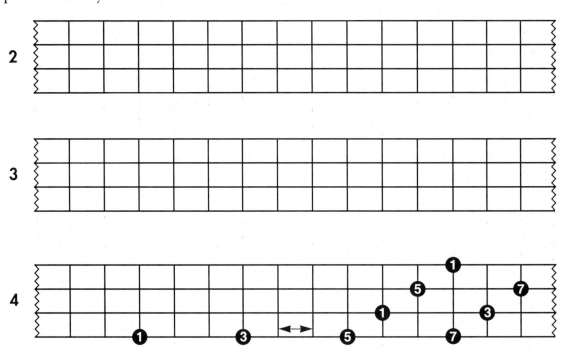

Exercise 8: dim7 arpeggio

Your own 8-note diminished scale and dim7 chord ideas:

The 8-Note Dominant Scale:

1. Interval construction:

The 8-note dominant scale is made up of alternating half steps and whole steps—exactly opposite from whole step–half step interval construction of the 8-note diminished scale.

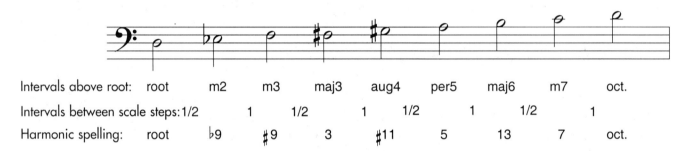

Intervals above root:	root	m2	m3	maj3	aug4	per5	maj6	m7	oct.
Intervals between scale steps:	1/2		1	1/2	1	1/2	1	1/2	1
Harmonic spelling:	root	♭9	♯9	3	♯11	5	13	7	oct.

2. Scale type and tonic chord:

The name says it all: the 8-note dominant scale is a dominant-type scale.

Its basic 7th chord is a plain 'ol dom7 chord—root, maj3, per5, and m7—just like the Mixolydian and the Lydian dominant modes. With the Lydian mode, the ♯11 has to be included in with the tonic 7th chord to be sure that the chord-scale relationship is described correctly: 7(♯11).

In addition to having a ♯11 in it, the 8-note dominant scale also contains altered 9's. To correctly describe the chord-scale relationship of this scale, one of the altered 9's must be included in the tonic chord. The most common chord symbols for the 8-note dominant scale are 7(♭9), 7(♯9) and 7(♭9, 13). If the melody calls for it, the ♯11 is added to the symbol—7(♭9, ♯11). In case the ♯11 is called a ♭5, the chord symbol would be 7(♭5, ♭9).

Some common polychords:

    a. The top triad is a maj6th above the bottom dom7th chord—B/D7

    b. The top triad is an aug4th or a dim5th above the bottom dom7th chord—G♯/D7 or A♭/D7

3. Most common uses:

- It's the "5" chord in either major or minor cadences.
- It's a great sounding tonic chord in rock, jazz and blues tunes.

4. Intervals above the root that define the 8-note dominant scale:

- m9th (♭9)
- m3rd (♯9)
- aug4th (♯11) or dim5th (♭5)
- maj6th (13)

5. Tetrachord construction:

The 8-note dominant scale is made up of two diminished tetrachords a whole step apart.

If you don't remember what a diminished tetrachord is, take a look at item 6 on page 190.

6. Four scales for the price of one – again!

I'm sure that you remember that the whole step-half step symmetry of the 8-note diminished scale allows you to create four 8-note diminished scales, a m3rd apart, from one scale. Well, the half step-whole step symmetry of the 8-note dominant scale allows you to do the same thing: to create four 8-note dominant scales, a m3rd apart, from one 8-note dominant scale.

Here are all four scales found in the B 8-note dominant scale:

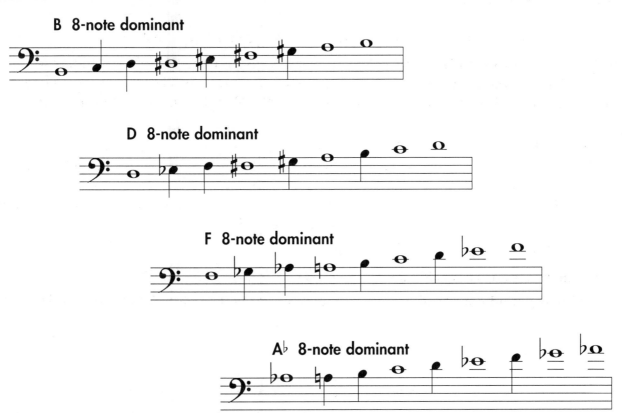

As one 8-note dominant scale produces a total of four like scales and chords, it follows that only three 8-note dominant scales, starting a half step apart, supply 8-note dominant scales and 7(♭9) chords covering all 12 semitones—15 when adding enharmonic starting pitches.

Here's the list:

    Group 1 – Starting with B: B, D, F and A♭ (G♯) – as above

    Group 2 – Starting with C: C, E♭, F♯ (G♭) and A – shown on next page

    Group 3 – Starting with C♯:   C♯ (D♭), E, G and B♭ – shown on next page

Group 2 – 8-note dominant scales:

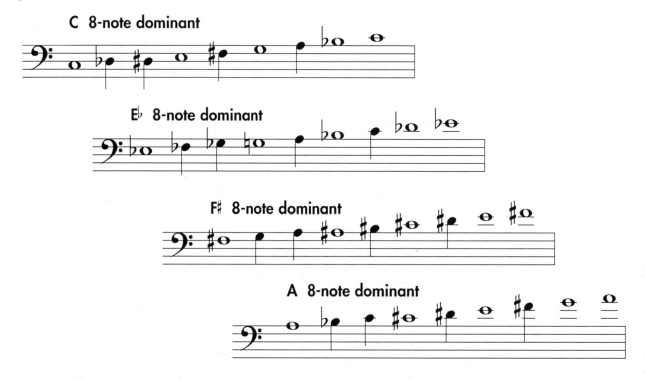

Group 2 – 8-note dominant scales:

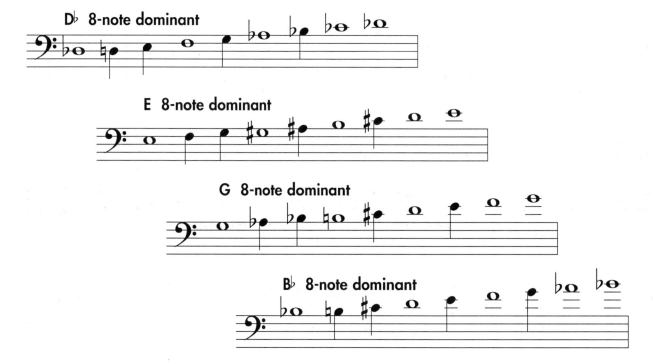

7. The spelling problem – again!

As with the spelling of the 8-note diminished scale, the spelling of the 8-note dominant scale is determined more by ease of reading and convenience than by technical accuracy. Three people could spell the same 8-note dominant scale three different ways! The differences are usually found in the spelling of the ♭9 and the ♯9. The C 8-note dominant at the top of the page is the only scale on pages 243–244 spelled with technically correct 9's. The rest use an enharmonic variation. Remember that *no matter how the scale is spelled, the function of each note remains the same.*

The 8-note dominant scale in the 1st position:

In Exercises 9-11, I've written two scales from each of the three 8-note dominant scale groups. Please figure out the rest of them as indicated. The exercises jump all over the 1st position, so feel free to improvise your own 8-note dominant stuff. Jump all over the 1st position!

Exercise 9: Group 1 – B and F 8-note dominant. Don't forget D and G♯ (A♭).

Exercise 10: Group 2 – C and E♭ 8-note dominant. Don't forget G♭ (F♯) and A.

Exercise 11: Group 3 – D♭ (C♯) and B♭ 8-note dominant. Don't forget E and G.

Exercise 12: 8-note dominant tetrachords in the 1st position

The 8-note dominant scale outside of the 1st position:

Here are some ideas for playing the 8-note dominant scale outside of the 1st position. Practice these and then come up with some of your own. Play over the entire fingerboard in every key.

1. Up one string – Starting with an open string

0   1   3 ◄►1   3   4 ◄►1   2   4

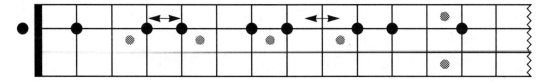

2. Up one string – Starting with a fingered note

1   2   4 ◄►1   3   4 ◄►1   2   4

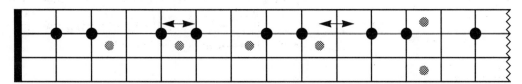

3. Two strings

1 ◄►1   3   4   1   2 ◄►1   2   4   or
1   2 ◄►3   4   1   2 ◄►1   2   4

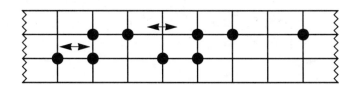

4. Three strings

1 ◄►1   3   4   1 ◄►1   3   4   1   or
1   2 ◄►3   4   1   2 ◄►3   4   1

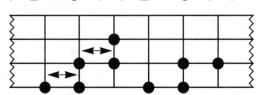

5. Two strings

1   2   4 ◄►1   3   4   1   2   4

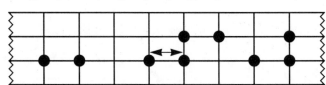

6. Three strings

3   4   1 ◄►1   3   4   1   2   4   or
3   4   1   2 ◄►3   4   1   2   4

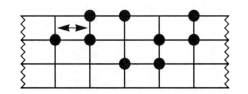

7. Two string pairs – F, B♭ and E♭ 8-note dominant

1   2   4   0 ◄►3   4   1   2   4

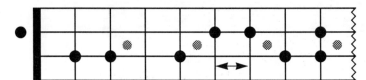

8-note dominant exercises outside of the 1st position:

Practice these exercises in every key. Use the list of starting pitches following each exercise to keep track of your progress. Play each exercise with as many of the fingerings on page 247 as you can. Be sure to retain the shape of the fingering you have chosen.

Exercise 13: 8-note dominant scale in four-note groups

More keys to practice: D   F   B♭   E♭   D♭   C♯   G♭   A   E   G   B   C

Exercise 14: 8-note dominant scale triads around the cycle of fourths

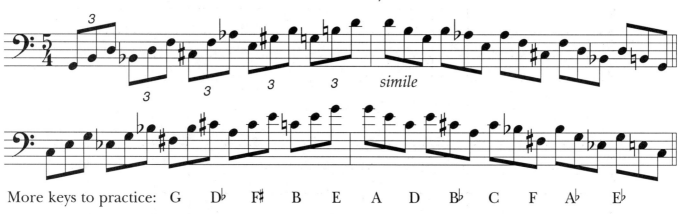

More keys to practice: G   D♭   F♯   B   E   A   D   B♭   C   F   A♭   E♭

Exercise 15: 8-note dominant scale in six-note groups – watch out for enharmonic changes!

More keys to practice: C   C♯   D   E♭   E   F   F♯   G   A♭   A   B♭   B

Two-octave 8-note dominant scales:

Again, Example 1 stays in the low end of the bass as long as possible. Example 6 gets to the top end of the bass as quickly as possible. Fill in the fingerboard charts with your own two-octave ideas for the 8-note dominant scale and practice them in *every* key.

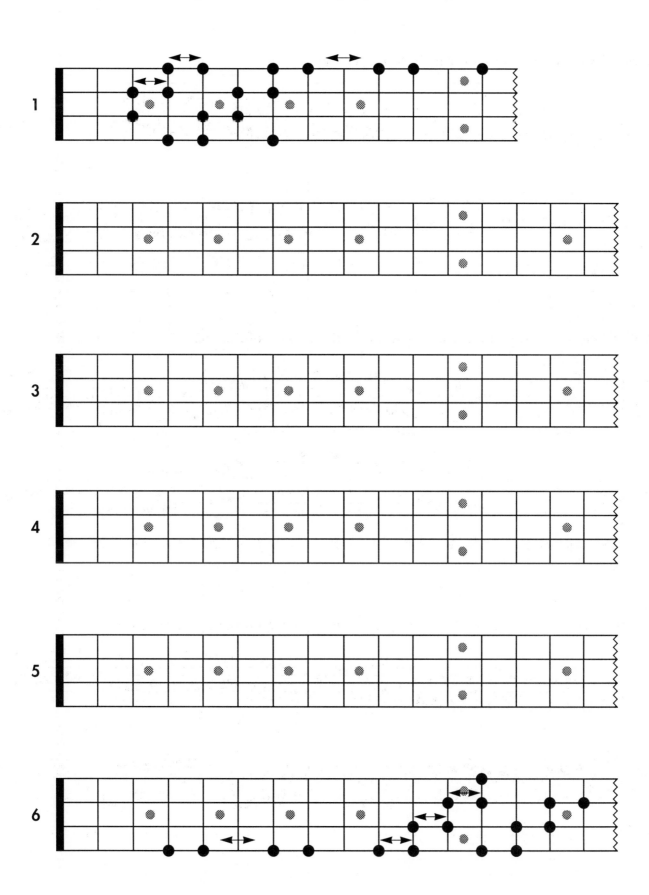

Your own 8-note dominant scale and dom7(♭9) ideas:

"Wait a minute! Isn't this the spot where we usually have two-octave arpeggios to deal with?"

"Yes, but since every note of this scale functions as an important chord tone, the exercises on the next few pages will get you better acquainted the sound of the 8-note dominant scale than arpeggio exercises. So, before you get to the exercises on the next few pages, come up with your own 8-note dominant scale ideas."

Using the 8-note diminished and the 8-note dominant scales together:

1. Because of the symmetric organization of half and whole steps in the 8-note diminished and 8-note dominant scales, when you play diatonically up or down either of them, one scale becomes the other. Below, in the E 8-note diminished scale, you'll find four 8-note diminished and four 8-note dominant scales all sharing the same notes. *Eight,* count 'em, eight scales for the price of one! On pages 252 and 253 you'll find the scales starting from F and F♯. Three pitches one half step apart produce 24 scales! It doesn't matter where you start!

E 8-note diminished

F♯ 8-note dominant

G 8-note diminished

A 8-note dominant

B♭ 8-note diminished

C 8-note dominant

C♯ 8-note diminished

E♭ 8-note dominant

8-note diminished and 8-note dominant scales starting from F:

F 8-note diminished

G 8-note dominant

A♭ 8-note diminished

B♭ 8-note dominant

B 8-note diminished

D♭ 8-note dominant

D 8-note diminished

E♭ 8-note dominant

8-note diminished and 8-note dominant scales starting from F♯:

F♯ 8-note diminished

A♭ 8-note dominant

A 8-note diminished

B 8-note dominant

C 8-note diminished

D 8-note dominant

E♭ 8-note diminished

F 8-note dominant

2. Since the scales alternate, so do the tonic chords—dim7, dom7($\flat$9), dim7, and so on.

    In the preceding exercise, you have Edim7, F$\sharp$7($\flat$9), Gdim7, A7($\flat$9), B$\flat$dim7, C7($\flat$9), C$\sharp$dim7 and E$\flat$7($\flat$9). The roots of similar chords and scales are a m3rd away from each other (more symmetry!) forming a diminished relationship.

    Here's the coolest thing about all of this. As all of the dominant chords found in one scale share the same notes, any bass line or solo material you play over one chord works with all of the others. The same is true, of course, for the diminished chords.

    In this example, which uses the first bar of Exercise 12-15, C7($\flat$9) or F$\sharp$7($\flat$9) may be used to resolve to F. The notes are the same although they function differently in each dominant chord. The 8-note dominant scale comes with built-in tritone substitutions!

C7($\flat$9)	root	$\flat$9	$\sharp$9	3	$\sharp$11	5	$\sharp$11	3	$\sharp$9	3	$\sharp$11	5	13	7	13	5
F$\sharp$7($\flat$9)	$\sharp$11	5	13	7	root	$\flat$9	root	7	13	7	root	$\flat$9	$\sharp$9	3	$\sharp$9	$\flat$9

3. When soloing, you may use dim7 licks over dom7($\flat$9) chords.

    Every 8-note dominant scale, dom7($\flat$9), has four 8-note diminished scales and dim7 chords in it which share the same notes. The 8-note diminished scales and chords are a half step, a maj3rd, a per5th and a m7th above the root of the dom7($\flat$9).

    The following example takes the example above and leaves off the first note of the first bar, thus creating a D$\flat$ 8-note diminished pattern. Using the C7($\flat$9) chord, the pattern starts a half step above the root—the $\flat$9 of the chord. With the F$\sharp$7($\flat$9), the diminished pattern starts a per5th above the root—the 5th of the chord. In both examples, the notes function the same way within the chords.

    Experiment using diminished scale and chord patterns a maj3rd and a m7th above the root of dom7($\flat$9) chords. This process helps you avoid starting solo ideas with the root of the chord which can get a bit boring after a while. Also, you create a lot of tension and release in your solo, which sounds great to the listener.

C7($\flat$9)	$\flat$9	$\sharp$9	3	$\sharp$11	5	$\sharp$11	3	$\sharp$9	3	$\sharp$11	5	13	7	13	5	$\sharp$11
F$\sharp$7($\flat$9)	5	13	7	root	$\flat$9	root	7	13	7	root	$\flat$9	$\sharp$9	3	$\sharp$9	$\flat$9	root

4. A dim7 chord may be thought of as the first inversion of a dom7 chord.

Adding a note a maj3rd below the root of a dim7 chord creates a dom7(♭9) chord. The root of the dim7 chord and the dom7(♭9) are both part of the same scale.

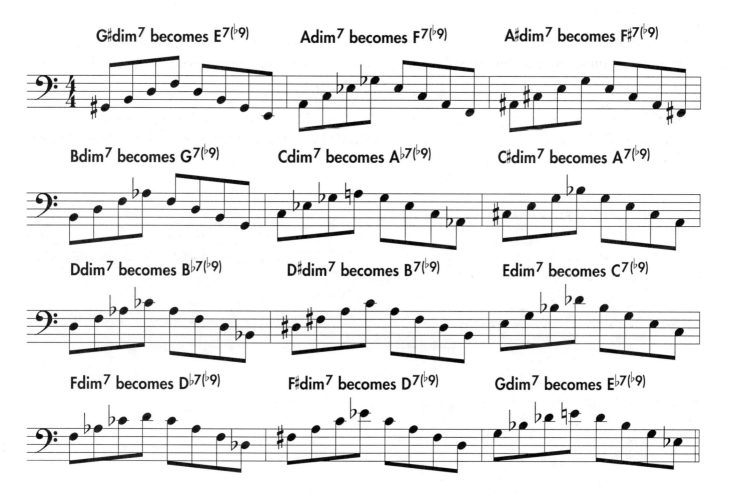

The next set of exercises is a collection of common "diminished" patterns. As you practice them, remember that:

1. Each pattern works with four 8-note dominant and four 8-note diminished scales.

2. Transposing each of the exercises up or down two half steps provides you with the remaining sixteen 8-note dominant scales and sixteen 8-note diminished scales. (Be sure that you know how every note functions in the chords.)

3. Any one or two bar portion of each of the exercises is good material for playing bass lines through or soloing over dom7(♭9) chords or dim7 chords. For example, using the one or two bar phrase as "5" chord material, resolve it to a note of the "1" chord.

4. Playing each exercise on the piano along with the four dominant and diminished chords that work with it will help you to hear how the line and the chords go together.

5. Casually playing any of the patterns in public real fast will truly amaze those around you—especially saxophone players! You know what to do.

Exercise 16: E, G, B♭ and C♯ (D♭) 8-note dominant

F, A♭ (G♯), B and D 8-note diminished

Exercise 17: F♯ (G♭), A, B and D 8-note dominant

G, B♭, D♭ (C♯) and E 8-note diminished

Exercise 18: F♯ (G♭), A, B and 8-note dominant

G, B♭, D♭ (C♯) and E 8-note diminished

Exercise 19: G, B♭, C♯ (D♭) and E 8-note dominant

A♭ (G♯), B, D and F 8-note diminished

Exercise 20: F, A♭ (G♯), B and D 8-note dominant

F♯ (G♭), A, C and E♭ 8-note diminished

Your own 8-note dominant and 8-note diminished ideas:

The Whole-tone Scale:

1. Interval construction:

The whole-tone scale, the third symmetric scale, is a six note scale made up of nothing but whole steps.

Intervals above root: root	maj2	maj3	aug4	aug5	m7	oct.
Intervals between scale steps:1	1	1	1	1	1	
Harmonic spelling: root	9	3	♯11	♯5	7	oct.

2. Scale type and tonic chord:

The whole-tone scale is a dominant scale. It has a maj3 and a m7 above the root as do all other dominant scales.

Like the Lydian dominant scale, the altered scale, and the 8-note dominant scale, the whole-tone scale has a ♯11 in it. More importantly, the whole-tone scale has a ♯5 in it just like the altered scale. The whole-tone scale is also like the altered scale in that it does not have a 13th in the scale; the Lydian dominant and the 8-note dominant do.

The only difference between the altered and whole-tone scales is that the altered scale, like the 8-note dominant scale, has altered ninths (♭9, ♯9) in it while the whole-tone scale has a natural 9 in it; the Lydian dominant does, too.

The tonic chord for the whole-tone scale is the augdom7. Other chord symbols that call for the whole-tone scale are augdom7(♯11), dom7(♯5), augdom9(♯11), and dom9(♯5).

3. Most common use:

- It is used as a "5" chord in major cadences.

4. Intervals above the root that define the whole tone scale:

- maj9
- maj3
- aug4 (♯11)
- aug5 (♯5)
- m7

5. Tetrachord construction:

The whole-tone scale is made up of two whole-tone tetrachords. Since this is a six-note scale, both tetrachords share the ♯11.

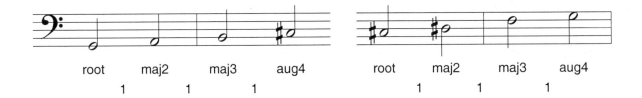

6. Six scales for the price of one!

The whole step symmetry of the whole-tone scale creates a unique situation. Starting from each scale step of any whole-tone scale, a new whole-tone scale is created—six new, complete scales that share the same notes or enharmonic equivalents. Here are the six scales starting from G.

Because six whole-tone scale are found in one whole-tone scale, it follows that any two whole-tone scales, one half step apart, produce whole-tone scales and dom7(♯5) chords covering all 12 semitones—15 when adding enharmonic starting pitches.

      Group 1 – Starting with G: G, A, B, D♭ (C♯), E♭ and F

      Group 2 – Starting with A♭:   A♭ (G♯), B♭, C, D, E and G♭ (F♯)

Whole-tone scales starting from A♭:

7. The spelling problem – for the third time!

As with the spelling of the 8-note diminished scale and the 8-note dominant scale, the spelling of the whole tone scale is determined more by ease of reading and convenience than by technical accuracy. The differences are usually found in the spelling of the ♯5. The B whole-tone scale on the previous page has a G♮ rather than an F𝄪. The F whole-tone scale on this page has a D♮ rather than an C𝄪. Remember that *no matter how the scale is spelled, the function of each note remains the same.*

The whole-tone scale in the 1st position:

Exercise 21: Whole-tone scales up chromatically in the 1st position

Exercise 22: Whole-tone scale tetrachords

Then F♯ G A♭ A B♭ B C C♯, then...

The whole-tone scale outside of the 1st position:

Here are some ideas for playing the whole-tone scale outside of the 1st position. Practice these and then come up with some of your own. Play over the entire fingerboard in every key.

1. Up one string – Starting with an open string

0 1 3◄►1 3◄►1 3

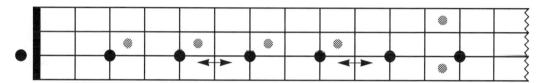

2. Up one string – Starting with a fingered note

1◄►1 3◄►1 3◄►1 3

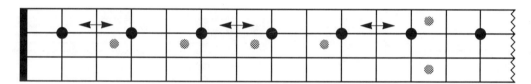

3. Two strings

1 3◄►2 4 1◄►2 4

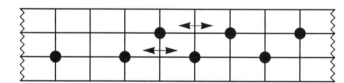

4. Three strings

4 1◄►2 4 1◄►2 4

5. Three strings

1◄►2 4 1◄►2 4 1

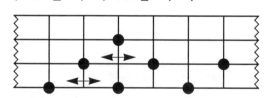

6. Four strings

4 1 ⋀ 4 1 ⋀ 4 1 3

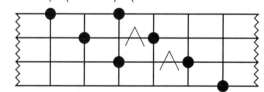

7. Two string pairs – F, B♭ and E♭ whole-tone scale

1 3 0◄►2 4 1 3

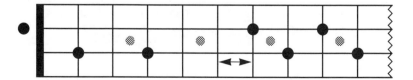

8. Three strings

2 4 1◄►2 4 1 3

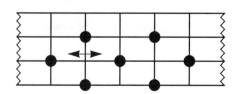

Whole-tone scale exercises outside of the 1st position:

Practice these exercises in every key. Keep track of your progress by using the list of starting pitches that follow each exercise. Play each exercise with as many of the fingerings on page 263 as you can. Be sure to retain the shape of the fingering you have chosen.

Exercise 23: Whole-tone scale in thirds

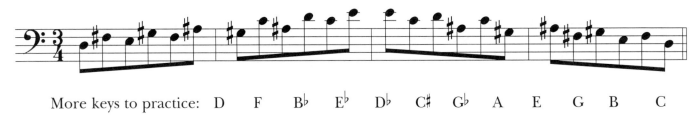

More keys to practice: D   F   B♭   E♭   D♭   C♯   G♭   A   E   G   B   C

Exercise 24: Whole-tone scale pattern

More keys to practice: B♭   E♭   A♭   D♭   F♯   B   E   A   D   G   C   F

Exercise 25: Diatonic dom7(♯5) chords

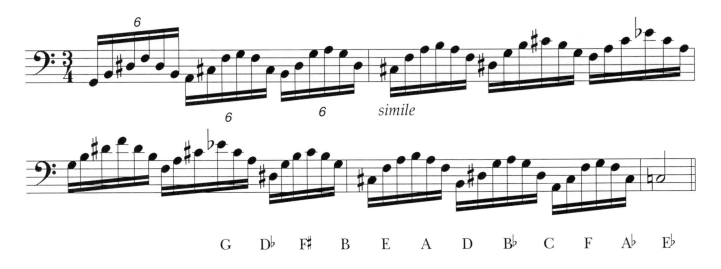

G   D♭   F♯   B   E   A   D   B♭   C   F   A♭   E♭

Two-octave whole-tone scales:

Example 1 stays in the low end of the bass as long as possible. Example 6 gets to the top end of the bass as quickly as possible. Fill in the fingerboard charts with your own two octave ideas for the whole-tone scale and practice them in *every* key.

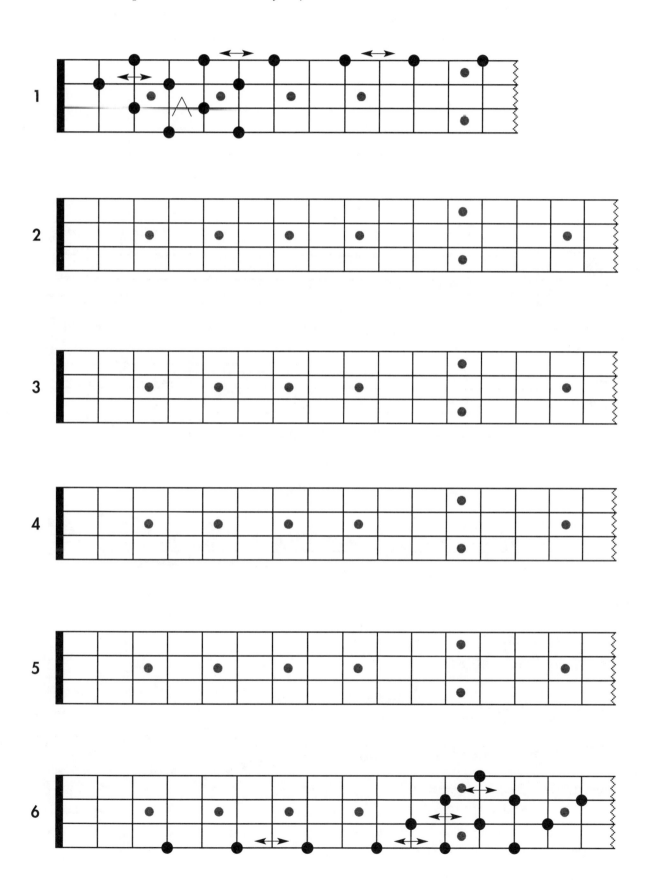

Two-octave dom7(♯5) arpeggios – Tonic chord – whole-tone scale:

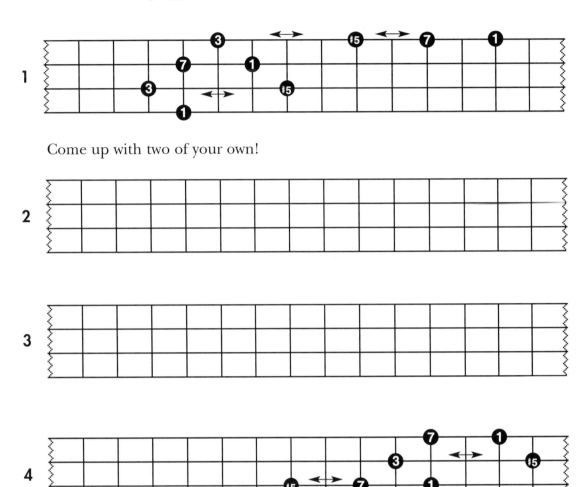

1

Come up with two of your own!

2

3

4

Exercise 26: dom7(♯5) arpeggio   Check out both fingerings.

1 Finger:	3 2 1 3 2 1 1 3	4 1 3 2 1 3 2 4	1 2 1 3 2 1 1 3
String:	E A D A D	A D G D G	D G D G
2 Finger:	1 2 1 3 2 2 4 1	2 4 1 3 2 4 3 2	4 3 2 4 3 2 4 1
String:	E A E A	E A E	A D E A D A D G

3 1 1 2 3 1 2 1	4 2 3 1 2 3 1 4	3 1 1 2 3 1 2 3
G D G D	G D G D A	D A D A E
1 4 2 3 4 2 3 4	2 3 4 2 3 1 4 2	1 4 2 2 3 1 2 1
G D A D A E	D A E A E	A E A E

Your own whole-tone scale and dom7(♯5) ideas:

The Last Chapter

Now that you've played scales and chords over every square inch of your bass in ways that are both familiar and new, you might be wondering what you've accomplished. A few things come to mind.

1. You have acquired the ability to negotiate the fingerboard in ways you never thought of.

All of the scale and chord patterns you practiced, especially those that cover 1, 2 or 4 strings, that were new or seemed a little strange to you, allow you get around the bass more smoothly and efficiently. No more big shifts unless *you* want one. You now have choices for the way you play things—even things you've played a thousand times.

2. Your left hand has gained a flexibility that it probably never had.

I'll bet you never thought your third and fourth fingers could become so important in playing music on the bass.

3. You have learned how to read notes if you didn't know how to before.

You now know where every note is on the bass.

Your knowledge of where notes are on the fingerboard increased a 1000% while you were playing those 100 or so exercises. Because there is more than one place to play any note on a 4-, 5- or 6-string bass—except for the very lowest notes—armed with this knowledge of the fingerboard, you are now able to look at a written part and quickly decide where to put your hand on the neck and to start reading. If that place isn't the best one, you can change it—options. Remember that if you are in a recording session and are handed a written part to play, the composer (who doesn't know as much about the physical challenges of playing the bass as you do and has written the bass part from hell) doesn't care about what you have to go through to read the part. All the composer wants to hear is the part played beautifully and played in the pocket. You can do this now.

Bassists who have difficulty reading notes, do so for a number of reasons. Among them:

a. *Someone said that reading notes is hard.*

More than likely, the person who said that doesn't know how to read! Don't forget that in the process of studying this book, you've read over 100 exercises that cover the whole bass in *every key*. Not bad.

b. *Someone said that reading isn't cool. "It gets in the way of creativity."*

Contrary to this notion, the ability to read encourages and actually speeds up the creative process. If you and all the players in your band could read, just think of how fast everyone would be able to learn the amazing new song you've written. That big chunk of time spent learning the song note by note can be reduced to minutes! No more will you ever hear, "Duh, would you play that note again?" The sooner your bandmates have the song in their heads, the sooner your ideas will be turned into real music. The arrangement, additions or corrections—*even new ideas*—can all be worked out in a quick, thorough and less frustrating way.

During the 20 years that I was a studio player in Los Angeles—where all musicians (even guitar players!) are expected to know how to read—I played on thousands of TV, movie, CD and jingle dates. I played over 5000 Tonight Shows! I also did a lot of playing in clubs with jazz, latin, rock and blues bands. In almost every instance, I was asked to read parts that contained notes, chord changes or both. If a part needed to be changed a little or a lot to make it either more interesting or more stylistically correct, I was able to come up with new ideas quickly because I already had the concept of the song in my head. (Don't forget that as bass players, we know more about how the bass fits into a song than a lot of writers do!) My ability to play the bass well combined with my ability to read well got me in the studio door. Once inside, there was no end to the creative things I could do. In the studio scene, not being able to read gets in the way of playing with some of the best players in the world and with the possibility of making a good living!

4. Your ability to read notes creates the ability to write notes.

You've seen and read a lot of notes, and know how the notes on the page relate to the bass—C, second space from the bottom in written bass music, is played either third fret on the A string or eighth fret on the E string. You've also read a lot of different rhythm patterns. Add all this to your ability to subdivide (Chapter 3, pages 35-36) and you've got all it takes to write down anything you hear. If you have never written notes on a page before, it does take some practice to get them to look just right. So, buy some music paper and get going. If you own a computer, get a program that will print out music for you.

5. You've significantly improved your ability to play by ear.

I'll bet you've done this a lot: You copied a bass line or solo from a tape or a CD just because you liked it or memorized the bass part to a new song by ear using a process of repetition without full comprehension of how the bass line or solo related to the chord progression of the song—*you heard it, you played it.* You've probably done this too: You tried to copy a bass line or solo, or tried to memorize a bass part and didn't have any luck because some of the notes seemed to be "too weird" or "too hard"—*you didn't hear it, you didn't play it.*

Now that you've played and heard every common and not-so-common scale and chord used in pop, jazz and classical music, nothing should sound "weird" or "hard" to you anymore. With every scale and chord you learned, you increased your sonic vocabulary. Your ability to hear something and to respond to it has grown dramatically.

6. You have learned how to interpret chord changes.

Major (maj), minor (m), augmented (+ or aug), diminished (° or dim)—kid's stuff. ♭5, ♯5; ♭9, ♯9; ♯11; ♭13—no problem! You know what *all* the numbers mean—yes, all those recent additions to your sonic vocabulary that add variety and spice to your chord progressions. You may, however, one big, burning question for which I've got the answer. The question is:

How do I remember all of these scales and chords?

It's easy.

All of the scales and the chords generated by them we've discussed may be separated into three groups which define both their basic sound and their function. The three groups are:

1. *Major scales and chords*

    All have a maj3rd and a maj7th above the root. They are usually used to define the key of a song ("This song is in G major.") or a new key-center within a song.

2. *Minor scales and chords*

    All have a m3rd and usually a m7th (sometimes a maj7th) above the root. They can also define the key of a song ("This tune is in G minor.") or a new key center within a song, or are used in chord progressions to establish a key (as the "2" chord in a 2–5–1 progression) or are used in place of major chords to give variety to a chord progression ("3" [Phrygian] is commonly substituted for "1" [Ionian] in jazz tunes).

3. *Dominant scales and chords*

    All have a maj3rd and a m7th above the root. They can define the key of a jazz or blues tune (*Straight, No Chaser* is in the key of F, the first chord of is F7—"This song is in F major.") or are used to establish a key (as the "5" chord in a 2–5–1 progression).

As long as you remember the harmonic spelling (how the notes of the scale function in a chord) for the basic scale from each group—the major scale for the *major scales and chords,* the Aeolian mode for the *minor scales and chords* and the Mixolydian mode for the *dominant scales and chords*—it's a simple matter of juggling some numbers around. For example, the Lydian mode, maj7(♯11), is only one note (read *number*) different from the major scale, maj7. You have only to respond to the numbers in the chord symbols to create bass lines that are at the same time melodically beautiful and harmonically correct. The harmonic spelling is given for the basic scale in each group. Only the number (note) changes are given for the rest of the scales in each group. It's easy.

Group 1: Major scales and chords

1. Major scale (Ionian mode – p. 33): Gmaj7

2. Lydian mode (4th mode – major scale – p. 87): Gmaj7(♯11) • Gmaj7(♭5)

3. Lydian augmented (3rd mode – melodic minor scale – p. 189): Gmaj7(♯5, ♯11) • Gmaj7(♯4, ♯5)

Group 2: Minor chord-scales

1. Aeolian mode (6th mode – major scale – p. 92): Gm7 • Gm7(♭13) • Gm7(♯5)

1   9   3   11   5   ♭13(♯5)   7   oct.

2. Dorian mode (2nd mode – major scale – p. 70): Gm7 • Gm6

maj13(6)

3. Phrygian mode (3rd mode – major scale – p. 82): Gm7 • Gm7(♭9, ♭13)

♭9

4. Locrian mode (7th mode – major scale – p. 98): Gm7(♭5) • GØ7

♭9   ♭5

5. Locrian ♯2 (6th mode – melodic minor scale – p. 211): Gm7(♭5) • Gm9(♭5)

♭5

6. Melodic minor scale (p. 179): Gm(maj7) • Gm(♯7)

maj13(6)   maj7

7. Harmonic minor scale (p. 163): Gm(maj7) • Gm(♯7)

maj7

8. 8-note diminished scale (p. 232): Gdim7 • G°7 • Gdim7(♯7)

♭5   dim7   maj7

Group 3: Dominant chord-scales

1. Mixolydian mode (5th mode – major scale – p. 77): G7

1   9   3   11   5   13(6)   7   oct.

2. Lydian dominant (4th mode – melodic minor scale – p. 197): G7(♯11) • G7(♭5)

♯11

3. 8-note dominant (p. 242): G7(♯9) • G7(♭9) • G7(♯9, ♯11) • G13(♭9) • G13(♯9)

♭9   ♯9   ♯11

4. Altered scale (diminished whole-tone, super Locrian - 7th mode – melodic minor scale – p. 218): G7alt • G7(♯5, ♯9) • G7(♯5, ♭9) • G7(♯5, ♯9, ♯11) • There is no 13th in this scale!

♭9   ♯9   ♯11   ♯5

5. Whole-tone scale (p. 259): G7(♯5) • G+7 • Gaug7 • There is no 13th in this scale, either!

♯11   ♯11   ♯5

6. Dominant ♭13 (5th mode – melodic minor scale – p. 204): G7(♭13)

♭13

7. Dominant ♭9, ♭13 (5th mode – harmonic minor scale – p. 171): G7(♭9, ♭13)

♭9   ♭13

Congratulations, you're done!